Turn Left at the Big Anthill

Rosemary Manchester

Turn Left at the Big Anthill
a memoir
Copyright © 2021 Rosemary Manchester

ISBN: 978-1-7354866-3-5

Author's contact information:
    roseisarose1950@comcast.net

Published by:
    Berkana Publications
    Sebastopol CA 95472 USA

Cover Design: Caitlyn Ottinger
Book layout: Berkana Publications

Printed in the United States of America

To my children,
Timothy, Peter, Mary Beth, and Martha

Acknowledgements

Deepest gratitude to the amazing team of Skye Blaine and Boudewijn Boom for their guidance, encouragement, patience, and skill in helping me finish the book. Thanks also to Laura McHale-Holland for her sensitive and meticulous editing. Special thanks to my beta readers, Kay Crista and Jane Huneke, and to the cover designer, Caitlyn Ottinger, my granddaughter.

I am indebted to Skye and our memoir group for their support and critique over the years: Mark Alarie, Nancy Baum, Arvada Darnell, Lanette Hunter-Reginelli, Mary Prisland, Jennifer Schoen, Amy Pane, Doug von Koss, Kay Crista, Ren Hjul, Christie Jones, and Andrew Delaney.

Thirty years ago, I joined the Anthology Group led first by Maudie Sell and Arie Reiser, later by Steve Boga, with Yvonne Wilcox, Terry Law, Cameo Archer, Louise Lambert, Gay Bishop-Brorstrom, Pat Rea, Thelmajean Edwards, Carolyn Doran, Garry Loveday, Raven-Light, Bob Thomas, and Chuck Kensler. Thank you for your wonderful guidance.

Jane Merryman and Lindajoy Fenley, thank you for inspiring me. Patricia Hempel thank you for helping me organize the story.

At the Sitting Room, a feminist library, thanks to J.J. Wilson, Karen Petersen, Clarice Stasz, Eloise Van Tassel, Barbara Lesch McCaffry, Michael McCaffry, Susan Bono, Robin Beeman, and Terry Ehret.

Special thanks to Mickey Pearlman who guided me to early publication, and to Robin Pressman and Suzanne Lang at KRCB.

At Bennington College, I studied with Susan Cheever, George Packer, Phillip Lopate, and Sven Birkerts, and later, Peter Trachtenberg. All thanks to them, and to my classmates.

Thanks to my friends at the Sebastopol Community Church who never gave up on me, especially Kathy Matthies.

Thanks to the Reading and Writing group at Burbank Heights: Judith Reimuller, Barbara Isaksen, Jim Stoops, Sandy Tate, Ron Harding, Ila Benevidez-Hester, Monique Pasternak, Charlyn Stetson, and others.

Thanks also to Jean LaCamera, Jane Love, Elizabeth Youngerman, Jon Gottlieb, and all others who supported my project. It takes a village. Thank you, thank you.

I'm sure I've missed some kind soul who assisted me along the way. Contact me, and in the next printing, I'll be happy to make the correction. See the copyright page for my email.

A Personal Note to Readers

During the year we lived in Belgium, Stewart and I wrote letters to our families every Sunday night after the children were in bed. We took turns at the Olivetti typewriter, which held five sheets of onionskin paper and four sheets of carbon paper. Our parents received a copy of every letter. Other copies went to family members and friends. We continued the custom on Sunday nights in the Congo, facing each other across the big desks in Stewart's office. We often used the blue Aerograms so popular in those years. I wrote about the children and Stewart wrote about his work. Everyone saved those letters, and when I decided to write my story I received boxes of them, five copies of each letter. I slipped them into clear plastic sleeves and filed them in binders, one for each year. They have enabled me to share with you my memory of the events of those years.

Fifty years after these events took place, the archives of the Royal Museum for Central Africa in Tervuren, Belgium were opened, giving access to details of the political history of the times.

Some names have been changed to honor people's privacy.

—Rosemary Manchester

1958

The Congo during the crisis 1960-1964
Jadotville is now called Likasi

Chapter One

The hollow whomp-whomp of a pile driver echoed across the fog-bound harbor. Rotterdam, virtually destroyed in the bombing raids of the Second World War, was recovering in the fall of 1957, twelve years after Germany finally surrendered.

The sky was grey with mist. The sea was greasy grey. The workmen on the piers seemed grey and listless. Dirty grey gulls hovered and squawked over dingy grey warehouses. Drops of moisture condensed on the rail of the *Nieuw Amsterdam*. Stewart and I stood silent, surrounded by our four small children, dismayed at the bleak scene. We'd sailed out of New York Harbor eight days ago. The August sun had warmed the deck of the great ship. September caught up with us during the voyage. Summer seemed a memory of long ago.

Flanked by a row of suitcases and carryalls, I shivered in my light-weight coat and helped Mary Beth and Martha button their sweaters. The stevedores shouldered the baggage down the ramp onto the pier. Warm coats, and all our worldly goods, were in those trunks and barrels.

Tim asked about the banging. He was six, the oldest. I explained, as best I could, the principle of the pile driver. I loved to explain things to the children. I recalled a conversation with his kindergarten teacher, back in West Hartford. I could still see her look of dismay when I shared with her our plans to transplant the family to Belgium and the Belgian Congo.

"Tim is one of the brightest children I have ever encountered," she said. "Does your family speak French?"

"Not yet," I said. We'll have a year of language study in Brussels. Tim will pick up the language."

She seemed dubious. Now, facing the reality of the Old World, my confidence ebbed away. What had I done?

Had it been only eight days since our emotional departure from Manhattan? On that sunny morning, Stewart's parents, sister, brothers, aunts, uncles, cousins, and several dozen parishioners from our church in Connecticut had come to wish us Godspeed. Stewart's mother wept at the prospect of losing her entire contingent of grandchildren. She held Martha, the youngest, just a year-and-a-half, in her arms. Martha sucked her thumb and gazed into her grandmother's face. Stewart's father swung three-year-old Mary Beth in his arms, high overhead. "Do it again, Grandpa," she pleaded. Five years would pass before they would be reunited, and she would be too big for their favorite game. Although he supported our adventure, he fought back tears. Stewart asked everyone to gather for a word of prayer. At least he didn't ask us to kneel on the deck. Public demonstrations of faith made me uneasy.

Deep horn blasts ordered all visitors ashore. Family and friends on the pier already seemed far away. "Wave to Grandma Lil," I said. Determined to set a good example, I smiled as the tugs pushed the boat away from the pier. I stepped up onto an iron bar for one last wave. The treacherous piece of metal rolled over onto my left foot. I bit my lip and waved. I hoped they couldn't see my look of agony. The tugs turned the ship, and we sailed slowly down the Hudson River. I limped away in search of the ship's doctor. No permanent damage, but it seemed an ill omen.

I was reluctant to leave the ship. Stewart searched for the driver who would carry us and our baggage to our home in Brussels. "I'll go find the guy," he said. "You and the kids can wait on the pier with our stuff."

"I'll go with you, Dad," Peter said. We'd celebrated his fourth birthday several nights before in our New York hotel room with Hostess Twinkies, not even birthday candles. I vowed to give him a real celebration next year.

We had put our lives in the hands of the Board of Missions of the Methodist Church. Over the years, the name of this body changed several times, but we would usually refer to it as The Board. I'd insisted I would not be separated from my children. I disapproved of the missionaries who sent their young children off to boarding school so they, the parents, could devote all their time to their work. The church fathers assured me my family would always come first. We signed on, and they revealed their true colors. Stewart and I were assigned six weeks of language school in Pennsylvania. No provision for childcare. We were told to "park our children somewhere" for the summer.

We had left our friends and all familiar things, and the parsonage, the only home the children had known. Even if someone in the family had been able to cope with four lively children for six weeks, I couldn't leave them. I was punished for my insubordination. Instead of going directly to Belgium to begin language study there, we were forced to wait for an August sailing when the fares were reduced. The authorities insisted it would be to our advantage to arrive in Belgium with no knowledge of French. That way, they said, we wouldn't have so much to unlearn.

Homeless, we spent a gypsy summer with family and friends. The children took turns in an outbreak of chickenpox. My mother and my sister managed the children for a week while Stewart and I attended a big conference at Purdue University in Indiana. We were officially ordained as missionaries. We met a couple who had just completed their year of study in Brussels. They raved about the apartment they had rented, the best place, the husband said, they had ever lived. He urged us to reserve the place right away. Brussels would be crowded because of the International Exposition. Too late, I discovered his reputation for hyperbole.

That apartment, at 20 Avenue de l'Equinoxe, Woluwe-Saint-Lambert, on the third floor of a five-story row house, was a snug fit for us. We were sandwiched into the middle of the landlord's family—*monsieur* and *madame* and their seven children—their living space below us, sleeping space above us. All rooms opened onto the well-trafficked common stairwell. Without a shared language, we were doomed. Our host family, described by the previous tenants as warm and genial, took an immediate dislike to us. *Madame* found my children *sauvage*, and we never reached a *rapprochement*. The first complete phrase I memorized, "*Cela ne vous regarde pas*," could be roughly translated, "It's none of your business." I resisted temptation and never said it to *madame*. We tolerated each other, but even as I began to speak her language, we were not friends.

Belgium had ruled the Congo since the 1870s. A year of study was required for all missionaries: teachers, preachers, doctors, nurses, administrators, builders, architects, pharmacists, accountants, mechanics. All were subjected to the official Belgian version of the history of their ownership of the Congo. I called it brainwashing.

Stewart attended classes at a school established by the Belgian government for missionaries to the Congo to learn French and colonial history. Madame Fortin was his fierce tutor in French. No longer the popular young pastor of an adoring flock, he suffered tremendous frustration. Eloquent in English, he stumbled in French. The congregation we left behind had sent us off with their blessings to a life of sacrifice and glory. They looked forward to sharing in our mission vicariously, thrilled and awed at the vision of their pastor saving heathen souls. The bishop to whom Stewart reported was less sanguine. Like Stewart's mother, he considered it a foolish move. But there would be no turning back.

I had fought for and won the right to devote my life to my children. Now I must keep my part of the bargain. Tim, Peter, and Mary Beth attended the local public schools. In French. Martha kept me company.

Peter and Mary Beth were assigned to separate classes in the neighborhood preschool. Peter, usually so full of fun, turned an uncomprehending face to his new teacher and clung to me with such tenacity I had to peel his arms away and stumble to the door. Mary Beth, almost three, followed, wide-eyed, her hand clutching mine. In her classroom, she was too frightened to speak or cry. She simply stood there in disbelief as I walked away. Martha howled in my arms. She assumed, no doubt, she would be next in line for abandonment. Tim, armed with only a few words of French, marched stoically into the first-grade class and took the place assigned to him by the stern and pitiless instructor.

The morning dragged on. Shortly before noon, I tucked Martha into her flimsy little blue canvas-and-aluminum stroller—so different from the deluxe chariots in which today's youngsters ride—and walked to the corner to meet the children. Trolley tracks ran down the center of the boulevard, between the lanes of cars and trucks. I never had much confidence in Belgian drivers. In those days, they were not required to have a license. I waited with apprehension for the children. I spotted Mary Beth in a *crocodile* of her contemporaries. She clung to the hand of the little girl beside her, eyes down, mouth clenched in her "I-will-not-cry" expression. She looked as though she had abandoned hope. She saw Martha and me, broke out of line, and ran to us. The teacher frowned her disapproval. I didn't care. Mary Beth and I hugged each other there on the sidewalk.

"I thought you'd given me away," Mary Beth wailed. "I thought I'd never see you again."

Peter appeared, not quite his usual jolly self. He'd made some friends, despite the lack of a common language. Tim came along then, not saying much. After lunch, the children discovered they were expected to go back to school. Another emotional scene followed. We all controlled ourselves on the street corner and the children rejoined their queues. This is the way it would be.

It rained almost every day. Martha and I looked out from our big front window at the apartment across the street. A somber woman and child stared back at us. Downstairs, across the cobblestone street, the grocer, a helpful soul, stood under his awning and watched the rain. He was patient with my pathetic efforts to ask for what I needed. He took time to teach me to pronounce *flocon d'avoine*, oatmeal. At the *Boulangerie* and the *Patisserie*, I could point to what I wanted. For the first time in my life, I felt stupid, confusing stupidity with ignorance. Ignorance can be corrected. Stupid or ignorant, I was humiliated. I had always understood humility as a Christian virtue, but it had never occurred to me humiliation might be a prerequisite for service.

A small radio, fixed to the wall of the dining room, was intended to be dedicated to my comprehension of French. I cheated and listened to the BBC news in English. One October morning, I heard the incredible announcement the Russians had tossed *Sputnik*, the *pamplemousse*, into orbit. The phlegmatic BBC commentator broke from his usual formality and crowed at the consternation of the United States at this unexpected setback. People in the neighborhood smirked their supercilious pleasure to see the Americans put in their place. Not that they liked the Russians. I never understood the anti-American bias. Icy stares in the shops. Sharp elbows in my ribs when Martha and I boarded the trolley. After everything we had done for them. The Marshall Plan, and all that. I was only twenty-nine, young enough to expect gratitude to follow benevolence.

On Sundays, we attended the English-speaking service at the Eglise du Champ de Mars. Thirty American families in the congregation were destined for the Congo, an assortment of what we described as mainline denominations: Presbyterians, Methodists, and Congregationalists. An island of ex-pats in an alien sea, we sought comfort in each other and in our common faith. I found solace in familiar hymns, belted out evangelical paeans of triumphant resolution. Stewart, appointed Assistant Pastor of the flock, delighted in the opportunity to conduct the service and preach in English. With less enthusiasm, I taught a Sunday school class of preschoolers. The children looked forward to Sunday school, not, goodness knows, for the lessons, but for the chance to be with their friends. After the service, the lively American boys and girls ran around the courtyard while the grown-ups lingered over coffee and compared notes on the degradations of the past week.

I wonder now at my conviction of the righteousness of our mission. My letters from those grey days reveal that, as my resolution hardened, I gradually yielded to the seduction of self-resignation and a kind of sick martyrdom. Surely my sacrifices and my unhappiness would be rewarded someday with *Stars In My Crown*.

Within the missionary community, we did our best to care for one another as the Scriptures instructed us. The year of study was a sort of limbo we must pass through on our way to sunny Africa. Most of the other missionaries lived in detached houses, *villas*, all to themselves, with even a yard for the children to play in. They encouraged us to move, reported available *villas* in their neighborhood. We were stubborn, committed to our poor choice.

Stewart bought a blue Volkswagen "bug" in Germany for $1,100, the first new car we had ever owned. On Saturdays, we toured the countryside. Waterloo disappointed, nothing like Gettysburg. Peter asked who had won the battle. I confessed ignorance. Stewart provided an impromptu history lesson for all of us.

The children settled into their school routines better than I had any right to expect. Through the fall, Tim brought home a perfect report card every week. Ten *(dix* in French), sometimes extra points for effort. He was conscientious about his daily homework and soon was able to serve as my interpreter at the neighborhood shops. Gregarious Peter made friends everywhere he went, and Mary Beth brought home stories of her *clique*. "My girls," she called them. Martha bloomed. She had my full attention while the others were in school, a new experience for her, the youngest of the brood.

Stewart's tutor praised him for his diligence. We entertained Madame Fortin for dinner, and she treated me to a concert of Mozart and Brahms at the Palais des Beaux-Arts. The following day she scolded me, furious that Stewart had spent several hours caring for the children while I went to the concert. I had no right, she said, to interfere with his studies.

I engaged a tutor of my own and got to work: *un, deux, trois, quatre, cinq.*

Mary Beth came down with the mumps and couldn't go back to school for twenty-one days. Martha's mumps case was more severe. This was the first time one of my children had been seriously ill. The mission doctors, Duvon and Phyllis Corbitt, were in Antwerp, in the Colonial Studies Program for Physicians. I phoned Duvon, told him about Martha's symptoms. He emphasized the danger of dehydration. I sat up all night in the rocking chair and held Martha in my arms. I gave her a spoonful of water every hour. The next day she was herself again, a miraculous youthful bounce of recovery.

We drove on Mardi Gras to Binche, two hours away, for Carnaval. Snow alternated with sunshine. I appreciated the wool socks hand-knit by Stewart's Grandma Cassie. The beat of the drums and bleat of horns guided us through the crowds of costumed villagers in masks and crazy hats, a city-wide Halloween party. One large contingent wore navy blue tunics, white pants, and feathered hats. Others dressed like Venetian gondoliers or American Indians. A crowd of children streamed by. Pierrots in miniature clown suits and pointed hats jigged along to the beat of the drum, accompanied by a priest, who also jigged. Everyone seemed to jump up and down. I had always considered the Belgians so dour.

Crowds followed the main attraction, the time-honored procession of the Gilles. Dressed in elaborate, traditional costumes with bells jingling and wooden shoes clacking on cobblestones, they clogged solemnly down the street. They looked warm enough, if a bit top-heavy, in padded suits of orange-gold fabric encrusted with heraldic designs in red and black, the puffy bodice topped with a wide lace collar with gold trim. They wore white knit caps with long tails coming down over the ears and fastened under the chin. Later, after lunch, many of them added a spectacular headdress of ostrich plumes. Each man carried a mesh bag of oranges—missiles, it turned out. Along with everyone else, we dodged the oranges, tried to catch them, chased them as they rolled down the street.

After Mardi Gras came Ash Wednesday, a day of penitence marking the beginning of Lent. We returned from Carnaval to learn that the children's school was closed because of an outbreak of diphtheria. One child had died. Our children were in no danger, as they had been vaccinated. I could hardly believe the Belgian children had not been inoculated. I was told that during the Occupation, the Germans forced vaccination on everyone. The Belgians, resentful at being told what to do, never forgave them.

All the school children reported for throat tests once a week. Mary Beth's first test showed her to be a "carrier." Carrier? I asked the missionary doctor, how she could be a carrier when she had been inoculated. He said the diphtheria germ is very hard to identify. He doubted very much she was a "carrier" and, even if she was, it didn't mean anything. We still had to comply with their regulations. Mary Beth couldn't go back to school for two months. Peter and Tim would need three clear tests in a row before they could rejoin society. The school itself was disinfected, closed for at least three weeks.

Bad news for me, in the depths of winter. I put my language study on hold and searched our supply of amusements for books we hadn't read, games they might have forgotten about, new crayons. The children helped me bake bread. A box of Valentine makings arrived, too late for the day itself, but just in time to divert us. We sat around the dining room table, cut and pasted, glued, and scotch-taped strings of hearts and doilies around the apartment.

The dismal weather kept us indoors. Four cardboard cartons entertained the children one day. They made a train, each of them in a box. They instructed Stewart where to cut holes for arms and legs and became a family of robots. Before they went to bed, they turned into turtles, just like robots, only on all fours.

The weeks crawled by. My cheery facade crumbled into fragments. The children and I grew impatient with each other. They quarreled and I snapped at them. The despair I tried to stuff down inside myself would not be contained. If we were at home in America, this wouldn't have happened. In memory, the cramped parsonage in West Hartford took on a rosy glow. I forgot the ugly wallpaper, the balky stove, the church ladies critical of my easygoing housekeeping habits, their disapproval of Cheerios on the carpet. Whatever made me think I could live in an apartment where the children were expected to be quiet, in a country where I couldn't understand what people said, or talk to them? Where my children had no place to play outside except the sidewalk, and there was no way for them to come back inside unless I went down two flights of stairs to open the door? And Madame scolded them. She had just washed the sidewalk. Washed the sidewalk! The Belgian children in the park were always perfectly dressed, the little ones in hand-knit outfits. When they played in the sandbox their mamas tied a plastic bag around their waist so they wouldn't get dirty. Not get dirty, in a sandbox? The Belgian children sat quietly, never ran around and hollered like normal kids.

My children hadn't asked to come here. It had been my idea. I was the one who had experienced a genuine call, like Samuel in the Old Testament. We had been sure the church fathers would never accept us, with four little children, but they did. They were that desperate. Here we were, in godforsaken Belgium, and it was all my fault.

Across the street at the *épicerie*, I waited in line to pay for my *flocon d'avoine* and some *speculoos*, crisp gingerbread cookies shaped like windmills. One of the women ahead of me said something about *les Americains*. I strained to hear. The Americans, she said, were responsible for the outbreak of diphtheria, for the death of the child, because they carried the germs. I set my groceries down and left the store. Were the

Americans responsible for everything bad that happened? And the obstinate Belgians still wouldn't inoculate their children.

At least we could still go to church and Sunday school. Then one of the mothers discovered her child had been in the same room with Mary Beth, a "carrier." She telephoned all the other mothers to tell them their children had been exposed to diphtheria. This was too much. One of the missionaries, for heaven's sake, an American. Didn't she know better? Was she as ill-informed as the Belgians?

A Belgian woman who spoke English came in occasionally to stay with the children when I could schedule a session with my tutor. She fell on the ice and suffered a brain concussion. While I searched for a replacement, my tutor called to say she was pregnant and would have to suspend our infrequent lessons for a while. I felt like a leper. Perhaps I should ring a little bell to warn people off.

Reading my letters home, written in those dark days, I trace my struggle not to give in to despair. I tried the light touch, mentioned the advent of spring, lilacs in bud. I invoked religion, admonished myself not to expect an easy road to glory. Surely it would all be better when we got to the Congo. I philosophized about discrimination against foreigners and hoped I had given others the benefit of the doubt back home in America. Nothing worked. I'm sure my letters didn't fool anybody. I was miserable and everybody knew it.

Lent melted into Easter, and the season of deprivation ended. Winter gave way to spring, and school reopened. Perhaps the Belgian parents were also suffering from the constant presence of their children. No more was said of throat swabs or carriers. I enrolled at the Alliance Française, moved quickly through the first level, and sailed into the second. Somewhere I have a certificate to prove that, at one time, I showed promise in French.

I farmed out the children for a day and went to the Keukenhof Gardens in Holland to see the acres of tulips in bloom. The shop windows in Brussels were filled with hyacinths. Crocuses bloomed in the park.

During the winter we'd followed the progress of the International Exposition. The site morphed from a muddy mess to a world-class attraction. The massive Russian Pavilion and the American Pavilion vied for pride of place. The Atomium towered above like an oversized toy.

We bought season passes. Stewart arranged to preach at the Protestant Pavilion, in the Belgian section, close to the Atomium. On opening day, a sunny day in April, we joined the crowds thronging the pathways. We commandeered a bench and unwrapped our sandwiches, watched the passing parade, and set aside our troubles. Flowers bloomed everywhere. Fountains splashed and murmured. Bands played. Everyone smiled. Americans recognized us by our clothes and Martha's stroller. "Where're you from?" we asked each other in the easy familiarity of Americans abroad.

We couldn't get enough of the American Pavilion. Apple trees blossomed and graceful fountains played. Attractive young college students welcomed the visitors and answered questions in an impressive number of languages.

Most of all I loved the carillon. The carillonneur sat at the keyboard in a glass booth—high up in a tower among the bells. He struck the keys with his fists to unleash the music. The bells pealed their glorious sonority. He played for an hour and descended the long, spiral stairway as though he were floating through the air.

June was a cold, rainy month. The children successfully completed the school year; Stewart failed to pass his exams. In spite of his diligence, he just couldn't overcome the handicap of coming into class with no prior knowledge of French. His professor commended him for his effort and suggested he stay on until January and re-take the exams, as many of the missionaries did. It was not unusual to fail on the first attempt. Madame Fortin was angry with him. Her students didn't fail. I shared Stewart's frustration, but the thought of six more months in Brussels was unbearable.

Stewart was not one to accept this judgment lightly. He smarted from his failure. He sent a cable to the bishop in Africa. We waited, with apprehension, for instructions.

Early one morning the doorbell rang. Stewart ran downstairs. "It's a cable from the bishop," he said when he caught his breath. "Listen to this. 'Come ahead as planned. We need you here to get the school year underway. The people are waiting for you. It doesn't matter about the exam.'"

He looked at me in wonderment. We hugged each other in excitement and relief. The children, still in their pajamas, looked on, wide-eyed in confusion.

"What's going on?" Tim asked.

"We're going to Africa," Stewart said.

The American Ambassador phoned to ask if we would like to attend the special Fourth of July celebration at the Expo. Stewart would represent the American Protestant presence at the concert by the Philadelphia Orchestra. I took his white dinner jacket and formal shirt out of the trunk and shook out the wrinkles. I looked through my wardrobe for something festive. I decided on a pale-yellow linen dress Stewart's mother had passed on to me.

On the gala evening, our special pass admitted us to the VIP parking area among the Mercedes and Cadillacs. We found our seats in the second row, behind the archbishop. I nudged Stewart. "Purple socks," I whispered. The American Ambassador introduced former President Herbert Hoover, a hero to the Europeans for his efforts on their behalf after both the World Wars. He stepped up onto the podium to the cheers of the crowd. He looked pretty good for eighty-three. He knocked over the music stand on which he had placed his notes, grabbed the papers in midair, and went right ahead with his speech. We were so close I could read his notes, underlined, printed in big letters.

The orchestra members moved their chairs forward to the edge of the platform, so close I could almost pat the cellos. When Eugene Ormandy came to the podium, I nearly fainted from excitement. Isaac Stern played Mendelssohn's Violin Concerto in E minor, Op. 64 with tremendous brio. He broke a string and tossed his Stradivarius to the concertmaster, who extended his own violin to Stern. Neither of them missed more than a note or two. I could see every drop of sweat on Stern's brow. When he finished, I leaped to my feet with everyone else and applauded until my hands stung. I shouted, "Bravo."

After the interval, the orchestra played the Brahms Symphony No 1 in C minor, Op. 68, one of my favorites. I dozed off, exhausted from the excitement. I woke up as the orchestra swung into "The Stars and Stripes Forever." During this year of self-imposed exile, I had become a patriot, maybe even a jingoist. Tears ran down my face as the orchestra tore into the coda, the horns blared, the tuba thumped, the piccolo trilled like a demented mockingbird.

In two months, we would be in Jadotville. Before we left West Hartford, we had met the family who would be our neighbors. We had seen snapshots of our home. Someone had sketched the floor plan, and the children had chosen their rooms.

I thought I knew something about Africa. I had read Joseph Conrad's *Heart of Darkness* and missionary biographies and autobiographies, most of them hagiographies. I'd just finished a terrifying book, *Something of Value* by Robert Ruark, about the Mau Mau uprising in Kenya. Surely he exaggerated. Anyway, they wouldn't murder missionaries, would they?

We had given only cursory attention to the African exhibits at the Expo. Now that we had a departure date, I found myself drawn again and again to the Congo Pavilion. We pushed our way to the front of the crowds, struggling to keep hold of the children's hands. Martha snoozed in her stroller. Pressed up against the low wooden railing, I stared at real Africans, twenty feet away, brought all the way from Africa for my entertainment, and displayed in a model village like lions in a zoo.

During the year, we had come to know several Africans who had converted to Christianity. They spoke excellent French and English and dressed as we did: the men in suits, white shirts, and neckties, the women in print dresses, stockings, and low-heeled shoes. They were nothing like these imported Congolese on view at the Expo, exotic in their bright wax-print costumes, a *tableau vivant* right out of *National Geographic* magazine, except that all breasts were modestly concealed in the yards of cloth in which the women wrapped themselves from head to toe. Secured by a multicolored wrap, the babies rode on their mother's backs. Their little heads bounced as the women pounded manioc roots—known in the West as cassava—into a coarse flour. Two women worked in tandem, chanted, alternately brought hefty four-foot pestles down on the manioc in a hollowed-log mortar with a thunk-thunk. They sifted handfuls of the flour into steaming cast-iron cauldrons with boiling water, balanced on stones over open fires. They vigorously stirred the thick porridge, *bukadi*, sometimes called *ugali*, with wooden paddles two or three feet long.

The men clustered under the trees, talking, occasionally calling encouragement to the women who performed the heavy labor and, I supposed, asking when dinner would be ready. The women dished up the porridge in large enamel bowls, and the families sat around on low stools and ate their dinner. Toppings included reconstituted dried fish, red-hot little peppers called *pilipili*, or chopped greens. Diners rolled lumps of *bukadi* into bite-size balls, made a depression with a thumb to scoop up toppings, and put them into their mouths. The mamas made little balls and popped them into the mouths of the babies. From time to time, the babies disappeared into the voluminous folds of cloth to nurse. All the Africans on display seemed oblivious to the close-packed spectators who commented on every movement in a babel of languages. Signs posted in several European languages identified the tribal groups represented.

The men brought out musical instruments, drums of all shapes and sizes, marimbas with dried gourds for resonators, rattles, and hand pianos. They sang in complex rhythms and harmonies and danced in repetitive moves, shuffled and stamped and jumped into the air. The women formed their own group as they, too, sang and danced and clapped in rhythm. My heart beat faster. I discreetly tapped my foot. I longed to call attention to myself, to let the other spectators know I was special, destined to live and work among these exotic folks.

Across the barrier, the Africans ignored the audience. I wondered if they had been instructed to do that. They seemed happy to be here. They had been under the close scrutiny of Europeans for years, and now, at the Exposition, they basked in friendly faces. What a fine opportunity for them to see more of the world, I thought, to see how *we* lived.

I recognize my complicity in the spectacle, but I thought then that my good intentions put me in a separate category. I wanted only what was best for the Congolese, to help them become more like us. Like me. I wasn't alone. Generations of well-meaning souls have fallen into that trap.

While I dreamed of the day we would leave dismal Belgium for the sunny Congo, the Congolese people retreated to their dormitories after hours on display at the Pavilion. In this unprecedented experience, they mingled with people of other tribes. They used their common trade languages, Swahili and Lingala, to get to know each other and exchange stories. Back home in the Congo, the Belgians had kept the people of various tribes isolated from each other. Here at the Exposition, aware for the first time of the puny size of the country that had made slaves of them, the Congolese found common ground. They explored the city, shopped, and ate in restaurants where they were served by white waiters.

So few had controlled so many for so long. The seeds of rebellion had begun to germinate here, under the noses of the Belgians, in the shadow of the Atomium that loomed over the Exposition grounds like a giant Tinkertoy.

Chapter Two

The little child, three years old, perched on a blue-painted stool in the sunny kitchen and watched her mother knead bread dough. Her mother put a lot of energy into it, leaned into it, rotated the mound of dough, leaned into it. The little girl's nose wrinkled with the fresh smell of yeast. The dome-shaped Philco radio on the counter poured out glorious music, Dr. Damrosch and the New York Philharmonic Orchestra, *The Music Appreciation Hour*. Violins shimmered; horns blasted.

"*The Ride of the Valkyries*," the mother said.

"What are *vawl kee rees*?" the child asked.

"Warrior maidens who carry the fallen warriors off to heaven."

"What do they look like?"

The mother smiled, plopped the dough into a brown crockery bowl, covered it with a dishtowel, and brushed the flour from her hands. She brought crayons and paper.

"Draw what the music tells you," she said.

The child drew a red-and-yellow angel flying into the clouds and entered a lifelong affair with classical music.

My mother saved my artwork. It's there, someplace, in a trunk with other important papers.

I sat with children my own age on small wooden chairs in the basement of the First Presbyterian Church. My dad was church treasurer. My mother served as superintendent of Sunday school. My older sister and her contemporaries occupied full-size chairs in another room. My little brother was in the nursery. My beloved Aunt Betsy held a placard on which were printed three letters.

"Who can tell me what these letters are?" she asked.

I wriggled in my chair and waved my hand. "I know! I know! It's J-O-Y."

Aunt Betsy beamed at me. "Yes," she said. "It spells J-O-Y." She pointed to each letter in turn. "To find JOY, you must put Jesus first, Others second, Yourself last."

I wanted to be joyous, like Aunt Betsy. Now I knew what to do. Somewhere in that trunk with the Valkyrie rested a crackled sheet of cardboard, festooned with stars, one for each book of the Bible. All my classmates are listed. I'm the only one to memorize all the names of all the books in the Bible—Old Testament and New Testament. Years passed before I heard the word "precocious." My mother worried about the sin of pride.

Six years old, I was the focus of all the ladies in my mother's afternoon reading circle. My mother had sewed my dress, with smocking on the yoke and a big sash. I dipped a perfect curtsey and recited a poem.

"I have a little shadow that goes in and out with me ..."

Eight years old, I followed my mother down the gloomy corridor of the Ripley Hotel. I had never been in a hotel. My mother carried a tray of ceramic cups of baked custard covered with a linen double-damask cloth, one of her best. A woman rested on a high bed in the darkened room, propped up by big pillows, General Evangeline Booth Demarest, daughter of General William Booth, founder of the Salvation Army.

"Bless you," the lady said in a gentle voice, so different from the dramatic voice in which she preached the evangelistic services every evening that week at the Presbyterian Church. And the singing! The singing! I had no idea the congregation could sing like that. "Praise the Lord! Praise the Lord!"

"God bless you for your kindness," the lady said. I never forgot the look of awe on my mother's face. I wondered what I might do, someday, to merit such a look.

My junior high school English teacher loved Shakespeare. She considered his work appropriate for adolescents. My pals and I adored her. We hung out in her classroom after school. I memorized great chunks of the Bard, on tap, still, in memory. I fell in love with iambic pentameter.

"Those friends thou hast, and their adoption tried ..."

The Second World War cast a grim shadow over my high school years. Boys I knew were drafted, or volunteered. Either way, they disappeared. Some of them died. I saved aluminum foil and rubber bands.

Debate was big in high school in Kansas, second only to basketball. Boys' basketball. No self-respecting girl would play by those dumb rules for girls.

I was recruited for the debate team when I was a freshman. Sassy, smart, competitive, I was born for this. My colleagues and I addressed serious subjects. We built our arguments with great care.

"Resolved: that the United States should join in reconstituting the League of Nations."

"Resolved: that the voting age should be lowered to eighteen."

I moved seamlessly from the affirmative side to the negative. It didn't matter what I believed. I could make a convincing case for either side. I came to understand the devious ways of politics and politicians. I rose through the ranks and became a star. We traveled on weekends to grapple with teams all over the state. In my senior year, our team won the state championships, and I had the highest speaker rankings. The basketball team came in second in the state finals that year. The school mourned. The awards ceremony was awkward. Debaters were not supposed to outperform athletes. Especially girls. Especially basketball players. In Kansas, basketball was king.

The boys on the debate squad looked forward to university, fraternities, preparing for careers as attorneys, professors, or preachers. My options were limited. I could be a teacher, a nurse, or a secretary. Or a wife. And mother.

I graduated from high school as the war in the Pacific ended. I was barely seventeen. I wanted to go to the University of Cincinnati and study archeology. No matter. I was predestined to attend the College of

Emporia, a small Presbyterian school in a town seventy miles from home on the Santa Fe line.

I majored in English literature. My favorite professor loved the Victorians, so, of course, I loved them too. Especially Tennyson, the rhyming schemes, the rhythm of the lines, the mystery and beauty of those luscious words, sweet in the mouth as hand-churned fresh peach ice cream.

"Come into the garden, Maude,
For the black bat, night, has flown."

My parents, the first college graduates in their families, met and fell in love at Fairmount College, now the University of Wichita, Kansas.

My mother's mother, Rose Belle Payne Hutchison, interrupted her education in Cincinnati to accompany her brothers to homestead in Oklahoma. I treasure a photograph of her on her horse, with her dog and her Winchester rifle. She married my grandad, a Texas Ranger and Indian Agent. He was a generation older, with grown daughters. They lived for a time in a sod house on the Osage Indian Reservation in northeastern Oklahoma. My mother was the oldest of four children. When she and her younger sister were ready for school, the family moved to a farm in Wichita. Mother and her younger sister, Marian, would have the education their mother had forfeited when she went to Oklahoma. They were brilliant students, Mother in mathematics, Marian in chemistry.

My dad interrupted his college education and joined the Army. It was called "The war to end all wars." Senior officers discovered that dad spoke both French and German. They hauled him out of the trenches and put him to work as a translator. He never talked about the war. Ever.

He and my mother married and moved into my grandfather's house in Newton, Kansas, in what was never intended to be a permanent solution. The Depression intervened. They raised their family, comprised of me, my older sister and younger brother, in the house my *grosspapa* had built. My dad was office manager and chief accountant for the Kansas Gas and Electric Company. He kept that job through the Great Depression and stayed with it until he retired. He rejected every opportunity for advancement. Better to be safe.

While my dad was overseas, my mother taught high school mathematics in a small town in Kansas. She coached the girls' basketball team, the boys' basketball team, and, finally, the football team. She'd learned team sports from her brothers. She didn't talk much about those years on her own. The high school yearbook pictures of her showed a young teacher who was beautiful, determined, and sweetly proud.

My dad came home from the war a broken soul. Mother devoted herself to his recovery. She had to give up her teaching career when they married. It's hard to imagine, today, that married women were not allowed to teach or coach in public schools. She found other opportunities to use her talent for instruction. She made sure I learned my algebra.

She taught Sunday school and women's Bible classes. She was a far better teacher than the men who taught the men's Bible classes. Many years later, she was elected an elder of the church, a great honor for Presbyterians. She was the first woman to hold that office in the local congregation. Years later, she was elected to the local board of education, another first for a woman. My dad was so proud of her.

The local Presbyterian church sponsored missionaries who lived and worked in India. Our family befriended them. The missionary family came home to Kansas on furlough every four years, and my mother and the missionary mom became close friends. Mother seemed to understand the impulse to serve God in faraway places.

You don't have to be a soothsayer to see what's coming. Bright kid, church-going parents, importance of education, and that wild-card grandpa, Texas Ranger and Indian Agent, another strand to braid in.

My first sight of Stewart stopped me in my tracks. My roommate and I watched from the window of our room in the college dormitory. "Who's that guy?" I asked.

"He's new," she said, "from back East."

I took an immediate dislike to his air of assurance. "Who does he think he is? And what's was he doing here? Probably thinks he's too good for Kansas," I said. "Look at him, arrogant snob, with his necktie and his tweed jacket." The other guys on campus wore blue jeans or khakis, open-collared sport shirts, athletic warm-up jackets.

Stewart wasn't taken with me either. He considered me an unsophisticated hayseed with an opinion on everything. My blue jeans offended him. He said they were inappropriate for campus wear.

Yet, thrown together on the college debate team, our scrappy antagonism made Stewart and me interesting partners. We engaged each other's minds and explored each other's intelligence. He knew about mythology, theology, politics. He didn't know anything about music. I boasted a lifetime of piano lessons and an impressive knowledge of classical music. I sang alto in the glee club, mixed chorus, and played timpani in the orchestra. Neither of us was interested in football.

We couldn't seem to leave each other alone. He was presentable, well-spoken, intelligent, tall enough. He liked the way I walked. Nobody had ever said that to me. He had a compelling voice and beautiful green eyes, shielded by horned-rim glasses. He had better manners than the boys from the farm. Destined for the ministry, he preached on Sunday mornings in a little country church nearby in Saffordville. He didn't plan to spend his life in Kansas.

We studied together in the library, sat across the table from each other. One evening he pulled an eight-by-ten black-and-white photograph from a manila envelope and pushed it across the table to present a formidable man, well past middle age, face like a bulldog, mop of white hair, immaculate stiff collar, necktie, vest draped with watch chain.

"Who's that old goat?" I whispered. The librarian looked up, shook her finger at me. Quiet in the library.

Stewart sat up straight, leaned away, frowned.

"That," he said, sotto voce, "is my father."

He let me sweat for a while before he confessed it was Raymond Baldwin, a politician from Connecticut whom he had met at the Republican National Convention.

"You were a delegate to the Republican National Convention?" I asked, impressed in spite of myself.

He laughed. "No, my uncle Harry took me along to experience the convention. We supported Robert Taft."

I rolled my eyes. "I met General Eisenhower once," I whispered. "He's from Kansas, you know. From Abilene."

The librarian glared at us and rapped for silence.

Off-campus on a debate trip, Stewart offered to give me some pointers on my chess game. We sat on the floor in his room in the hotel, the chessboard between us. I looked into his eyes, saw a spark I hadn't seen before. We leaned forward into a kiss, set the chessboard aside and my life changed. I fell in love with Stewart. My mother had told me I'd know when the right one came along.

The Dean of Students liked us both and had congratulated us on our engagement. "You make a good team. And you'll never be bored."

Side by side on the scratchy seats on the train, we were on the way to my home for Thanksgiving weekend. My parents adored Stewart. They couldn't believe I had captured such a prize. The train smelled musty. Hot, dry air puffed out of the ventilator at my feet. I slipped off my shoes. The monotonous clickety-clack, clickety-clack of the wheels on the rails reminded me I was working against time. After we finished college, Stewart looked forward to the seminary. There was no wife in that picture. After graduation, when he had his own pulpit and congregation, it would be time to think of marriage and a family. Yet here he was, ambushed by an attractive, determined young Presbyterian virgin from a respectable Midwestern family, who would expect wedlock to follow as the night the day. Sometimes I felt sorry for Stewart, sideswiped on his way to his own intended destiny. He never knew what hit him, not then, not now, after thirty years of marriage and forty of divorce.

I was eager to show off my engagement ring with its tiny diamond chip. This Thanksgiving would be an ideal time to set the date for our wedding. My parents would be so pleased. My mother would need time to make my dress. I glanced over at Stewart. He was reading.

"Stewart, have you thought about when we might get married?"

He didn't look up. "No need to rush. Being engaged is about all I can handle right now."

I stared out the window at fields of wheat stubble sticking up through the snow. Cattle stared stupidly at the train. Restless, I wanted to talk. Stewart was absorbed in *The Confessions of Saint Augustine*. I wondered what sins the saint had to confess.

"I think we should discuss our plans for the wedding."

He looked over the top of his glasses at me and put his finger in the book to mark his place. "I need to get on with this reading assignment. There'll be plenty of time to talk about marriage."

I pouted. "You don't love me," I accused.

"Don't be ridiculous."

I sulked. He relented. We compromised on a June wedding, twenty months in the future, after graduation. He went back to his book. This wasn't the way I had imagined it would be. Weren't we supposed to be giddy with joy and expectation?

We were married in the sanctuary of the red brick Presbyterian church in which I had spent every Sunday of my childhood.

Marriage was one thing; parenthood was something else. When the doctor confirmed my pregnancy, I rushed home to our basement apartment, eager to share the excitement with Stewart. He was not pleased.

"You know I'm getting ready for seminary," he reminded me, as though I might have forgotten. He had a full scholarship. He had never pictured himself entering those hallowed halls with a wife, let alone a pregnant wife. "Are you sure you're pregnant?"

"Of course I'm sure. I didn't do this all by myself, you know. You were there. It takes two."

Stewart persuaded me to delay joining him at Perkins Theological Seminary at Southern Methodist Seminary in Dallas until after the baby was born. I would wait out the pregnancy at home with my parents.

My mother and dad were kind and considerate and asked no questions. They cared for me as though it was the most natural thing in the world to have a newly married pregnant daughter in the house. Tim was born two days after our first wedding anniversary.

When he was two weeks old, he and I joined Stewart in Texas. We moved into the dormitory for married students with children. It was hot. Tim never wore his cute little baby clothes. Even a diaper seemed too much. The following summer I was pregnant again. Tim was fifteen months old when Peter arrived. Stewart finished the seminary in an accelerated course and accepted an invitation from a church in West Hartford,

Connecticut, near Winsted, where his family lived. We loaded the boys and everything we owned, mostly cartons of books, into our station wagon, a classic old Chrysler "Woodie."

In West Hartford, Stewart came into his own. The congregation was primarily Swedish. He won their hearts and minds. The parsonage sat close by the church, separated by a narrow corridor of sidewalk. The pastor would be on call at all times. A committee of church ladies responsible for overseeing the upkeep of the parsonage found fault with my casual housekeeping. The congregation resented my demands on their adored pastor. Who could blame him if he preferred their admiration to the complaints of a nagging wife and the needs of two lively little boys? Oh no. Pregnant again. Mary Beth's sunny, blue-eyed blondeness delighted the Swedes.

In 1955, a disastrous hurricane and flood swept through New England and wiped out Stewart's father's business. Their home on the hill was undamaged, but it would be years before the town recovered. For Stewart's mother, my fourth pregnancy was one more disaster. "First the flood," she said, "and now this." Martha Rose completed our family. There were no more babies.

Resigned to the fecundity of the pastor's wife, the church ladies organized childcare during the worship services. Word reached the missionaries-in-training at the Hartford Seminary, less than a mile away, and young families showed up at our church. Their enthusiasm for service overseas was contagious: "Come join us. The need is great, especially in Africa."

You would think the needs of four small children would be sufficient, but my early attraction to foreign missions was rekindled. There were advantages to consider: a sunny climate and no parsonage committee.

Stewart's career trajectory didn't include service overseas. He had just persuaded the burgeoning congregation to relocate and build a large new sanctuary. They were deep in architectural drawings and financial prognostications.

Missionaries like to tell stories about their call to service, dreams, visions, visitations. For some, it's a gradual awareness of people in need. Others are called to save heathen souls from eternal damnation. Some just seem to drift into it. As a child in Sunday school, I learned about Samuel, the boy who heard a voice calling in the night. He responded, "Speak, Lord, Thy servant heareth." Heady stuff for an imaginative child.

And so it came to pass that I had a dream, or a vision, and God spoke to me. In my dream, I saw the continent of Africa, as though I were floating high in the air. It was night, and beyond the solemn blackness of the Sahara, a few tiny lights twinkled on the dark continent. I sensed a Presence beside me, and I marveled at the mysterious sight. I recognized my destiny: to go there. I don't remember any words. I felt an upwelling in my heart and overwhelming gratitude, as though I had been given an extravagant and unexpected gift. I felt chosen, blessed.

The flickering lights faded from my vision. Nothing like this had ever happened to me before, nor has it since. I could not possibly comprehend the magnitude of this change.

Breakfast at the parsonage was not the time to share my deepest thoughts. The children dribbled milk and orange juice onto the placemats and scattered cereal on the floor. Martha, in her highchair, banged her spoon, demanded Cheerios. Stewart finished his coffee and stood up.

"Could you wait a few minutes?" I said, "I have something to tell you."

He turned pale. "You're not ..."

I laughed. "No, I'm not pregnant. It's something else."

Stewart shepherded the children out to the sun porch to watch cartoons on the little black-and-white television. I sat at the table, dreaming. He came back into the kitchen, frowning, apprehensive. He hated surprises.

"I had a dream last night, more like a vision, I guess. God is calling us to go to Africa."

Stewart sat down, put his briefcase on the floor, and stared at me. He studied me as though I were a problem to be solved, a look with which I came to be too familiar. Why had I thought he would be pleased?

"Don't you think," he said at last, "if God wanted us to go to Africa, he would have spoken to me?"

I couldn't argue with that. God had called me, and I had taken for granted it included him. And the children. I didn't know what to say.

Stewart stood, picked up his briefcase. "People are waiting for me at the office. We can talk about this later." From the kitchen window, I watched him cross the narrow passage between the parsonage and the church and disappear from sight.

Back in our courting days, Stewart's first gift to me was a leather-bound copy of *The Cloister and the Hearth*. Him for the cloister, me for the hearth.

I went about my chores. I cleaned up the kitchen, carried dirty clothes to the basement, and loaded them into the washing machine. I made the beds, picked up clothes, settled arguments, wiped noses, made peanut-butter-and-jelly sandwiches. I felt again an inner glow, rekindled. I had been chosen for a higher calling. I washed the lunch dishes, trying to decide which ones we would take with us to Africa and which ones I would give away. I ironed Stewart's weekly allotment of eight white shirts, two for Sunday, a fresh one for the evening service. Every so often I did a sort of inner check, and yes, the voice was still there inside me.

Stewart was patient and reasonable. He reminded me of his own calling, how difficult it would be for him to leave the congregation just as the building program was getting underway. His people depended on him, looked to him for guidance and comfort.

"Have you thought about the children?" he asked. "Our children?"

"Of course I've thought about the children. How could I not? I think about them constantly. I spend every waking hour taking care of their needs. I know, the timing seems off, but we can work it out. Lots of other families do."

"I don't know. It just doesn't make sense to me."

"But what about the voice? The Call."

He didn't have an answer for that. To his credit, he never said I must have been imagining things. My call to Africa filled up a lot of space in the house. We couldn't ignore it, and we couldn't seem to settle it. I became desperate, as though there were some urgent task I must perform.

I told Stewart's father we were going to Africa. He was appalled, as well he might. These were his only grandchildren, and they had a mutual adoration society with him. I held out for two weeks, but the drops of water failed to make an impression on the stone. Stewart maintained his busy schedule and waited for me to get over it.

I was never very good at prayer. "Could you just go over that part again, God? Did I hear that right?"

One night after the children had finally gone to sleep, I collapsed into a comfortable old chair on the sun porch to watch *Oedipus Rex*. As the drama unfolded, there seemed to be a message in there for me, the dangerous power of obsession. If I didn't give up this notion of going to Africa, I would ruin our lives. I felt a bleak sadness and grief for what might have been.

Stewart came home. I told him, "It's over. We don't have to go to Africa."

I thought he would be relieved. I felt a sick nobility, the seductive satisfaction of self-denial. He put his briefcase aside, sat down, and stared at me. He looked exhausted.

"I spent the evening calling on new people in the neighborhood. I get a monthly list from the Welcome Wagon, you know, prospective church members. Everywhere I went, several other ministers had been there before me."

I was not surprised. Two other Methodist churches lay within a mile of ours.

"I thought about that," he said. "Why should we compete with each other for members when those people in Africa have nobody? I can't get those needy Africans off my mind. Maybe we should talk to The Board. With all these little kids, they'll probably turn us down anyway, but we could try."

And we did.

The application process went smoothly. If The Board had concerns about so many small children, they didn't mention it. Bishop Newell Booth, presiding bishop of the Southern Congo Conference, would have the final say. Bishop and Mrs. Booth arranged to come to West Hartford to meet us, the latest new candidates for Africa. Eager to make a good impression, I invited them for dinner.

The bishop preached the morning service. His eloquence held the congregation spellbound. He described the work of the Methodist mission in the Katanga province of the Congo. He named the cities where the Methodists had established churches and schools: Elisabethville, Kolwezi, and a mining city called Jadotville, home of the central-processing plants for one of the richest aggregations of strategic minerals in the world: copper, cobalt, and uranium. The Congolese were crying out to hear the Good News of the Gospel, and the mission desperately needed a minister to supervise the African pastors who served the one hundred and twenty churches in the huge Jadotville district. Most of those pastors had only rudimentary training and longed to learn more. The mood of Stewart's congregation, determined to hold onto their pastor, shifted to excitement about the great task to which we planned to pledge our lives.

Before the church service, I'd put a roast in the oven and an apple pie. I set the table with the lace tablecloth and our best dishes. We gathered around the table. Martha, only a few months old, woke from her nap. Mrs. Booth held out her arms for the wailing baby, soothed her, and offered to feed her while Stewart carved and served the roast. Bishop Booth told us about the home that waited for us, a large comfortable house with three bedrooms, designed and built by Victor Longfield for Bishop and Mrs. Springer—the pioneer bishop and his wife—in 1928.

"That's the year I was born," I exclaimed.

The bishop passed around pictures of the house, small black-and-white photos with deckled edges. "It's a good place to raise a family," he said.

I glanced around the cramped dining room of the parsonage, the garish wallpaper with deep-purple cabbage roses and creeping vines. I had not been consulted about that wallpaper. Outside the windows, dirty snow covered the ground. No more snowsuits, I thought, no more wet mittens on the radiator. No more interminable winter colds.

I cleared the table and carried in the pie, redolent of cinnamon and nutmeg, the golden-brown crust fluted around the edge as my mother had taught me. I basked in the murmurs of appreciation as I levered the first slice onto a dessert plate. My heart sank. The flour-dusted apple slices lay in gooey grey liquid, not baked long enough for the luscious syrup to form. I groaned. Stewart looked up from his conversation with the bishop.

"The pie isn't done," I said.

"It looks all right to me," the bishop said briskly, holding out his plate. "Apple pie is my favorite. Mrs. Booth often bakes a pie like that."

She raised her eyebrows in surprise.

The Booths were famously successful in recruiting missionaries. When they first came to the Congo in 1944, only four families were serving in his area. By 1960, there were fifty missionaries, three of whom were the children of early volunteers.

I served the pie, and we ate it. "Good pie," the bishop said and smiled at me. I decided then and there I could trust Bishop Booth with our lives. This proved to be true.

Why did I go to Africa? You could say it was all because of an apple pie.

Chapter Three

A plume of fine red dust drifted up behind the car and settled into the trees. We crept down the long driveway toward the house and parked beside the low hibiscus hedge.

"Wake up, kids," Stewart said. "We're home."

Mary Beth and the boys sat up, rubbed their eyes, and stared out the windows. Martha slept in my arms, her blue traveling dress of polished cotton wrinkled and scrunched up, her curls matted with perspiration.

The house looked exactly like the snapshots Bishop Booth had shown us two years before. Mellow, antiquated, it had survived many storms and would shelter our family through many more. The wide over-hang of the red corrugated-metal roof shaded generous windows set deep into weathered brick walls. Not American bricks: hand-size, hard-edged, symmetrical. Oh no. These were African bricks: dried in the sun, irregular, formed of the same soil from which the red dust floated. A thrill of deep satisfaction ran through me. At last, home.

Had it been just yesterday that Tim and Peter had led the way, scampering up the aluminum stairs to board the Sabena plane for Elisabethville? Mary Beth had gripped my hand and Stewart carried Martha in his arms. Comfortable seats, smiling attendants, menu choices. We had survived the Grey Year. The engines roared. We lumbered down the runway and rose into the sky—on our way, at last, to sunny Congo.

The Swiss Alps scrolled by far below, then the boot of Italy and the Mediterranean Sea. The sun set as we landed in Tripoli to refuel. The plane droned on in the dark, southward, ever southward. Clusters of lights marked towns and villages, then fewer and fewer isolated lights—campfires, maybe—until, finally, nothing below us but blackness and the vast desert. I felt as though I had been here before. My long-ago dream of Africa. I slept, woke, and slept again.

Dawn came; passengers began to stir. The children stretched, looked around. The endless green of the jungle unrolled below. "When are we going to get there?" Peter asked.

I smiled. "Soon."

The flight attendants collected pillows, folded blankets, brought coffee, milk, and little rolls. It seemed like a dream. We gathered our belongings, stumbled up the aisle and down the stairs onto the tarmac. Bishop and Mrs. Booth stood outside the terminal, surrounded by a cluster of missionary families. Our family for the next few years.

Stewart carried a sheaf of papers through a door marked Immigration. Then, with luggage loaded into cars and station wagons, we drove through town to the mission.

Upon our arrival, I couldn't take it all in: a kaleidoscope of images, a crowd of faces, moms, dads, and children. In somebody's living room, Nescafé in delicate china cups. Coffee cake. A babble of voices. Names flitted through my head. I was supremely happy. What if we hadn't responded to God's call? Would my heart have been heavy for what might have been?

Later, Lynn DeMoss drove us to our home in Jadotville, seventy kilometers away. He was one of a group of young college graduates sent by The Board to serve three-year terms. A few years younger than Stewart and me, Lynn seemed like a kid brother: brash, funny, not at all pious, and desperately homesick, yearning for his fiancée.

"Enjoy the paved road. After Jadotville, it's all dirt." He chattered on, offered candid opinions of the various missionaries. No longer able to keep my eyes open, I dozed.

Stewart's voice alerted me. "We're almost there. That must be the anthill they told us about, where we turn left."

A landmark anthill. "Those ants must be really big," I said.

Lynn laughed. "Actually, they're not ants. They're termites. People eat them. They're considered a delicacy. Good protein."

We rattled across the bridge over railroad tracks. Jacaranda trees lined the streets. Their pale blue flowers fluttered down onto the pavement. Flamboyant trees flaunted banners of crimson blossoms. We turned in at the sign, *Mission Methodiste*, and stopped in front of the house.

"Can we go in, Dad?" Tim asked.

"Sure, looks like the door's open. They must be expecting us."

Martha woke up and looked around, confused. "We're home," I whispered.

I followed Stewart into the big, screened porch. I visualized long afternoons in those wicker chairs. Two front doors, side by side. The one on the right opened into Stewart's office. He was already in there, inspecting two large desks, pushed together, back-to-back. Those desks must have been there since the house was built, too big to have come in through the front doors. I imagined Bishop and Mrs. Springer facing each other across the wide expanse.

The door on the left opened into the living room. The house, unoccupied for several years, smelled of abandonment. The walls cried out for paint. I'd bring life into these empty rooms, fill them with color and comfort and music and laughter and the smell of fresh bread. I sat down on the couch, inspected the chairs, upholstered, like the couch, in sturdy vinyl, easy to care for.

In the dining room, a stage setting for family dinners, birthday parties, Thanksgiving, a large Danish-modern table was surrounded by six chairs. Just right.

Beyond the dining room, the kitchen. I'd get to that later. A big back porch—screened in—stretched across the width of the house.

Jim and June Decker and their children lived in the other residence on the compound, a much newer house, close to the road. We had come to know them in West Hartford. For the first time, I heard *"Hodi?"* at the front door. That Swahili greeting would soon become second nature to me. June was pregnant, due to give birth in January. Their children sidled in. Greg was the same age as Peter, and Sondra a year older than Tim.

Martha wriggled out of my arms, and Sondra took her hand. A perfect galaxy of children, they trooped outside to play on the swing set.

June had prepared the house for us, made the beds, hung towels in the bathroom, stocked the refrigerator with milk, butter, eggs. She set a loaf of fresh bread on the counter beside a bowl of fruit.

"I'll leave you to settle in. I've made lunch, come on up to our house when you're ready. And you're having dinner with us this evening."

Lynn carried in the suitcases. "I can't stay, "he said. "I've got to get back to E'ville."

We had already picked up the habit of shortening the name of Elisabethville. Mary Beth said, "When we say the Lord's Prayer, we always say, "Deliver us from E'ville. Is that a bad place?"

Lynn laughed. "That's a good one, Mary Beth. Well, I've got to get back to bad old E'ville." He assured us we would see him again soon. I stood outside for a few minutes, listening to an industrial racket. The hum, roar, toots, and whistles from the Union Minière ore processing plant would be my soundtrack, all day and all night. Would I ever become accustomed to the inexorable sounds of industry? The unimaginable wealth the Belgians were determined to keep under their control? The railroad, adjacent to the mission property, added to the cacophony. Freight cars shunted endlessly back and forth.

My kitchen was a work in progress. New L-shaped cabinets were strewn around on the back porch. They didn't fit the space for which they were intended. The upper and lower units formed right angles, and the kitchen walls did not. This was, after all, one of the older mission houses. In days to come, we would push the lower cabinet into the crooked corner as far as possible, leaving ample space behind for lost silverware and utensils. The mission carpenter later mounted the upper cabinets on a frame. Somehow, the system worked.

I unpacked a suitcase or two, hung clothes in the closets. Deep voices echoed through the house. Stewart called from the study. A group of African preachers and teachers had come to welcome us. Others came and went, calling "Hodi" to announce their presence. I greeted each one. The exhaustion of the overnight flight caught up with me. I excused myself and went back to settle in. The breeze carried the children's voices and rhythmic squeaking of the swings, hidden behind a hedge between the two houses.

I marvel at that first evening with Jim and June, the four of us around a table set with an immaculate white linen cloth and fine china. Candles shed a soft glow. The children had their own table in the hall. The cook, Nawej, dignified in a white jacket, brought in the roast beef for Jim to carve at the table. The mashed potatoes were smooth and fluffy, the gravy like silk. Later we heard Nawej in the kitchen, singing hymns under his breath as he washed the dishes.

I turned to June. "What a wonderful dinner."

"All the credit goes to Nawej," she replied. "We're so fortunate to have him. He's a famous cook, much sought after."

Jim said, "I've taken the liberty to line up some candidates for you to consider for your own staff. I hope you don't mind."

"We don't call them servants," June said. "They are helpers."

"I've never had household help," I said. "I can manage the big house, but I'm not sure I could manage a helper."

Stewart glanced at Jim. "This might be a good time for us to reconsider," he said to me.

"We're obligated to provide jobs and income for the Africans," Jim said. "It's important to expose them to the ways of the missionaries."

I had anticipated the need to adjust to new ways, but not this.

"It's late, we must go," I said. Peter, Tim, and Greg glanced up from their books, *The Adventures of Tintin*. Sondra was reading to Mary Beth and Martha, *How the Elephant Got His Trunk*. I've always loved Kipling's *Just So Stories*. Perhaps, one day, we might see the "great grey-green, greasy Limpopo River, all set about with fever-trees …"

It had been a long day. Jim walked with us under brilliant African stars. He pointed out the Southern Cross. "You won't see the North Star. It's just below the horizon. During the rainy season, we can see some of the Big Dipper."

Across the valley, the refinery hummed and rumbled, the sound punctuated by whistles and hooting horns. I breathed the cloying sweetness of frangipani blossoms, heavy as tuberoses. The scent didn't quite cover the rank smell of urine.

Jim explained. "That passage on the other side of the hedge, the pedestrian bridge over the railroad, is a convenient place for people to relieve themselves on the way to and from town. When you get used to that smell, it's time to go home to the States."

We said goodnight, and Jim turned back. The children scampered down the road. Jim called after us, "Watch out for snakes. They like those mango trees. Sometimes they drop down on people passing underneath."

I shuddered. "Maybe we should warn the kids."

"They'll be all right," Stewart said.

Jim accompanied Stewart to enroll the children in the Athénée Royal de Jadotville, the government school. Jim's French was impeccable, and Stewart's was not. First impressions would make a difference. Tim went into second grade, Peter in first grade, along with Greg Decker. Mary Beth entered preschool, described, with pride, as *Froebelian*. All the teachers at the *athénée* were Belgian. A few African children attended classes, under a government policy that encouraged the development of an African middle class, called *evolués*. Most African children competed for places in the mission schools operated by the churches. The Roman Catholics dominated, with Belgian clergy, nuns, and teachers. At the *Mission Méthodiste*, the teachers, all African, got by with minimal equipment and barely adequate textbooks. The mission's elementary school across the playground from our home provided lively background sounds, shrill young voices on the playground, singsong chanting in Swahili in the classroom. Rote learning prevailed throughout.

Baba Samuel came to us to do the things I didn't want to do. I cooked, and Baba cleaned up the kitchen. He kept the house spotless, mopped the red concrete floors every day, and waxed them once a week. I sent him home to his family at five o'clock. After supper, I stacked the dishes in the sink. He cleaned up the kitchen in the morning. He washed our clothes in a concrete tub. The Maytag, the old-fashioned model with a wringer, was on its way from New York by freighter, along with our household goods. When our baggage arrived in Kolwezi, a mining town fifty miles west, Stewart took the train to claim our stuff and take it through customs. He paid $40 duty on the Maytag. "Worth every penny," he said.

The long-awaited shipment came by train to Jadotville a few days later. It was delivered to our door by the ancient mission truck. Wooden boxes, trunks, and metal barrels, packed over a year ago, had been stored in a warehouse in New York while we were in Belgium. It felt like Christmas. Lamps, blender, toaster, waffle iron, and juicer. Dishes, pots, and pans. Only one glass was broken. (My packing skills are awesome.) Sheets and blankets and pillows. Books, pictures, clothes, toys, birthday presents wrapped and labeled. Sears had confused our order for an ice cream freezer and two scoops. They sent two freezers and one scoop. Or were they just being generous? We would be much in demand at parties and picnics.

Baba Samuel had never seen anything like the miraculous Maytag, much bigger and more efficient than the machines from Europe. He would have preferred a more prominent placement for the machine, rather than hiding it in the laundry room off the back porch. The machine went immediately into service. Stewart plugged in the transformer, tossed in some dirty towels, and stood back as the agitator churned the suds. In no time at all, the wash water turned red like the soil. Baba Samuel showed great respect for the wringer as it snatched the clothes from his hands. He hung our things outside to dry and ironed everything to kill the eggs of the formidable insects that spawned while the laundry hung in the sunshine. Those insects could do a lot of damage, burrow under the skin and lay their eggs, causing fearsome rashes.

Baba Samuel and his wife and children lived in a tumbledown mud-brick house out of sight in a grove of banana trees on the back of the mission property. The *boyerie*, it was called, a term left over from the old days, still used by the Belgians. To them, servants were "boys." I warned the children never to use that term. I avoided the *boyerie* and seldom visited Baba and his family. I was embarrassed to keep an employee in such a rundown place, unable to offer anything better.

The Belgians preferred to send their cooks to shop at the open-air market for fruit and vegetables, with a *toto*—usually a child of one of their servants—to carry the baskets. I did my own shopping and conscripted my own children to carry baskets.

A local shopkeeper offered Sears Super Kem-Tone paint. I bought eight gallons. This wasn't the parsonage. I could choose my own colors. Sunset rose for the dining room, caprice yellow for the kitchen and bathrooms, linden green for the living room, hall, and office. In the bedrooms, starlight gold for Stewart and me, apple blossom for the girls. The boys' room was Wedgwood blue, trimmed in white, in homage to City Temple in London. Workmen slapped the paint onto the walls. I hung pictures, put books on the shelves.

A bewildering procession of Africans passed through our study and living room: pastors, teachers, and laymen. They wore khaki trousers and long-sleeved cotton shirts, or suits passed on to them by the missionaries. "*Hiyambo, bwana,*" the pastors said to Stewart. To the teachers he was *Monsieur*. "*Hiyambo, mama,*" the pastors greeted me, respectfully taking my hand. I served them Nescafé in our colorful plastic cups and saucers, and *petit beurre* cookies from the Bon Marché, the grocery store downtown. Church members came to greet me. They brought small gifts, a few eggs, some mangoes.

We waited for our car to arrive. Stewart borrowed a bicycle and rode around town. His district comprised an area three hundred kilometers long. He was responsible for the supervision of African pastors in 104 preaching places, ranging from village huts to brick churches in the towns and cities. The first new church would be built in Kambove, a mining center in the hills nearby, where Union Minière had uncovered a huge deposit of copper ore. The company set aside four acres for a church and a school.

In the montage of new faces, one caught my attention: Pastor Joab Mulela. Joab had presence. The men deferred to him. He stood tall and observed the scene. Joab looked directly into my eyes, talked spontaneously to me, not shy or hesitant, no hint of subservience. His grizzled, grey hair hinted at his age. He must have been in his seventies. The older Africans didn't record birth dates or celebrate birthdays. Joab had been with the mission since the earliest days. When I first knew him, a renegade snaggletooth protruded from his mouth. It spoiled his looks but somehow added to his distinction. His English was good, colloquial. He had a natural facility for languages and dialects. He claimed fluency in twenty-two of them. It never occurred to me to doubt him. In 1960, he came to the States as a delegate to the General Conference, a worldwide gathering of Methodists. While he was there, a dentist fixed his teeth. He was more handsome, but I missed that outrageous incisor.

He also had the most wonderful laugh. Of all the Africans I came to know, he alone would joke with me and laugh without restraint, throwing his head back with a guffaw. Through everything that happened during the years I was in Africa, Joab remained my steadfast friend.

Stewart and I turned our attention to language study. Every morning, after the children went off to school, we met with our Swahili teacher, *mwalimu* Jules Samuel, a gentle soul who spoke better French than either of us, as well as excellent English. He taught at the Teacher Training Institute at Mulungwishi, the large mission about twenty kilometers northwest of Jadotville on the unpaved main road. Lots of fine red dust.

The three of us sat around the dining table, closely observed by a crew of workmen outside who scraped flaking paint off the window frames. Stewart and I counted on our fingers, *moja, mbili, tatu, ine*. Through the open windows, we could follow enough of the workmen's conversation to hear them question the wisdom of the church sending them *wazungu* who didn't even know how to count. Jules chewed his lip as we laboriously sounded out phrases and practiced the names of the objects in the room. *Ni kitu gani?* (What's this?) *Ni meza* (Table). *Ni kitabu* (Book).

Swahili is not a difficult language. It's completely phonetic, a trade language imported from coastal areas on the Indian Ocean. Each vowel and each consonant has essentially its own sound. Swahili is one of the few languages with no gender.

The Baluba people, the most prominent tribe in our region, spoke their own tongue among themselves. Lingala was used in the Northern Congo; a variety of tribal languages were spoken in the interior. People preferred to speak their own tribal language, their true language, the language in which they spoke to each other, their children, and to their God. Or Gods. Swahili was a compromise, useful for communication between members of the various tribes, and with the *wazungu*.

Stewart and I were just beginning to put sentences together when Jules's responsibilities at Mulungwishi increased. Our studies languished when he could no longer take time to work with us, and though we promised to continue on our own, we slacked off. Stewart, impatient to get to work, decided to learn on the job. He became famous for his colloquial Swahili. His early sermons must have baffled the congregation. Joab kidded Stewart about the time he appeared to have told the congregation not to brew beer in the bathtub.

I found plenty of excuses not to study. While Tim, Peter, and Mary Beth were at school, Martha spent her days at home with me. There were always meals to prepare, curtains to hem, letters to write. And books to read.

One afternoon, a group of about thirty women, members of the Kipendano (those who love one another), came to formally welcome me. They assembled in the schoolyard and paraded over, baskets and enamel pans on their heads. "*Hodi*," they called. "*Karibu* [Come in]," I responded.

We sat on the screened porch. June joined us and helped me with the Swahili. She was gracious. I followed her example. Some of the women had walked several miles in the hot sun. They brought gifts, tomatoes, potatoes, cabbages, celery, and eggs. Lots of eggs. They knew the missionaries liked eggs. We were always asking in the villages if anyone had eggs to sell. Some thought we had no eggs in our own country and had come to Africa for eggs. The women piled everything on the table, the vegetables, the eggs, their gifts for me, to thank me for coming to work with them.

They wore floor-length dresses of wax-print cotton in acid green, all shades of red, orange, bright blue, with imaginative repeating prints, dizzying arrays of palm trees, bananas, pineapples, huts, geometric designs. An extra length of cloth held babies on their mothers' backs. Toddlers stayed close to their mothers and stared at me. Most of the women had a child or two, a shy toddler hiding in the mother's long skirt, a baby tied onto her back. I looked away from the children's runny noses. When I was just a girl and announced my intention to be a missionary, my mother told me I'd better get used to children with runny noses.

They sang a hymn, clapped their hands in rhythm, and one of the women prayed. There was a speech of welcome, which June translated for me. "We are all one in Christ, and we work together, regardless of color."

They were glad I had come to work with them. They had an additional gift for me: twenty-five francs, about fifty cents, left over after they bought the eggs. I didn't want to take the money, but June said I must. I managed to say, "A*sante sana* [Thank you very much]." They lined up in the front yard for a photo.

Stewart took the photo. Everybody wanted a copy. He tried to explain it was a slide. No copies. They walked away, empty baskets on their heads, babies and toddlers peeking at the *wazungu* in fear and wonder.

"*Kwenda vizuri* [Go well]," I murmured, over and over.

"*Bakia vizuri* [Stay well]," they responded.

The Kipendano women were all business. They spoke to me in loud voices, as though I were deaf. They asked when sewing classes would start. I was expected to follow the example of Mama Libby, who had taught them when she lived here. They made sure I knew when the Kipendano meetings were.

Why did I resist their invitations? They were bossy, but no more so than the church ladies back in the States. I gave myself a stern little lecture. Isn't that what I came there to do? Stewart encouraged me to get involved, to learn the language as he was doing, by using it. Martha accompanied me to the women's meetings, carrying her little basket of coloring books, crayons, dolls, and doll clothes. The women greeted me, "*Hiyambo, mama*," and made room for me in their circle on the ground in the shade of a mango tree. I struggled to understand their rapid Swahili, answered inappropriately, saw dismay and confusion on their faces. The women asked me to lead in prayer. I stuck to the basics: "*O Mungu Baba, tunapiga akisante sana kwa* … [O God our Father, we thank you for …]" I attached a list of everything I could think of the name for. Only God knows what I said.

They asked me to preach. I deferred, pleading lack of fluency in the language. They kept after me about sewing classes. They wanted me to drive them downtown to the *commerçant* who sold cloth, buy it for them at wholesale prices, and help them with their sewing. They would pay for the cloth. They didn't bother with patterns; they just cut the fabric and sewed seams on a hand-cranked machine, the left hand feeding in the cloth, the right hand spinning the wheel. Why was I so reluctant to help them?

I couldn't get past some exalted notion of what it meant to be a missionary. I'd imagined myself seated on a chair under a palm tree, the center of attention, reading the Scriptures to simple souls who hung on my every word. Instead, I sat on the ground among outspoken, impatient, strong-minded women who expected me to take them to the store and help them sew dresses. Ants crawled up my legs and bit me. My legs cramped, my back ached. I couldn't understand what they said. Martha shared her crayons with the runny-nosed toddlers, who thought they were candy. Why did I ever think I could do this?

Stewart was a natural. He took to his work as though it were what he had always wanted to do, no hesitation about language or discomfort in unsanitary conditions. He loved village work. He sat around with the elders, organized services, preached, served communion, passed little aluminum cups filled with grenadine. He never hesitated when it was his turn to share the common cup. He came home from days in the bush filled with enthusiasm and plans for the future. An unexpected opportunity opened for him to teach evangelism and church doctrine in the pastors' school at Mulungwishi.

A large plot of land—1,800 acres—along the railroad, about twenty miles north of Jadotville, was purchased in 1940 from a local farmer for the Springer Institute at Mulungwishi. Over the years, a church, dormitories, and classrooms were built on relatively flat land, and missionary residences nestled into the hills. A steep hill overlooked the site, crowned by a thirty-foot-tall cross, made of metal barrels welded together.

The School of Theology graduated its first class in 1954 and continued to send African pastors to establish and serve churches throughout the region. Primary schools and the Institute de Moniteurs reflected the emphasis on education by and for the Africans.

In the same manner, the Girl's School, built in 1955, preceded the Domestic Science School, where African women learned sewing, cooking, and childcare, as well as how to conduct meetings and plan programs. This became the foundation of the Kipendano.

Occasionally, at his urging, Martha and I went with Stewart for a day. I hated being stared at. The grass roofs of the mud-brick huts offered some shelter from the sun and rain, but the huts were dark and smelled of dried fish. Goats wandered about, picking through the garbage. The children crowded around Martha. I blanched at their hacking coughs, their wicked sores. Martha hid behind my skirts. The women prepared strong tea, wiping out the cups with the same cloth with which they wiped runny noses and dusted off the chairs. Stewart said I was too squeamish.

The dozen missionaries who lived at Mulungwishi came into Jadotville frequently to shop for groceries, visit the open-air market, have their cars serviced, and meet with pastors and teachers. I especially welcomed the families whose children were too young to be sent to boarding school. People stopped by our house for coffee or to use the bathroom. I always invited them to join us for a meal. Stewart sat at one end of the table, and I sat at the other, nearest the kitchen. After the children had been excused and gone off to play, the adults sat around the table talking and drinking Nescafé.

I organized picnics, afternoons at the local swimming pool, birthday parties. We became famous for our hospitality, and the Mulungwishi people reciprocated by including us in their social events. Could it be that, for now, this was my mission? To serve the missionaries?

The European nations that carved up the continent of Africa in 1850 had claimed vast areas for themselves. The churches followed suit, staked out their territories, and agreed to respect the boundaries. Belgium was overwhelmingly Roman Catholic, and the Congo reflected that dominance, but the Protestants did well for themselves. The Methodists claimed most of the Katanga Province and a good chunk of the Kasai to the north. The Presbyterians took over a large section of the area farther north. The smaller fundamentalist denominations, the Garanganzes, the Plymouth Brethren, and even some of the Baptists, respected no boundaries. They planted and maintained outposts as directed by a Higher Power. This must have created some confusion among the Africans, but that wasn't a topic of discussion.

Bishop Springer, the pioneer of Methodist work, was now in his eighties and in retirement at Mulungwishi. The colloquial name for the

Methodists, "Splingers," was universally recognized and generally honored. Old Bishop Springer took a fancy to Martha. He loved to take her onto his lap and recite for her enjoyment a long poem by Rudyard Kipling called "The Sons of Martha." She gazed up at him, speechless in wonder and adoration.

The evangelists held the highest places in the hierarchy of missionaries. Their mandate was clear and unapologetic: they were here to save souls.

Over the years, Stewart flirted with soul-saving. He was an eloquent preacher, and it must have been exhilarating to exercise that kind of power—to call people to the altar, watch them kneel, and hear them cry out their sins. He mastered the vocabulary and found the Africans receptive, eager to confess their sins and follow Jesus. The evangelists welcomed him, but with reservations. He was, after all, a Yankee.

On matters of doctrine, I kept a low profile. As a wife and mother, I was not expected to have an opinion on theology. Everyone assumed I shared Stewart's beliefs. They knew they were always welcome at my house, where they could count on a good meal and interesting conversation.

One Saturday morning, a Chevy station wagon I hadn't seen before drove into the yard, and an attractive woman climbed out of the car. She wore a stylish cotton skirt and blouse, sleeves rolled up and fastened with little buttoned tabs. She pulled back her blonde hair with a blue ribbon. Betsy Morgan had arrived, just when I needed a friend. Betsy and her family lived at Mulungwishi. They were my first Californians. Betsy worked in the mission dispensary with Amos, a capable young African nurse. Together they had started a well-baby clinic and a nursery for premature babies. Her husband Bob, an architect, designed and built houses, schools, and churches.

Betsy was a gifted nurturer of all living things. Plants, animals, and children thrived in her care. She had an unusual affinity with all animals. They sought her out. They knew they were safe with her. The Africans brought her animals in need of nursing, orphan baby monkeys, a miniature antelope—called a *dik-dik*—with a broken leg. She often had a bush baby, an adorable little lemur, tucked into her pocket.

Betsy taught their sons, Chris and Norm. Their older daughter, Kitty, was in boarding school. At the moment, Bob was in the hospital across the street from the mission with a severe case of hepatitis. Betsy agreed to leave Chris and Norm with me while she visited Bob. It was easy to fold them into the flock. Mary Beth and Norm, both four years old, decided right away to marry each other when they grew up.

Betsy was a treasure, a kindred spirit. Neither of us shared the rigid fundamentalism of many of the other missionaries. We each admitted to some unease about this, as though we didn't quite measure up. We were both determined to keep our children with us as long as we could. I envied her language skills and her ease with the Africans. She respected them too much to look upon them as lost souls in need of salvation. We kept our opinions to ourselves and ignored the patronizing attitude of the evangelists toward the laity.

I loved going to the market with Betsy and our coterie of children. She introduced me to the routines. Every Saturday, African farmers, men and women, brought produce to town by truck, bicycle, or on foot. The women balanced enormous loads on their heads. They rinsed the red dirt from the produce in a concrete trough and arranged everything on concrete tables. Early in the afternoon, the market opened. Local Africans came first, to buy manioc tubers, dried fish, plantains, *pilipili*, and greens.

At three o'clock, the official in charge of the market blew a shrill blast on his whistle, and the Europeans began to shop. Dried fish and manioc were put aside, fruit and vegetables moved into prominent positions. Prices doubled or tripled. Belgian ladies in smart cotton dresses, accompanied by their cooks, greeted each other formally. Young *totos* carried their baskets. Upwardly mobile African families, in European clothes, spoke French as they selected vegetables.

Betsy and I filled our baskets with lettuce, spinach, tomatoes, onions, green beans, peas, potatoes, scallions, mushrooms, celery, parsley, oranges, lemons, guavas, mangoes, avocados, and, surprise, strawberries. Sometimes asparagus. We washed the vegetables in the kitchen sink and Betsy heaped the colorful mixture in my largest china bowl. We filled the pitcher with fresh lemonade. Our families feasted. I still think of it as California salad. In Kansas, salad was a slab of iceberg lettuce drenched with Thousand Island dressing. Or wilted lettuce with bacon bits and a chopped hard-boiled egg.

"How are you getting on with the Kipendano?" Betsy asked me one day.

I sighed. "I just can't seem to get the hang of it."

"The Jadotville women are tough. They have a reputation for being difficult. Mama Libby spoiled them. It's a shame. You know, Bob and I studied French in Brussels and spent our first three months here learning Swahili. You and Stewart were just expected to go right to work, learn on the job. How come you never went to language school like the rest of us?"

I told her about that first summer, after we signed up, when The Powers That Be told us to find someone to take care of the children while we went to language school in Pennsylvania. I wasn't about to start our service with The Board by parking the children somewhere, and we had nowhere to park them, anyway.

"We asked The Board to send us on to Belgium so we could start learning French," I told her, "but they preferred to wait until late in August when the price of the steamship tickets went down."

"That doesn't make much sense," Betsy said.

"We had to get out of the parsonage to make room for the new occupants, and all our stuff was packed to go overseas. Stewart's folks took us in for a few days, but their house was awfully small, and the kids came down with chickenpox. That took a while. Finally, we went on the road, drove to Kansas, stayed with my parents. We were gypsies."

"That's awful."

"I know," I said, with a sigh. I seemed to be sighing a lot. "I think the people at The Board were mad because I refused to leave the children. I had already made it clear I wouldn't be sending them away to boarding school. They were punishing me for not bowing to their will."

"So unfair," Betsy said.

"I try not to think about it, just work on my Swahili every day. It's so easy to get distracted."

Stewart found a place for me to be of service. The church in Likasi, in the section of town in which most of the Africans lived, had long contended with a noisy bar just across the street. The owner put the bar up for sale. The church bought it and converted it into a social center. The teachers asked for evening classes in conversational English. I said I'd try.

I stood behind what had been the bar in the dimly lit room and faced thirty young African men. They wore dark slacks, white shirts, ties, shoes, socks, and carried briefcases. They spoke good French and burned with resentment at the condescension of the Belgians. We practiced polite conversation in English. Weeks passed, and we progressed into an exchange of ideas. The men longed for the time when their country would achieve independence from the Belgians. They asked provocative and insightful questions.

"Why do the missionaries have cars and refrigerators, and we don't?"

"Why don't the people in America send cars and refrigerators to us?"

"You tell us it's wrong to fight. Didn't America fight for its freedom?"

"You tell us it's wrong to have more than one wife. In America, men divorce their wives, leave them, and take another wife. Isn't our way better?"

None of them had more than one wife, of course, but we failed to treat the traditional ways of their people with respect. I answered their questions as best I could. I agreed with them that divorce was ridiculous and unfair. I told them what little I knew of the American Revolution. My answers had no weight. I was only a woman, a wife. I had no power or status in the Mission, and they knew it.

Two years later, after the country gained its independence and these men were in charge of the schools, they posed these same questions to the missionary men who, in turn, accused me of having encouraged insurrection. This was not the first time I got into trouble, or the last. Later, in the States, I had to give up teaching Sunday school because I encouraged the young people to ask questions and express opinions rather than just swallow the stories whole. The parents called Stewart to complain. "Can't you control your wife?"

To his credit, he said, "I don't even try."

Chapter Four

The oppressive October heat settled in. High humidity left me sticky and testy. Mice ran around all night in the attic. Bats squeaked, scooped up the pesky mosquitoes. The Rhodesians called it the "suicide season." Everyone was cranky, on edge.

Finally, the longed-for rains arrived and cleared the atmosphere. A procession of storms rolled through. Thunder crashed and boomed. Torrential rain pounded the metal roof. Around the dining room table, we had to shout to be heard. The rains scoured the dust from the trees and shrubs. Intervals of intense sunshine dried deep ruts in the muddy clay. New leaves appeared. The landscape changed from brown to green. Flowers bloomed in unexpected places. Amaryllis pushed up through the hard clay soil. Delicate red flowers adorned the flamboyant trees.

The rains were predictable, unlike the stream of visitors from the United States. We were expected to build a network of support for our work. Bishops, prominent ministers and evangelists, church bureaucrats—most of them accompanied by their wives—and ordinary church folks on tour sat around our table, dining on plastic dishes. Had I known, I would have brought the good china.

The two grocery stores in town offered almost everything at prices that stretched my meager budget. Over the years, I developed recipes and menus. The visitors preferred simple, familiar food: macaroni and cheese, spaghetti and meatballs, potato salad and ham, New England baked beans. They raved about my homemade bread, biscuits, and pineapple upside-down cake. They loved my signature dessert, fresh fruit from the weekly market: sliced strawberries, mangoes, bananas, and oranges, presented in a hollowed-out pineapple decorated with sprigs of fresh mint.

Visiting clergy trotted out their favorite sermons, and translation was a challenge. Lynn was pressed into service for his awesome Swahili. I loved to watch him in action. Occasionally, he improvised. Who would know?

"… and God wrapped a rainbow around His shoulder," the preacher from America declaimed, tracing the arc with his right arm. He turned to his translator. Lynn hesitated, scratched his head.

"What's the Swahili for rainbow?" he asked, *sotto voce*. I shook my head, shrugged. The preacher waited, eyebrows raised. "I already told them that," Lynn said, with an encouraging smile.

At that time, in 1958, Albert Schweitzer was still at work in his hospital at Lambaréné on the Little Ogowe River in Gabon. We grew accustomed to our visitors' rhapsodic tales of *le grand docteur*. I learned to anticipate their words.

"And then the great *pirogues* came across the river, the paddlers singing and dipping their oars in unison."

I confess I was impatient with their stories. We had nothing like that to offer.

I served biscuits with real butter, a special treat.

"Dr. Schweitzer serves margarine," one of my guests gushed, with a condescending smile. I wanted to snatch that precious butter right out of her hand.

The observance of Halloween might better have stayed behind in another culture, but the children begged to trick or treat. June said, "It's okay. My kids dress up in weird stuff every year." Tim was a wicked pirate, Peter a cowboy. Mary Beth chose to be a ghost in a pillowcase, and Martha was an angel. Baba Samuel was astonished. We took the kids out to Mulungwishi, where the Americans admired the costumes and passed out candy. The African students and teachers seemed to enjoy the spectacle. They had seen it all before. How strange, to bring ghosts and cowboys and pirates to their doorsteps, while our mission was to deliver the Africans from alien spirits.

June and I joined forces with Nawej to prepare for Thanksgiving. No turkeys anywhere. Betsy sacrificed two ducks she had raised and gave them to us for the feast. Nawej roasted them perfectly, with oranges in the stuffing. June found a can of cranberry sauce. I had a can of pumpkin. I took great care with the pies. The Belgians didn't sell pumpkin or cranberry sauce in their shops. We set a separate table for the children and dressed up in our best clothes for the traditional feast, celebrating the holiday by overeating in a hungry land.

The following Sunday, in an act of contrition for our gluttony, the children and I went with Stewart to one of the smaller village churches in his jurisdiction, a place too small to support a pastor. The schoolteacher conducted the service. He suffered from chronic rheumatism. Many villagers manifested signs of poor health: horrendous coughs, inflamed eyes, scabies. We joined in the lusty singing of unfamiliar words to familiar tunes. I puzzled out the translations. In time, the old ways would be encouraged, and drumming and dancing would once again be incorporated into the worship service.

Here in this poor village of mud huts, grass roofs, no electricity or running water, the African children stared at our well-dressed, well-fed family, and our blue Volkswagen. One woman had made mother-daughter outfits from the same cloth for herself and her girls. A woman's long string of plastic beads broke when her baby tugged at them. The beads rolled everywhere. My children scrambled with the others to collect beads and carefully place them in her lap.

Martha sat upfront with her dad, facing the congregation. Restless, she wandered out to play with the village children. They picked up stones and arranged them into patterns. I was pleased to see her join in the game, but the runny noses and open sores were hard to ignore.

Stewart asked the teacher if they might celebrate Holy Communion. One of the men went down the hill to fetch water. I tried not to think of the source of that water. The teacher poured some grenadine syrup into the jar, and a cracked enamel cup was shared around. Stewart read the service in Swahili. Was the power of the Holy Spirit sufficient to protect us from germs and diseases? I felt ashamed by my lack of faith.

We drove back to our pleasant home and enjoyed Sunday dinner. I couldn't forget the poverty of those villagers. I never resolved these conflicts. When I compared our lives with those of most of the Africans, we were rich. Compared with the Belgians, and people back in the States, we were poor. Stewart was impatient with me. "Of course, the villagers are poor. That's why we're here, to bring them into awareness of another way of life, to show them the good life, the Christian life." I kept my doubts to myself.

As missionaries, we had access to the hospital across the street from the mission, operated by the government-owned railroad. Duvon Corbitt, the mission doctor who had advised me in Brussels when Martha had the mumps, was now stationed at Piper Memorial Hospital, five hundred miles north of us. There was no phone service, and the shortwave radio connection was unreliable.

Although my primary concern was for the children, I would be the first to sample the local medical services. I dragged around for a week or two, tired all the time, and depressed. No appetite. Maybe it was the heat. I complained, just enough to get Stewart's attention. "There's a hospital right across the street," he pointed out. "There's bound to be a doctor there who can see you."

Desperate, I followed his advice. The doctor spoke no English, and my pathetic French was inadequate, but we managed to communicate.

"How long have you been in the Congo?

"Since September."

"*Voila!* Sunstroke. You must rest."

He sent me home with some pills. "Let the servants do the work," he advised.

Every day I felt worse. I went back to the doctor.

"Give it more time," he said.

He gave me more pills. They didn't help. I felt worse than ever.

Several days later, I glanced at the mirror and a yellow face looked back at me. Not even the doctor could miss these symptoms. "*Voila, c'est la jaunisse* [See, it's hepatitis]."

He prescribed some different pills, told me to rest, and let the servants do the work. It became a sort of litany. Eventually, I recovered.

Obviously, I would not be able to depend on local medical care for my family, even in an emergency. What would I do if the children were injured or had appendicitis? I underwent an appendectomy when I was twelve and I could never forget the agony of waiting for the doctor.

Saint Nicholas arrived at school on schedule, on December 5th, in a vintage yellow Chevrolet convertible, sweating in his red satin suit and long white whiskers. He was accompanied by his counterpart, Zwarte Piet, in blackface. We had met the same characters the previous Christmas in Brussels. Belgian children didn't hang up stockings, they put their shoes by the hearth on Christmas Eve. Naughty children found coal in their shoes on Christmas morning. Here was Zwarte Piet again, in the Congo, enjoying his role.

Mary Beth's class sat wide-eyed as the jolly old Saint Nicholas, watched closely by Zwarte Piet, took out a large book. He called each child by name and distributed toys and sacks of candy. Mary Beth curtsied and thanked him, in French, for his gift, a miniature stove with tiny pots and pans. The younger children received chocolate bars. Martha held onto hers for a while and smeared the soft sweetness all over her white dress. We followed the crowd to the boys' school, the *athénée.* Mary Beth called it the "Matinée." Peter, handsome in his white shirt and long pants, grinned from the front row of primary school students. Saint Nicholas called his name, told him to keep up the good work, and gave him a wind-up train. Each little girl received a doll. Tim's class, second graders, waited impatiently until they, too, received their trains and dolls. Saint Nicholas promised to come in a helicopter next year. He asked the kids to leave a glass of Simba, the local beer, for him, and to make sure Papa didn't drink it.

The children had made elaborate presents for their parents, doggies and kittens and ashtrays, molded of plaster of Paris. Their teachers placed great emphasis on perfection. They re-worked the kids' offerings, corrected inaccuracies, and removed excess paste and crayon for neatness and conformity. I treasured the gifts the children made but regretted the suppression of their individuality, messy though it might have been.

At the mission school across the way, another Saint Nicholas and Zwarte Piet stepped out of a small black sedan. Saint Nicholas wore a shabby red robe. Zwarte Piet glared at the children lined up in the yard, who held out their hands for some cheap candy. The kids cheered with the same enthusiasm as their counterparts in the government schools.

The African churches spent months in preparations for Christmas Eve, the Protestant version of Midnight Mass. They competed to produce the longest and most elaborate depiction of not only the Nativity, but favorite stories from the Old Testament: Noah and the Ark, Daniel in the Den of Lions, David and Goliath, Moses, and the Ten Commandments. Sometimes these services went on all night.

We walked over to the church next door for the pageant. Angels wrapped in white satin surrounded the crèche. Shepherds with long crooks herded a flock of "sheep": children crawling down the aisle, covered with sheepskins, baa-ing loudly. After an hour or so, we took our children home and tucked them into bed. Their longest stockings hung by the fireplace. Tim waited until the others were asleep.

"Mom, is there truly a Santa, or do the parents fill the stockings?"

"I think you've figured out that the parents help."

"Don't tell the others," he said. "They really like believing in Santa."

Lynn was now one of the family. He often stayed over in the primitive guest house and showed up for meals. He liked my cooking. He played with the children for hours. They called him "Uncle Lynn," the customary honorific among the missionaries. They giggled when he teased them and chased them and called them "hairy monsters." Restless, he was eager to finish his term in a few more months and return to his fiancée in Michigan.

I asked him, "What are you going to do if the plane can't take off?"

"Bicycle to control tower," he grinned.

He and I gossiped about the other young people and their inevitable romances, which would lead either to heartbreak or the altar. Intimacy before marriage was not an option. Lynn disclosed that a certain couple had set the date for their wedding, and we would be invited. As it developed, the entire missionary community was invited, as well as African teachers, pastors, students, and friends of the bride and groom.

We drove to Elisabethville on a Saturday morning. The groom hosted a potluck picnic lunch for everybody. The bride was present, her hair in pin curls. We changed into our best clothes and gathered at the church. The men, Africans and *wazungu*, wore "church clothes": dark suits, white shirts, city shoes, neckties. The women wore polyester shirtwaist dresses, some with full skirts, some with slim skirts, not too tight or too short, in subdued colors and, in spite of the heat, nylon stockings and shoes with little heels. Some of the Africans wore outfits previously owned by the *wazungu*.

The bride's parents had sent a traditional white gown and veil. Mary Beth and Martha and all the little girls, in their best frilly dresses, were enraptured. The bridesmaids, one white and one black, wore gowns and carried bouquets of frangipani and ferns. The groom was flanked by two attendants, one white, one black. When the couple walked up the aisle together, their students broke into cheers and whistles. At the reception, we nibbled fruitcake and sipped sweet fruit punch. The children ran around and played tag. I could hardly wait to get into comfortable clothes.

I asked the bride, "How long have you known each other?"

"Long enough," she replied. "He loves Jesus and I love Jesus." What else could matter?

Lynn tied old shoes to the getaway car. The bride and groom left in a shower of rice, and we cleaned up the church for services the next day. The young couple returned to the States six weeks later for graduate study. They planned a lifetime of service in the Congo.

The Kipendano ladies made themselves comfortable around the dining room table. I served tea and cookies. Mama Louisa Ngoi, the District President of the Kipendano, chaired the meeting. Everyone loved and admired Mama Louisa, a hard worker, who was capable, smart, and diligent. I hoped to get to know her better, to be friends. She and I didn't have many opportunities to be together. She taught in the Women's School at Mulungwishi and was already the mother of five children.

Today she was uncomfortable. She looked as though she could go into labor at any moment. Her blouse stretched tight across her belly. I recognized the feverish restlessness that comes during the final days of pregnancy when you wonder how much longer you can bear this burden. I tried to find a comfortable chair for her. She was gracious, as always. She never complained. She planned to give birth in the hospital across the street. I wished her well and asked her to send word when she went into labor.

She took us rapidly through the agenda, to plan the annual district meeting. The women kept their reports brief in consideration of her discomfort.

Mama Louisa died in childbirth. The baby did not survive. I would never be able to nourish a closer friendship with her. I cried for her motherless children. Her many friends would comfort them and care for them, raise them as their own, but, still, to lose your mother was a great sorrow for a youngster to bear.

Louisa's brother, Alfred, was the popular pastor of the Mulungwishi church, as well as a fine musician and composer of hymns. Louisa's husband was another story. I didn't care much for him. He was pleasant enough, but he lacked ambition and had barely managed to finish secondary school. The Springers employed him to do odd jobs.

Stewart and I drove the four local pastors to Mulungwishi for the funeral. We waited together in the church. An hour passed. Birds chirped and flew around in the rafters. There were murmurs of conversation. We sat quietly waiting, grieving.

One morning before the street riots began, when we were still new in Jadotville, Stewart and Pastor Joab and I sat around the table, with cups of Nescafé. We heard a commotion out in the street. Drums banged, people wailed. Stewart hurried to the front door. "I want to see what is going on," he said.

"It's a funeral procession," Joab said. He could tell from the sound of the drums.

"Oh, boy," Stewart said. "I've been hoping to see one of those." He grabbed his camera and ran out to the street. It was the custom for African women in mourning to bare their breasts and cover themselves with white powder. Joab looked at me, raised his eyebrows. "Don't you want to see it, mama?"

"Not really. Funerals aren't a spectacle for *wazungu* with cameras."

He regarded me thoughtfully, head tipped to one side. "That doesn't stop the other missionaries."

"I know."

We smiled at each other. From that day, there was a special bond, unspoken, between Joab and me.

Long-standing cultural differences became most apparent at the time of a death, especially the death of a church leader. Traditionally, mourners gave full vent to their emotions: they screamed and sobbed, tore their clothes, and beat their breasts. The missionaries had brought a new format: the stoic repression of grief so deeply ingrained in the Western world. Foreign customs prevailed. It pained me to watch the African Christians struggle to conform to the expectations of the missionaries. A compromise can't please everybody and usually pleases nobody.

The mourners came down the hill from Louisa's house, singing. They had spent the night there, praying and singing and wailing together. Emotions that poured out during the night-long vigil would be suppressed during the long service in the church.

Men carried the two coffins on their shoulders into the church and placed them before the altar. I wondered why they hadn't tucked the baby in with Louisa, rather than in that tiny coffin.

Months earlier, here in this church, we had attended another funeral. The dignity of the service was shattered when workmen came forward, closed the coffin, and pounded nails into the lid. Dreadful blows clanged, echoing through the sanctuary.

Today, the coffins at the front of the church were already securely closed. There would be no unseemly hammering. Pastor Alfred maintained his composure as he presided at his sister's service. He preached for a long time. We sang Louisa's favorite hymn, "*Mungu anateke Ndege* [His Eye Is on the Sparrow]."

The women wailed and sobbed aloud, giving way to uncontrollable grief. The pastor urged them not to be sad. Louisa had gone to be with the Lord. The widower sat stunned and silent, surrounded by his weeping children. Pastor Alfred reminded us death can come at any time. We should all be ready. You never know what will get you: a car, a train, or a snake out in the bush.

We walked with the crowd out of the church through the tall grass to the nearby graveyard. The two coffins were set down beside two shallow pits. All of a sudden, I heard a rumbling sound, like an earthquake. People stampeded, shoved each other aside in their frenzy to get away from the graves. On the fringe of the crowd, I moved farther back to get out of the way. The word *nyoka* was repeated, over and over. *Nyoka*. Snake. A snake had fallen into the grave, just a tiny snake, but a powerfully bad omen. A man jumped into the hole and stabbed the snake with his shovel. A woman comforted a small boy who was trampled in the confusion. People calmed down. Pastor Alfred's voice rose in prayer. The little boy wept in his mother's arms. Who would comfort the five motherless children?

The coffins were lowered into the grave. It was the custom for the men to shovel dirt onto the coffin. This time, the women moved forward and picked up the shovels, scooped up the red clay, and pitched it into the grave. The dirt settled onto the coffins until they were covered. The men took the shovels and finished the job.

We stood silent, uncertain what to do. The quiet seemed ominous. The snake, a symbol of evil, had invaded the sacred ritual and planted a profound unease in our souls.

Pastor Alfred pronounced the benediction. He assured us we would see Louisa on the Day of Resurrection.

Chapter Five

If the Methodist mission of the Southern Congo had been a monarchy, I would have crowned the doctors, Duvon and Phyllis Corbitt, king and queen. The evangelists might have argued with me about that. They dealt in the salvation of souls, while the physicians held the power of life and death.

The doctors reigned at Piper Memorial Hospital, deep in the bush, three hard days' drive north of us. Duvon was a star, a gifted diagnostician and surgeon, an accomplished raconteur. He performed surgery, delivered babies, and supervised the staff—a Danish nurse and three African male nurses. More young men were in training, and three young African women were preparing to be midwives. When Duvon was on the road at the wheel of their battered station wagon, or in the air piloting a Piper Cub, Phyllis carried full responsibility. They were a formidable team. They had two small children.

In addition to his mandate to serve the Africans, Duvon was responsible for the health of the missionary families. Northern Rhodesia offered excellent doctors and hospitals within a day's drive. Major surgery required a consultation with Duvon. He, in turn, petitioned the physician-in-chief in New York for permission to proceed. In years to come, this protocol would complicate my life in ways I could not have imagined.

We had intermittent contact with Duvon by shortwave radio. One morning he announced that he was on the road, on his annual tour of physical exams for all the missionary families. Several days later he breezed in, ready for action. He brushed aside my offer for coffee.

"Later. I've got a lot of ground to cover. Children first," he barked. He lined them up, eldest to youngest, gave them a quick check, and brought their inoculations up to date. The sight of needles sent Peter into his favorite hiding place in the garage, but there was no escape. I rewarded the children with homemade popsicles.

Duvon never developed much of a bedside manner. He motioned to me. "You're next. Go in the bedroom and take off your clothes." The children stared at him. Their popsicles dripped onto the floor. Stewart shooed them outside to play. I sat on the edge of the bed, naked, light-headed with embarrassment. Duvon marched in and closed the door. "Any complaints?"

I tried to match his nonchalance. "Just the usual, pre-menstrual cramps, some occasional heavy bleeding. Nothing serious."

He frowned. "Let's take a look. Lie down."

It seemed like an order. I complied. I studied the ceiling while he examined my vagina. "Everything seems okay. I'll be on the lookout for fibroid tumors."

"I don't like the sound of that."

"Nothing to be concerned about," he assured me. "Just part of being a woman. Eve's curse and all that." His impersonal hands moved across my breasts. He hesitated, intent, silent, serious.

"What is it?" I asked, unable to endure the silence.

"Something, definitely something," he murmured. "I can't quite tell." His fingers continued to palpate my left breast. I held my breath, sick with dread.

"Without a biopsy, I can't really tell," he said at last. "I'll have to talk to your husband about this. Go ahead and get dressed and we'll go over your options."

I trembled as I put on my clothes and brushed my hair. I could hear their low voices in the dining room. They fell silent when I came out of the bedroom.

Baba Samuel brought a tray of cups, saucers, a tin of Nescafé, a pitcher of milk, a bowl of sugar, and a steaming kettle. I spooned coffee crystals into the cups, poured in hot water, and stirred in milk. The plastic cups and saucers were the colors of Campbell's soup: tomato, cream of celery, split pea. For once, I found no comfort in the ritual. I looked past Stewart's shoulder and out the window where the children played on the swings. I could hear their voices and the squeak of the swings. Duvon stirred his coffee, cleared his throat.

"There's a lump in your breast. You need a biopsy. I can make a referral for you to the government hospital in Johannesburg. You can fly down there. It's the best medical center in Africa, with modern equipment, fine surgeons, specialists. They'll do the pathology there."

He must have seen my look of dismay. "Or you can come up to Kapanga. I do this surgery all the time for African women, under a local anesthetic. We don't have general anesthesia yet. I can send the tissue to Johannesburg for analysis." He waited. "Nothing to worry about," he said. "It's minor surgery. I'm sure we caught this in the early stages."

I wished I were so sure. I looked at Stewart. "What do you think?"

"It's up to you," he said.

"Couldn't we go to New York?"

Duvon winced. "The Board won't let you do that. Their policy is to use the mission doctors. They give us a lot of special training, and they feel we're qualified to take care of the missionaries, as well as the Africans."

"Oh, Duvon, you know I don't question your capabilities. Everyone knows what a fine surgeon you are. It's just that I've never been to Kapanga, and it's hard to picture the facilities there." I turned to Stewart. "Why don't we all go?"

He frowned. "I'm just getting into the work. Starting these new schools and churches. It wouldn't be good for the children to take them out of school. It's a great opportunity for you to see the bush country. Maybe you could fly up on the mission plane."

"Or you might be more comfortable in Johannesburg," Duvon offered.

"Forget it, Duvon. I won't even consider going to Johannesburg," I sputtered. "South Africa is the last place on earth I'd go, even if they have good hospitals. For white people. The whole apartheid thing is evil. I won't even buy peanut butter from South Africa. Or apples."

Stewart looked uncomfortable. He wanted this settled. "It's your decision."

"I guess I'll have to go to Kapanga by myself, then."

Duvon interrupted. "But you won't be alone. Betsy Morgan needs to come up to the hospital for some female problems. You can drive to Kapanga together. She knows the road."

"And I'll take care of the kids," Stewart said. "You can take the Volkswagen. I'll borrow a mission car. Or ride the bicycle."

"What about my class?"

Stewart looked blank.

"My English class. The teachers. They're doing so well. I hate to miss a session."

"I'd probably just give them time off until you get back. You won't be gone that long."

The men looked so pleased with their solution to my problem.

We sat around the supper table that evening. "Your mom's going up to Kapanga for a few days. It will be like a vacation for her."

"Can we all go?" Tim asked. "I heard there are hippos up there."

"Not this time," Stewart said. "Dr. Corbitt wants to do some tests."

"What's the matter, Mom?" Mary Beth asked, concern on her sweet face. "Do you have an infection?" She knew about infections. Every mosquito bite, every abrasion developed into a nasty sore on her tender skin.

"Not exactly an infection," I said.

"Well, Stewart said, "it's sort of like an infection."

"Where is it?" Mary Beth asked. "Can I see it?"

I smiled, to reassure her, and myself. "No, Sweetie. It's inside. We're not quite sure what it is, but it's nothing serious. I won't be gone long. I want you kids to mind your dad and work hard at school."

"We'll be fine," Stewart said. "Baba Samuel will have the kitchen to himself for once. And I can cook, too, you know."

The children looked thoughtful. "I like Mom's cooking," Peter said.

It seems incredible now that two white women drove five hundred miles into the bush, over primitive roads, unescorted, for three days.

Betsy and I were prepared for every emergency: fallen trees that blocked the road, mud holes, flat tires. We made room in the little Volkswagen for an ax, shovel, cables, gas can, tire pump, tire patches. We knew nothing about auto repair. We would depend on heaven's protection and the kindness of strangers. Most of the rudimentary road consisted of little more than parallel sandy tracks through tall grass. After we passed Kolwezi there were no motels and no gas stations.

We had an easy first day, seventy miles to Kolwezi. We spent the night in the hotel, La Bonne Auberge, and treated ourselves to a steak dinner. In the morning we got an early start, filled the gas tank, and set out for the long, long drive to Sandoa. We had our instructions. If our car hit a chicken or goat, we should not stop. We would have just provided dinner for the villagers. If we hit a person, we must not even slow down. Our lives could well be forfeited. Betsy and I tried to decide what we would do in an actual emergency. We hoped to avoid such a draconian choice.

We met only two cars as we drove north all day on the sandy road, the main road to Léopoldville. It didn't look like the main road to anywhere. Oncoming drivers were supposed to give way and pull off into the grass. They often differed on whether to pull off to the right or to the left. We drove slowly through the center of dozens of villages and small towns, passing ramshackle mud houses with tin roofs or thatch, tumbledown roadside shops advertising Coca-Cola. Flocks of frantic chickens and black goats, and sometimes children, ran into the road, narrowly missed by our car. People ran out of their huts to cheer and wave at two white women passing through in a blue Volkswagen. We waved back, steered the car carefully down the dirt track, red dust flying behind us. At noon we stopped, spread our picnic blanket in front of the car in the narrow road, and ate our sardine sandwiches.

Through the long afternoon, we took turns at the wheel, driving through the monotonous landscape. A lone giraffe watched us from a distance. Troops of monkeys chattered in the trees, and baboons loped along the road. The sun worked its way across the sky. We came to a wide river with no bridge. Betsy tooted the horn to alert the attendant sleeping on the far bank. The makeshift ferry drifted toward us. It was just a bunch of boards thrown across a cluster of dugout canoes attached to a cable that sagged across the river. Betsy was a pro. She maneuvered the car up two narrow more-or-less-parallel planks onto the shaky platform. We drifted slowly across, propelled by the sluggish current.

Late in the afternoon, the shadows lengthened. In the brief dusk, we drove down the lane into the agricultural mission near Sandoa village. Alerted by shortwave radio, the missionaries were expecting us, and the guest house was ready.

Gallons of water were on the boil in a barrel over a charcoal fire in the yard. A servant carried the buckets into the bathhouse and filled the tub. We took turns. What a luxury, to soak ourselves and wash off the dust of the road. Refreshed, in clean clothes, we joined the family for dinner. Like most of the men up-country, Keith was a hunter. Lucille served antelope steak. She set a lovely table with Franciscan china, the old-fashioned Desert Rose pattern.

"Anybody you'd like to talk to in the States?" Keith asked, eager to show off his shortwave radio. He tossed the antenna high up over the branches of a mango tree. "I usually get pretty good reception at night. Let's see who I can find to patch you in." He picked up a strong signal in Rhode Island. Betsy asked about a connection to her grandmother in East Longmeadow, Massachusetts.

"I grew up in East Longmeadow," our contact replied enthusiastically. In no time at all, we heard a quivery voice.

"Hello, Betsy?"

Keith and I went inside to give them privacy. They talked for about twenty minutes. The signal faded before I had a chance to call anybody. The conversation meant everything to Betsy and her grandmother. Her grandmother died before she and Bob went home on furlough.

We looked forward to an easy day, just four hours to Kapanga. More rivers to cross. At the Lulua, one of the big ones, Betsy steered carefully onto the rickety ferry. We heard frantic honking and shouting, and a huge heavily loaded truck pulled up behind us. Betsy inched forward to make room, and the truck lurched onto the little raft. We hung over the front of the platform, and the truck hung off the back. Halfway across we surprised a pod of hippos. My first hippos! They opened their enormous jaws, showed their formidable teeth, and sank back under the murky water until we could see only their bulging eyes and piggy ears.

Duvon and Phyllis welcomed us and directed us to the guest house, where bathwater warmed on a fire outside. We joined the family at the dinner table, hippo pot roast from Duvon's recent hunting trip, fresh vegetables from the garden, and pineapples that grew in abundance in the sandy soil. Lovely tablecloth, nice china.

Drums sounded through the night. The hospital and mission were on the outskirts of Musumba, one of the largest villages in the Congo, an important center in the upper Katanga Province, and the home of the *Mwant Yav*, the Paramount Chief of the Balunda. Sixty thousand people were subjects of this dignitary. Bishop Springer founded the mission there in 1912, and the then-current *Mwant Yav* asked him to send a doctor. Dr. and Mrs. Piper arrived a year later, and construction began on the hospital, a rambling mud-brick one-story structure bearing their name.

Phyllis gave us a tour of the overcrowded hospital. A metal roof had only recently replaced the traditional thatch. We enjoyed the legendary stories of diners holding umbrellas to deflect the chaff and insects and occasional snake that tumbled down from overhead. A noisy generator provided electricity during the day. At night, kerosene lanterns shed their dim light.

The hospital had a primitive laboratory, but neither a blood bank nor an X-ray machine. There were two hundred beds, no sheets, no blankets, no mattresses. Patients brought their own bedding or wrapped themselves in whatever they had. A recent epidemic had overwhelmed the hospital. Patients lay two to a bed, on blankets on the floor, in the aisles, and under the beds. They were recovering from surgery, or pneumonia, or complications of chronic bronchitis or malaria. Entire families brought their sick. They camped nearby and prepared food over open fires for themselves and the patients. There was no kitchen. The families slept on the ground. Everything smelled of wood smoke.

I asked Phyllis about an elderly woman who was nursing a baby. A grandmother, she said. When the baby's mother died, the grandmother made medicine from herbs that allowed her to lactate. She would raise the child as her own. The identity of those leaves remained a secret, respected by the *wazungu*.

The village children, ever on the lookout for excitement, saw soldiers from the post mowing the field. The helicopter was expected. The men made a huge circle in the grass with white powder, A crowd gathered. Several weeks ago, two white women, wives of Belgian officials, had come to the hospital to give birth. They stayed in the government guest house. The babies were born in quarters less grand than Betsy's and mine. We'd called on the new mothers and admired their infants. Now the helicopter would take them back to their homes.

In time, that grassy strip would be leveled and mowed so small planes could come and go. This would be not only a convenience for Duvon and the other mission pilots, but a lifesaver when the country rose up in civil strife after Independence.

The doctors turned their attention to Betsy and me. One morning, promptly at nine o'clock, I walked resolutely into the hospital and climbed onto the operating table, a sturdy wooden table padded with folded blankets. I looked up at the faces surrounding me, black and white: Duvon, Phyllis, and the three African nurses. Duvon led a prayer in the local dialect, a sibilant language unknown to me. The generator outside thundered into life.

He rolled up his sleeves and asked, "Ready?"

I nodded. I just wanted to get this biopsy over with. Jo'burg might have been a more prudent choice after all. Too late now, here came the needle, local anesthesia. I dreaded being conscious through the process. In case I wanted to watch, the concave reflector on the overhead lamp mirrored a grotesque image of the scene. I closed my eyes. Blood trickled down my armpit. I tried to be a good patient. I was stoic. I whimpered a bit near the end. Duvon removed a piece of flesh the size of the end of my little finger and brandished it in his forceps for my approval.

"It looks good," he said. "I'm sure there's no malignancy. I'll send it to Jo'burg, just in case." He sewed up the wound with black thread.

"As long as you're here on the table, I might as well do a D and C, scrape that uterus." I wasn't even sure what a D and C was. Had he discovered something else when he examined me in Jadotville? Is that what he and Stewart had been talking about when I came into the room?

"In a modern hospital the procedure would require general anesthesia," Duvon remarked casually. I certainly would have preferred to be unconscious, or at least numb. Or not having the procedure at all. I can't forget the sound, like scraping carrots. Two of the African nurses carried me to an army cot in the corner of the "recovery room," behind a screen.

"Special treatment for you," Duvon said. "My African patients climb off the table and walk away."

I drowsed while Betsy was on the table. The nurses carried her over to join me on the cot, and I scooted laboriously to one side to make room for her. We lay there, head to toe, groaning and giggling weakly and dozing for an hour or so until we felt strong enough to get up and walk slowly back to the guest house.

Betsy spent several days in bed. When she felt better, I felt worse. I developed an awful rash all over my body, and a terrible case of hives. The doctors treated me with everything they could think of, but nothing helped. I resorted to sleeping pills at night. And Duvon had bragged on me as the one with no nerves at all.

We were eager to get back to our families, but the doctors were not ready to release us. When Betsy felt stronger, we started sewing projects. Occupational therapy. We intended to earn our keep. I stitched the seams and tossed the work to Betsy for handwork. We made four skirts, a blouse and two dresses for Phyllis. We learned to say, "Thank you very much" in the Lunda language, *Kwajikitish nakash.*

Two more *wazungu* patients were in town, Belgian women, wives of officials, to consult the Doctors Corbitt about complications of pregnancy. They stayed in the government guest house, tended by their servants. These two showed no respect for the local people. The condition of the wife of the District Commissioner was considered too complicated for the small mission hospital, and Duvon and Phyllis were relieved when the government helicopter zoomed in to take her to the District Hospital in Kamina, the nearest city.

Phyllis stopped by one morning as Betsy and I finished our breakfast. "The *Mwant Yav* is coming home. He's been in Elisabethville for a big palaver on *Independance*. I'll walk over with you. You don't want to miss this."

We joined the procession of people and hurried toward the landing field. "Can you hear the difference in the drums?" Phyllis asked. "Those are his special drums. There are still a few old men who understand the language of the Talking Drums, but everybody knows the sound of the drums of the *Mwant Yav*."

Above the clatter of the helicopter, as it touched down, I heard for the first time the unforgettable spine-chilling shriek of the women, an expression of praise and adulation. The *wazungu* had a word for it, *ululation*. That word never felt adequate, or appropriate. I needed an African word for an African sound.

Like most doctors I have known, Duvon and Phyllis routinely discussed their day's work at the dinner table. Symptoms and diseases, details of surgery, babies delivered—cesarean and otherwise. No place for the squeamish. Betsy loved it. I tried not to listen. I felt a sudden dampness and looked down to see my white blouse drenched in blood. Duvon leaped up, startled. I squealed, "Oh, doctor, I've been stabbed."

"That was an awfully lame joke," Duvon said. He hustled me into the bathroom, mopped up the blood, and tossed the bloody towels to soak in the bathtub. "These things happen every so often," he said, to reassure me. "The skin heals, a clot forms inside and the skin suddenly gives way. Nothing to be concerned about. I'll see if Phyllis has a clean blouse."

I could tell he was rattled. We returned to the dinner table as though nothing had happened. Duvon chuckled. "Oh, doctor," he said in falsetto, "I've been stabbed." I had secured my reputation as a wit and an unflappable patient.

"Suppose that had happened on our way home," I said later to Betsy. "What would we have done?"

"I have no idea." She and I had expected to be back with our families by now, but the doctors needed to make sure my wound healed properly. Finally, they pronounced us ready to travel. We had been there almost two weeks. We returned the books we had borrowed and distributed the rest of the treats we had brought: tins of tuna, boxes of Oreo cookies, Cracker Jacks, Kool-Aid.

We started early. Against all instructions, we drove all the way to Kolwezi that day. No complications on the Lulua ferry this time. The hippos were somewhere else.

The last couple of hours were no fun at all. Betsy and I were exhausted. It grew dark and we struggled to stay awake. We sang all the songs we knew and then sang them again. It was after ten o'clock when we checked into the hotel, La Bonne Auberge. I had a cup of tea and a warm bath and plunged into a deep sleep.

In the morning, I delivered Betsy to her family and arrived home at noon. I tooted the horn, and Stewart and the children came running. Home at last, a joyous reunion. So much for each of us to tell.

That night I fell asleep to the noise of the processing plant, not nearly as effective a lullaby as the hypnotic village drums. I missed the soft air, the easy interaction with the villagers, and, most of all, birdsong in the early mornings.

Six months later I ran into Duvon at a district meeting.

"Oh, by the way," he said, "your results came back from the pathologist in Jo'burg. You're okay."

Chapter Six

My children moped around the house. "There's nothing to do." "There's nobody to play with."

Sondra, mistress of games, and Greg, ready for any adventure, would soon be on their way to America with their parents and baby sister, officially on furlough. The family never returned to the troubled Congo.

Not for the first time, or the last, the end of the school year brought a wrenching loss of friends and playmates. Peter and Tim had some consolation when Greg gave them his pet monkey, Popo Kidogo. Their hearts broke when someone stole the affectionate little monkey. I worked hard to conceal my relief. Mary Beth and Martha complained that there were no kittens. I took the girls to the Union Minière pool almost every afternoon. It wasn't enough.

We endured a week of what we called African flu. The doctor across the street prescribed not only pills, but suppositories. The children, indignant, protested. Their fevers abated. Pale and listless, they sulked.

"Stewart, we need a vacation," I said. "I need to get away, to go someplace."

"What do you mean?" he said. "You had that nice trip to Kapanga."

"I wouldn't exactly call that a vacation. And that was months ago. We're entitled to take a month off. You need a break. We all need a break. The children are driving me nuts. We need to go somewhere and rest."

"You make a good point," he said. "I can't take a month off, though. Too much to do. We could go someplace for a week. We had a good time in Northern Rhodesia. What did you have in mind?"

"I was thinking of Lake Munkamba. A lot of missionaries have cottages there. We might be able to rent one for a few days. I'd love to go somewhere where we could swim." Lake Mukumba was one of the few lakes in Africa free from bilharzia, a dangerous disease carried by snails. It is highly infectious and difficult to treat.

"What's wrong with the Union Minière pool? You can swim there any time, for free."

"I'm going to see if there's anything available at the lake. The kids would love it."

I made some phone calls. It was a long shot, high season, the missionary children home from Sakeji School. On impulse, I called Bishop Booth.

"Of course you can use our cottage," he said. "Mrs. Booth and I will be in the area, and we have a few days when we'll be on the road. You are more than welcome. I'll send directions and let the caretaker know you're coming."

A jerry can of gas, just in case, took much of the space in the Volkswagen. It would be a long way between gas stations. Stewart added the usual shovel, ax, tow rope, jack, spare tire, teddy bears, battered dollies. I replenished the first-aid kit. Luggage-wise, we each had one small duffle, with swimsuits, jammies, shorts, tee shirts, sandals, long pants, and sweaters for cool evenings. All this in the blue tin trunk tied on top of the car. Barely room for the picnic basket and water jug. Nobody could change position without a lot of negotiation. Stewart drove, of course; I was the navigator, arbitrator, and enforcer. Our hand-written instructions offered confusing landmarks. Odd-shaped anthills. Grove of trees. Fork in the road. We arrived after dark, found the cottage, ate cold cereal with canned milk, made up the beds, and collapsed.

We woke in paradise. The rising sun glittered across the water. We scrambled to find our suits and jumped into the lake. What joy: the clear water, the sandy bottom of the lake, the early sun through the trees! We spoke quietly, not to disturb the stillness.

The calm was suddenly shattered. Was that a powerboat coming our way? The noise stopped abruptly. The boat drifted closer. A young boy held the tiller. A tall man stood up between the thwarts. He wore a baseball cap with the words "Arkansas Razorbacks." The boy gunned the motor and the man sat down abruptly. They slowed down and made a big circle around us.

"Howdy, how y'all doin'? We heard y'all were comin'. I'm Ed, and this here is my son, Mark. We're from Calico Rock, Arkansas." He pronounced it *Arkkinsaw*. "We heard you come in last night and thought we'd come over to get acquainted. Pat's cookin' breakfast for all of us. Git in the boat."

Peter stared in awe. "Where'd you get that boat?"

"Well, there's a story there, for sure, but it'll have to wait until after breakfast. Pat's makin' biscuits."

Pat had everything set up on the deck: a pot of coffee, orange juice, scrambled eggs and bacon, and, sure enough, hot biscuits and honey. "You were pretty late getting in last night. We figured you'd be hungry."

Mary Beth and Martha shivered in their swimsuits. "Lordy be," Ed said. "Those little girls are freezin. Go get some of those big towels, Mark. We got to get them warmed up. And bring a towel for their mom. Get a plate, y'all. Let's eat before it gets cold." To be with Ed and Pat was like standing in the sunshine on a chilly day.

"Now I'll tell you how we got that boat," Ed said. "We were on furlough at our home church in Arkansas. One of the deacons asked us what we'd like best for our work. Mark here piped up and said we'd like a motorboat. By golly, if they didn't just get us one." There it was, tied to the dock, bouncing a little in the current. "Purty, isn't it? Y'all can use it anytime. Mark, why don't you take these boys for a ride?"

"You guys want to go water skiing?" Mark offered.

"Will the boat go that fast?" Tim asked.

"Sure, go ahead and get in. I'll get the skis."

They zipped across the lake and back, taking turns at the tiller and on the skis, their joyous cries audible over the roar of the motor.

"When they come back, we'll take the boat and run you over to the grocery store," Pat said. "You probably need some supplies."

We bought bread and jam, oatmeal, and powdered milk. Back at our cottage, the watchman made the beds, brought in pails of water, and fired up the kerosene stove to boil our drinking water. The bishop's cottage lacked formality. Cast-off furniture, unmatched china, battered pots and pans, lots of teacups, only one with a handle. I stared in wonder at an unusual architectural feature, a carved mahogany pillar on which an ascending procession of people and animals spiraled up the ceiling. Who could have carved it? Why was it here? Surely the Booths' official residence in Elisabethville would be a more appropriate setting for this magnificent work of art, I thought.

The two tiny bedrooms suited the children. Stewart and I slept on an ancient fold-out couch in the living room. We had no privacy. "Aw, come on," he whispered. "They won't hear us; they're sleeping."

"No, they're not. Let's wait a while," I whispered back. We fell asleep before the children did.

In the water, the boys grew more daring. Mary Beth remained cautious, while Martha leaped fearlessly into "dat swimmin' pool." I kept watch, lest she wandered into deep water.

We skipped Sunday morning service. I hadn't packed any Sunday clothes. We had the lake to ourselves. Voices raised in familiar hymns drifted across the water. The music faded. A post-church promenade passed by: men in seersucker suits and white shirts, women in cotton dresses, stockings, and pumps. Some of the men were smoking cigarettes. I was shocked. I turned to Stewart.

"Can they do that?"

"Oh, yes, Presbyterians are allowed to smoke."

"That doesn't seem right."

One of the Presbyterians must have overheard our conversation. He stopped, turned to a colleague.

"Look at that," he said, in a loud voice, "those Methodist sinners, swimming on the Sabbath. For shame."

They smiled—or was that a sneer?—and walked on. I parsed the definition of sin. Which was worse: to break the Sabbath, or to smoke? In any case, I felt morally superior.

In anticipation of the Booth's arrival, we restored the cottage to order. I teased Esma about the china.

"If I had known you collected cups without handles, I would have brought you some of mine." She was not amused.

There have been a few times in my life when I wanted to stop the clock and prolong the present into infinity. This was one of those times of peace and contentment. The days had slipped by like dreams. We hoped to come back another time. It was not to be. The following summer, the violence of Independence was unleashed. Rebel soldiers trashed and burned the cottages. The Booth's faithful watchman was hacked to pieces, as was that magnificent mahogany column, people and animals wending upward, heaven bound.

Chapter Seven

Mary Beth and I came home from Saturday market. Our baskets brimmed with summertime bounty: lettuce, green beans, carrots, potatoes, green peppers, peanuts, and a special treat, strawberries. I filled the sink with cool water. Martha climbed up onto the kitchen stool and swished the vegetables around.

Stewart was at work in his study. I heard him whoop and turned off the faucet. He came into the kitchen, clutching a telegram, Peter and Tim close behind.

"So, what's up?" I asked.

"How would you and the kids like to spend some time in the real Africa?"

That was our code for the bush, for rural Africa, picture-book Africa. How could our house, with electricity and running water, in a town with paved streets and industrial noise, compare with that?

"Danny Elliott invited us to Camp Meeting at Samusamb," Stewart said, "I've been asked to preach."

Samusamb was famous, an annual get-together and revival meeting, organized by the old-timers, the veteran missionaries upcountry. With this invitation, Stewart received their seal of approval.

"We've got a week to get ready and show up in Kapanga. That's the jumping-off place for Samusamb."

Our little Volkswagen again scarcely contained our family and luggage. Each of us had a small duffel for the journey packed with a swimsuit, pajamas, sweater, toothbrush, a change of clothes.

Nothing had changed since Betsy and I had driven this road to Kapanga. Same parallel tracks in the sand, very little traffic. Goats and chickens ran into the road from the same small villages. It was a new experience for Stewart and the kids. At the Lulua River, he tooted the horn several times to summon the ferry—visible on the far shore—and skillfully maneuvered the little car onto the precarious platform. Upstream a group of hippos sported, bobbed to the surface every few minutes, a first sighting for the children. Hippo eyes and ears appeared, their great heads emerged, and their enormous jaws swung wide to reveal curved tusks and an impressive mouthful of fist-size teeth. The jaws snapped shut, the heads sank out of sight with a whoosh, down into the muddy river. The children stared in silence. The real Africa, at last.

In the front yard of the guest house at Kapanga, a fire smoldered under a barrel of bathwater. We took turns, washed off the red dust.

The next morning Stevie, twelve years old, stood at the stove in his mother's kitchen, his lanky frame wrapped in the cook's white apron. Doughnuts sizzled in a huge kettle of hot oil. Stevie turned them with a long-handled wire fork. He and his brother spent nine months of the year at Sakeji, the boarding school for missionary children in a remote section of Northern Rhodesia.

"I bet your mom will be sorry to see you go back to school," I said.

"Yes ma'am, I know she misses me, and so does my dad, but they're doing the Lord's work. I like school. We have a good time. Will Tim and Peter go to Sakeji next term?"

"No, they're doing just fine at the *athénée* in Jadotville. I think I'd die if I had to send them away." He looked over at me. Not for the first time, or the last, I wished I could call words back into my mouth.

Young Stevie was gracious. "Well, it's hard, all right, but it's not so bad when you know it's the Lord's will."

His mother came into the kitchen. "How are you getting on with those doughnuts, Stevie?" she asked. She turned to me. "We've got four kinds of cookies ready—peanut butter, chocolate chip, oatmeal, and ginger. I still have to make brownies and bake this yeast dough." She raised the corner of a white dishtowel and poked her finger into the mound of dough.

"I can do that for you, Diane," I offered. "How would you like it, pan rolls, dinner rolls? Large, or small?"

"Some of each, I guess. Let's see." She counted on her fingers. "There will be eighteen of us missionaries, counting all the kids. My boys will be with us for two days, and then Danny will take them to Sakeji School. He'll take the Cartwright boys too. That's four big appetites. I hope we have enough food."

"There's enough here to feed an army. I don't know how you do it."

"When you live three hundred miles from the grocery store, you get really good at planning."

Stewart eagerly accepted Duvon's invitation to visit the hospital and observe the daily surgery. "Nothing fancy this morning," the doctor said. "Just some routine stuff, hernias and such."

Duvon reported later to me. "Well, during the first operation, your husband tied his shoes four times, pulled up his socks twice, and then just bent down to touch his toes. But he stayed through the whole thing. He's a good sport."

At noon our caravan set off for Samusamb, a hundred miles away over deplorable roads. Stewart drove Danny's station wagon. We called it the fastest vacuum cleaner on the road. It sucked all the road dirt into the car. All the boys rode with him in the big car crammed with camping equipment and supplies.

I drove the Volkswagen. Diane navigated. The four little girls, two of hers and two of mine, chattered in the back seat, content to share paper dolls cut from the Sears Roebuck catalog. African drivers drove the two heavily loaded mission trucks. Danny had left early that morning on his old bicycle, riding with a host of African men on their ancient, dilapidated bikes.

"Danny rides his bike along with them, so they won't get scared and turn back," Diane said.

"A hundred miles is a long way on that bicycle."

"It's a Cadillac compared to what the Africans ride. Danny doesn't mind. He loves sharing the journey, fixing their flat tires."

We drove for a while in silence. Diane turned to me. "When do you and Stewart plan to send your children to Sakeji School? You know, they like to get the children when they are small, to break them to their system."

I shivered involuntarily. It would be a long drive to Samusamb. "So far they're doing well at the *athénée*. They're more comfortable now in French, and they're making friends with the local kids."

"How are you coming with your French?"

"I wish I were better at it. I don't seem to find time for language study."

"Well, if you sent the children to Sakeji, you'd have time."

I was trapped in my own car. Diane didn't let up. "You know, when you go home on furlough it will be hard for them to adjust to American schools. Sakeji's on the British system, and at least they speak English."

This wasn't the time to explain that I wanted the children to be bilingual. My inability to carry on a conversation in French was a constant embarrassment. The boys often translated for me. Maybe someday I'd find time to work on my French. Maybe even master the subjunctive.

I sighed. "Diane, God gave me those children. They are the most important thing in my life. I just can't imagine sending them away. I don't know how you and Danny do it."

"The Lord gives us strength," she said sternly. "My boys know it's God's will for them to be at Sakeji. Actually, they like it there. It's a good, safe, simple life. They have tons of friends. They dammed the river for a swimming hole, the boys love that. And the teachers are all good Christians. Susie can hardly wait to join her brothers."

In the rear-view mirror, I watched Susie, six years old, the eldest of the four little girls in the back seat, holding catalog cutouts in each hand. Her little sister, Cindy, was the youngest.

"Here's the mama, and here's the daddy," Susie said. "Mary Beth, have you got the baby buggy?"

Mary Beth's blonde head bent over the cardboard tray. I couldn't imagine sending her away when she was six. I winced to think of empty chairs at our dining room table. Was I selfish to want my children at home? Maybe they would be happier at Sakeji. Had Diane and Danny set up the travel arrangements so she could have this conversation with me?

Enough of this. Time for a subject change. "Tell me about Samusamb," I said.

"It's a beautiful place. Big old trees. The Lulua River runs between huge rock walls. At one point it's so narrow you could jump across it." I looked at her in surprise. The Lulua was a big river. "Don't worry, Chief Samusamb will make sure nobody tries to jump across the river. He is responsible for our safety. Not that many years ago, the region was cannibal country, and the Africans were deathly afraid of it. They refused to go anywhere near the place. The missionaries started the annual Camp Meeting there to prove our God was stronger than the evil spirits."

The road continued to deteriorate. Stewart, comfortable behind the wheel, led the way deeper into the bush. We followed close behind, choking on the dust that billowed around us. The girls napped in the back seat. We were quiet, thinking our own thoughts. Diane broke the silence.

"We are all so pleased with the way you and Stewart are settling into the work. Stewart has a real rapport with the Africans. He has already brought so many to Christ. I'm just thrilled you could come to Samusamb with us."

Stewart had accomplished a lot during our first year. He'd traveled constantly over the district, encouraged the pastors. He'd started a pastors' school, managed the district schools, supervised the erection of new buildings for churches and schools. Uninhibited by his elementary Swahili and stilted French, he preached in several different churches every Sunday. He got on well with the bishop and the other missionaries. He'd won the approval of Danny and Keith, important men in the Conference. He'd been reluctant to leave West Hartford for Africa, and the year in Brussels was a nightmare of failure and disappointment for him. Yet he wasn't discouraged. Chastened by his example, I resolved to be more supportive, to find my own way to contribute to The Work.

The road disintegrated into parallel tracks through waist-high dry grass, then over slippery rocks on the edge of a deep ravine. I drove slowly, cautiously, and pulled up behind Stewart. The girls woke up, rubbed their eyes. "Are we there?"

One after another, they stumbled out of the car.

"Don't wander off, girls," I called after them. I stifled my panic as they waded into the tall grass and disappeared. "Stay where I can see you."

Diane laughed. "You don't have to worry about them getting lost here. The Africans will know where they are. The only thing to worry about is crocodiles. They move really fast."

When she described the place, had she mentioned crocodiles?

We followed Danny to a clearing. Three shoulder-high grass shacks stood in a row, bundles of dry grass tented together to form walls, one side open. Peter and Tim hoisted duffels and sleeping bags from the car and tossed them into the nearest hut.

"That's handy storage space," I commented.

"That's more than storage space. Those huts are the guest rooms. We sent out an advance crew to set up camp. You brought cots, didn't you?"

I looked at Stewart, raised my eyebrows. Cots?

He looked sheepish. "I didn't think we had room for them."

"Oh, that's all right. We brought an extra air mattress. I'll find someone to pump it up for you. You'll be surprised how comfortable you'll be. Just pile lots of dry grass on the floor." She introduced us to the latrine, a hole in the ground, screened by woven reeds.

"You brought insect repellant, didn't you? You have to watch out for spiders."

And snakes, I thought. And don't forget the crocodiles. Mary Beth and Martha heard "spiders" and decided to sleep in the car. They fit comfortably in the Volkswagen, one across the front seat, one in the back.

The other missionaries were veterans of bush life. In their well-organized compound, camping equipment lined the walls of the big tents. Sleeping bags were unrolled on camp cots, clothing stashed in wooden boxes, lawn chairs and camp stools set up. Lanterns hung from low branches. "Come," Diane said. "I'll show you the kitchen."

In a field of trampled grass, supplies were piled on two long aluminum folding tables: sacks of flour and rice, boxes of spaghetti, baskets full of crusty loaves of bread, big aluminum bowls of mangoes, pineapples, and papayas. Ice chests formed a line under the tables. The camp stove, the round surface of half a steel drum heated by a brisk fire, was crowded with generous saucepans and skillets. I greeted the African cooks, most of whom I recognized from the mission kitchens. Wrapped in white aprons, the crew bustled about in high spirits. They sang as they chopped, stirred, stoked the fire, brought more wood, split kindling. The air was redolent with the irresistible scent of onions and meat frying and spaghetti sauce bubbling. All of a sudden, I was ravenous.

A red-flowered plastic cloth covered another long table. "Lunch in ten minutes," Diane announced. She directed us to the washstand under a nearby tree. We filled our plates, poured Kool-Aid, and found places on the rough benches. Keith said grace. I sprinkled powdered Kraft Parmesan cheese on my spaghetti. "The Africans have their own kitchen," Diane said. "They're cooking *bukadi*. We bring tons of manioc for them."

Manioc, a dependable food source that thrived in poor, drought-resistant soil, was the staple of the African diet. Women dug up large tuberous roots and put them to soak to leach out the cyanide poison. The roots were dried on mats in the sun and pounded to a coarse flour by women wielding strong, heavy wooden paddles. We had first seen this done at the International Exposition in Brussels.

The veteran missionaries tried to convince me that the *bukadi* in their area was sweeter, tastier. They claimed to enjoy it. They agreed that it offered very little food value but many of the Africans didn't have alternatives. Meat was scarce. They craved substantial food to quench the pangs of hunger, and *bukadi* met that need.

"And we promise them meat," Keith said. "They need protein. That's how we get them to come. We'll go hunting tomorrow and try for a big hippo that will feed the whole crowd."

Stewart and the boys stared at him.

"Can we go on the hunt?" Tim said.

"Of course," Keith said. "We'll all go."

"What does hippo taste like?" Peter asked.

"It's delicious," Lucille said. "Just like roast pork. I'm sure you'll like it."

Peter looked dubious. He asked for seconds on spaghetti.

Exhausted from the drive, I longed for a nap. "The services will start soon," Keith said. "You don't want to miss hearing Stewart preach."

Several hundred people had already gathered in a natural amphitheater among the huge rocks. The children and I found a place in the shade and spread an old quilt on the ground. It was hot, without a breeze. Flies circled around. Insects crawled over us. Stewart's voice rang through the clearing, echoed off the rocky cliffs. He urged repentance from sin. Danny and Keith took turns, translating into Chokwe. We had left the Swahili-speaking region when we crossed the Lulua River.

Stewart preached for an hour. Mary Beth and Martha laid their heads in my lap and went to sleep. I shifted about, tried to get comfortable, not to disturb them. At last, Stewart brought the sermon to a close. He invited the congregation to come forward, confess their sins, and seek forgiveness. A ragged crowd surged to the altar as we sang a hymn. *"Bwana Jesu, Bwana Jesu."* Men and women, young and old, wailed under the weight of their transgressions, cried out for salvation. They fell to their knees and sobbed and gave their hearts to Jesus. Ecstatic, the women threw their arms in the air and ululated, *yeee, yeee, yeee,* a shrill startling noise, the sound of real Africa. Babies bounced on their mothers' backs, wide-eyed, their heads bobbing from side to side. The crowd milled about crying, reluctant to disband, singing, and praising Jesus. *"Yesu ni Bwana* [Jesus is Lord]."

I reflected on my own transgressions. I coveted my neighbor's army cot. I placed my children above The Work. Were these sufficiently grave to require repentance? Other people's sins surely sounded more interesting.

Mary Beth and Martha woke up. I stretched my aching limbs, and we walked back to the huts and tents. Stewart and Danny, drenched with sweat, caught up with us.

"Who wants to go swimming?" Danny asked. "You brought your suits, didn't you?"

I asked about the crocodiles.

"Diane must have told you." He ignored Diane's dirty look. "The girls always worry about the crocodiles. Leave it to me. I'll take care of them."

"Danny shoots his gun every half hour or so," Diane said. "He claims that scares them away."

Mary Beth looked at me to see if I was scared. I tried for nonchalance, like the others. But I couldn't let it rest. "Don't you worry about bilharzia?"

Diane lost patience. "The snails avoid swiftly running water. We swim below the waterfall."

The waterfall? What next?

In the grass hut, Stewart and I peeled off our sweaty clothes. Crouched under the low thatch of the makeshift roof, we struggled into our swimsuits, ducking and dodging to avoid the sharp stems of dry grass. I put my skirt and shirt back on to spare the Africans the sight of my bare legs. African standards of modesty contrasted sharply with European customs. African women wrapped layers and layers of colorful floor-length cloth around their waists and hips, careful to keep their legs covered at all times. I had long since become accustomed to their natural, unselfconscious manner as they bared their breasts to nurse their babies. No European woman would think of exposing her breasts, yet many didn't hesitate to expose their legs in provocative shorts and short skirts. I wore skirts of mid-calf length, as the other missionary women did. My modest one-piece bathing suit didn't set off any alarms, but I was uncertain how I would be regarded here. I'd take my cues from Diane and Lucille.

The path through the trees to the river ended at the brink of the falls. The water plunged thirty feet. Noise and spray permeated the air. There were no Africans at the river. I needn't have worried about embarrassment. The *wazungu* would bathe unobserved.

We climbed down the rough track to the pool below the falls. The river was fifty feet wide here. Diane was right about the strong current. Keith and Danny carried their guns down the cliff. Keith fired his gun to scare away the crocodiles. The noise echoed through the canyon. "Don't go into the river yet," he said to the impatient boys. "We'll give the crocodiles ten minutes to vamoose." It seemed ages until he gave the thumbs-up. The boys cannon-balled in, hollered, and splashed each other. I eased into the clear, cold water and paddled gingerly around, alert for the crocodiles' ugly snouts and beady eyes. Mary Beth and Martha stayed close to me. The men stood waist-deep in the water, planning the hunting trip for the next day.

Diane and I lay on sun-warmed rocks and let the late afternoon sun dry our tired bodies. The little girls shivered, their lips blue with the cold. We wrapped them in towels, rubbed them vigorously, dried their hair. The boys' shouts resonated as they dunked each other, floated on their backs, and spit jets of water into the air. Keith blew his whistle, time to go. We climbed the trail to the top of the falls. I heard a shot. The men and boys came into view. Stewart carried Danny's gun. "I think I got a crocodile back there," he said. He tried not to look too pleased with himself.

Keith said, "Yeah, you got him all right, no question. Good shot. Good practice for the hunt tomorrow." I was pleased to see Stewart accepted into the fellowship of hunters. It was important for Tim and Peter to see their dad holding his own with Keith and Danny. Guns made me uneasy. I knew nothing about hunting. My dad renounced guns forever when he left France after the First World War.

Danny said it was time for us to meet Chief Samusamb. We'd change out of our wet swimsuits and all go together. The real Africa for sure.

The chief, a small man, wrapped in a sort of sarong, wore a jaunty pith helmet. His keen eyes examined us. His council members, dressed in trousers and shirts previously worn by *wazungu*, stood by in respect. I couldn't help but be impressed by the natural dignity of the chief. Solemnly he greeted Danny and Keith and their families, and we visitors were introduced and welcomed. Stewart thanked him for his hospitality. Keith translated. We followed the chief and his retinue to the place where the mighty Lulua River poured swiftly through a narrow channel a strong man might, indeed, jump across. Nobody was going to do that today. I wondered if Keith or Danny had ever tried it. Probably not. The chief would have heard about it, and that would have been the end of Camp Meeting.

The chief asked Danny if the *wazungu* would like to see the talking drums. Would we ever! Danny gave us a brief preview as we walked along the path. The various tones and rhythms sent messages to those who knew the language. Everyone in hearing distance understood the message as it was transmitted. Drumming—an endangered art—had proved far more reliable than the telegraph. Few young men were willing to serve the long apprenticeship.

The great drums stood in a clearing, huge logs about six feet long, bark removed, the underside flattened for stability. Danny described the process by which the narrow slit is made along the length of the log. A burning stick is repeatedly pushed into the top surface to char the wood and hollow the log for resonance. The slit, several inches wide, extended deep into the log. I couldn't imagine the time and patience this required.

The drummer appeared, a wiry man in ragged shorts and shirt. He held two stout sticks with a glob of hard rubber on the end of each one. He saluted the chief and waited respectfully for permission to play. Keith announced that we would hear the "March of the Paramount Chief of the District." The drummer stepped up to the side of the waist-high log, paused for a moment, drew a deep breath, and attacked the drum. He pounded his sticks vigorously on different surfaces and produced an incredible variety of tones and sounds, a veritable symphony. I couldn't analyze the complex rhythm, an unmistakable message of awesome power and majesty. Summoned by the thunder of the great drum, men and women ran into the clearing and stood transfixed, perhaps transported to an earlier time when the power of the great chief was indeed paramount. The echoes died away. Spellbound, nobody moved.

There would be an encore. Instructed by the chief, the drummer played the "Call to War," which summoned his men to bring their spears and guns, and the women to take the children and hide deep in the bush. The hair rose on the back of my neck. More men ran into the clearing, high on adrenalin, surprised, ready to fight for their chief. He smiled at them, gazed intently at the crowd, waved his hand to calm them. No need for those spears and guns today. Just a practice run. The spell was broken. The power of those drums. I'd be terrified to hear that booming, crackling thunder in earnest. The chief nodded to the drummer to put away his sticks. I shook off my trance and looked around at the respectful crowd, all eyes on the chief and his drummer. The chief calmly accepted our homage. He invited us to approach the impressive drum. It seemed almost sacrilegious to lay my hands on it, to tap the surface here and there for a variety of tones. I was transported back a hundred years, to the Africa of David Livingstone and Henry Morton Stanley. Farther back, to the time of Prester John.

Another songfest occurred that evening around a huge bonfire that crackled like gunshots. The fragrant smoke plumed up into the trees. The men's voices rose, rich and deep in intricate harmonies and complicated rhythms. The women's voices soared to an accompaniment of gourd rattles and small drums and the clink-clink of bits of metal on empty bottles. My children, in warm pajamas and sweaters, couldn't keep their eyes open. Stewart and I picked up Mary Beth and Martha, and the boys stumbled after us down the path. We tucked them into their sleeping bags, Mary Beth and Martha in their preferred spot in the Volkswagen. Tim and Peter had spread their bags on the grass piled deep on the floor of their hut. Stewart and I, in the other hut, laid our sleeping bags atop the slippery air mattress and crawled in under the mosquito nets. I hoped all the spiders and snakes were already asleep. The sound of singing drifted our way, with the scent of the campfire. The drums sounded through the night. Magnificent stars shone through the open spaces in the roof of the hut.

Early sunlight filtered through the walls. Alarmed by a rustling noise, louder and louder, I sat up. Something big was approaching through the dry grass. "Stewart! Wake up! Something's coming."

He sat up, rocked the air mattress as he reached for his glasses. "What's the matter?"

"I think it's a crocodile," I wailed. Helpless, trapped in the tangled bedding, frozen with fear, I listened as whatever it was coming closer. For the first time, I wished Stewart had a gun. At least the girls were safe in the car. But what about the boys? And me? And Stewart? Why hadn't I married a hunter?

A big, clumsy black dog broke through the side of the hut and jumped up onto the air mattress. He panted and slavered as he clawed his way, his big feet slipping and sliding. Danny's hunting dog, ecstatic, licked my face. I shoved him away. He was heavy. His breath made me gag. Bits of straw stuck to his fur. Stewart laughed. I felt foolish, having been terrified by this harmless hound making his morning rounds. It wasn't funny yet: the sudden change from abject fear to relief—and embarrassment. Stewart pulled on his clothes and went in search of breakfast. I could hear laughter. I dressed slowly, dreading the merciless teasing I knew would come. I was among some accomplished teasers. I took a deep breath and walked to the breakfast table.

Danny went first. "I hear you're scared of my ol' hound dog."

"Yeah," Keith said, "that hound doesn't look anything like a crocodile."

I tried a tight smile, helped myself to oatmeal, sliced a banana, and poured reconstituted powdered milk over it. Then I put slices of fresh pineapple and hot rolls fresh from the improvised oven on my plate, added evaporated milk to a cup of lukewarm Nescafé, and took my place on the bench. The conversation had already moved on to the proposed hunting trip.

The morning preaching service was less intense than the day before. The crowd seemed distracted, restless for the hunt. No souls were saved. After an early lunch, the men set out on foot through the forest for the river, Danny, Keith, and Danny's dog in the vanguard. Stewart and the boys followed the crowd toward their destination, a deep pool several miles down the river, where hippos congregated in large numbers.

A hippopotamus is a huge animal, but a small target. The only vulnerable spot in the inch-thick hide is a small area near the eye. The herd spends the day slowly bobbing up and down in the water, randomly coming up, one by one, every few minutes to breathe. Protruding eyes and little piggy ears break the surface of the water. If the coast is clear, the entire head emerges, the enormous jaws open wide on their hinges for an audible intake of breath, the jaws close and the head disappears. All this takes less than half a minute, a challenge for the hunter, who seldom gets a chance for more than one shot before the animal disappears under the water. A dead hippo will float to the surface in an hour or so, as the gas in the stomach expands. The hunting party discusses whether or not the hunter has hit his target. Perhaps the hunter missed, and the hippo has escaped death this time, swimming away under water followed by the whole herd. If the hunter is successful, or lucky, a great cheer goes up at the sight of the floating carcass.

Hippos are extremely dangerous. Their heavy tusks can turn an ordinary boat into kindling. A prudent hunter shoots from the shore or uses a boat with a double hull or a hollowed-out teak log. At night, the entire herd comes ashore to graze. They decimate great areas of vegetation with their scissor-like tusks, grinding the greenery between their fist-sized molars. These testy herbivores will attack humans, maim and kill them, and leave them as lunch for crocodiles.

The afternoon shadows lengthened as we waited for news of the hunters. We were too far away to hear gunfire. The little girls played with paper dolls. Happy to have some time to myself, I read *Cry, the Beloved Country*, Alan Paton's classic story of South Africa. I had already read it several times, but books were scarce. I liked the sad story and the mysterious Zulu words, *Umfundisi, ixopo, ndotsheni*.

It would soon be dark. What could take them so long? Diane seemed unconcerned. She'd been through this many times. The sun disappeared on schedule, about six o'clock, the sudden dark of the tropics. We built a small campfire for warmth and comfort. Lucille rummaged through the food boxes. "There's spaghetti sauce left over from last night. I'll put on some rice to boil. We can make a salad. If the men bring meat, we'll grill some steaks. They're bound to be hungry after all this time and that long walk." At last, we heard deep voices. Lanterns moved through the trees. Diane called out, "Did you bring home the bacon?"

Danny emerged into the firelight, his dog padding along at his heels. "Not exactly. We won't know for sure how much bacon there is until tomorrow morning. We took the big dugout canoe onto the river and I got a pretty good shot at a big hippo. We waited forever to see if it would surface. You know how the Africans talk it over, did I hit it or not. Some said *Bwana* Danny missed this time. It was almost too dark to see. It finally floated and they gave me a big cheer. We waded in and I got a rope around it, tied the carcass to a big rock. We left some men to guard it against the crocodiles. We'll go back in the morning for the butchering." Stewart and the boys came out of the woods. They looked exhausted. They gulped cup after cup of water. Lucille served them plates of rice with spaghetti sauce, and salad.

Danny turned to me. "You and the kids will want to come in the morning. It's quite a sight, you won't want to miss it. We'll go out early, take the truck to bring home the meat. You all come in the car after you've had breakfast. It's too far for the girls to walk."

Stewart crunched a piece of bread. I could see his grin in the firelight. "Danny gave me the first shot, but I missed. Then he took a shot and hit it. Wait till you see it, it's huge. Enough meat to feed the crowd for a week." I tried to imagine it. I was pretty sure I'd never seen that much meat.

At first light, Stewart and Danny and all the boys crowded into the back of Keith's ancient pickup, along with as many Africans as the truck would hold. Keith liked to say the truck ran like a good Christian, by faith alone. The fellows never went anywhere without picks and shovels, axes, a wheelbarrow, a block and tackle. You could always count on trouble on the road.

An hour later, we followed. Diane drove the station wagon while I steered the Volkswagen. We soon came upon Keith's truck, stopped in a clearing by a small creek. Men bustled around, carried logs and stones and large branches. Keith waved and walked over to where we had pulled up.

"What's going on?" Lucille asked. "Did the truck break down already?"

"Not this time. Take a look. We're building a bridge."

In Africa, things seldom go as planned. The builders of this bridge had failed to finish the job. Stout upright posts anchored a sturdy log frame on which they'd laid sawed-off logs. The wood that formed the roadway wasn't secured in place, and there were no access ramps. The squared-off bridge sat forlorn, about five feet above the level of the road, like a child's drawing of a work in progress, short a pair of hypotenuses. The men were building ramps. Keith thought the bridge looked strong enough to support his truck, and if he drove slowly, the loose logs would probably stay in place. "We couldn't possibly get the meat this far without the truck. It's going to take a while. Find some shade and make yourselves comfortable."

Keith, Stewart, Danny, and all the boys toiled along with the Africans. They shoveled dirt, chopped logs, and tamped down earth and stones as the ramps took shape on each side of the bridge.

I sat in the shade and watched. I shooed away the flies while they worked and sweated. Gradually, the approaches grew higher and longer. Several hours passed before Keith announced it was time for a trial run. "Wish me luck," he said, and swung into the cab of the truck. "Say a prayer."

He drove slowly forward, then paused so the men could move stones and shovel more dirt. The front wheels rolled onto the bridge. Keith gunned the motor. The truck thumped and rattled its way across the loose branches and inched its way down the other side. Everybody cheered.

Keith got out and walked back, and carefully examined the structure. At his thumbs-up, the men loaded their tools into the bed of the truck. Keith cautiously drove the station wagon to the other side.

Surely the lightweight Volkswagen would have no problems. Stewart climbed in behind the wheel and the little car, the focus of all eyes, crept up the ramp. The station wagon had knocked some of the logs on the bridge out of alignment. Stewart accelerated, eased the front wheels up and over. The car stuck there, stranded like a turtle, teetering on the logs, wheels spinning, going nowhere. Half a dozen men ran up behind the car and hoisted up the rear bumper. The front wheels engaged, the car moved forward, the back wheels bumped down, and Stewart rolled across the bridge and down the other side. The men trooped across, shouting and laughing.

We formed a sort of caravan. Keith's truck led; the station wagon followed. The Volkswagen brought up the rear like a caboose. After several miles, the bush track through the forest ended abruptly in a clump of trees. "We'll walk from here," Keith said. "It's not that far to the river, about half a mile."

The Africans jumped down from the bed of the truck, eager to get to the kill. As we approached the river, I could hear the excited murmur of the crowd. Men stood waist-deep in the water and pulled the dead hippo toward the shore. The ropes broke and broke again. The beast, as big as a Volkswagen, was finally dragged onto the beach. Men grabbed machetes and hacked into the carcass, intent on their work. We kept back at a safe distance. They knew what they were doing. Nobody got hurt. They worked fast, slashed off wide strips of the thick hide, and laid them on the ground, skin side down, fat side up, to make a sort of clean carpet onto which they tossed hunks of meat. Dark blood spouted, ran down their arms and legs, oozed across the pale carpet of fat, and drained into the river. They carved out the six-foot-long tenderloin and presented it to Mama Diane. She crammed the meat into an insulated picnic carrier, twenty kilos of tenderloin, enough to feed the missionary gang for the rest of the week.

When the men whacked into the stomach of the hippo, they released a cloud of noxious gas. We retreated into the trees, gagging and retching. We couldn't escape the foul odor.

"Eeugh," Peter said, "I'm not going to eat anything that smells like that."

I suggested we hike back to the car. "Good idea," Lucille said. The children and I had gone about ten feet down the path when a great shout went up from the crowd back at the river. Oh, no, I thought. Those machetes. They must have killed somebody.

"*Bwana!* Look, *bwana!* More hippos!" The herd bobbed up and down in the river, oblivious to our presence. In their midst was an enormous hippo. "*Bwana!* Shoot it, *bwana!* Shoot it!" Danny and Keith huddled, talked it over. They carried extra licenses, in case they found more game. The District Commissioner issued the permits, forty dollars for each hippo. Danny had a second permit. They could use the meat. They had a big crowd this year, and the people could always take some home with them. Danny, intent, walked along the bank, kept pace with the unsuspecting herd as it drifted slowly downstream. He disappeared around a bend in the river. The crowd grew quiet. Another family of hippos, old ones and young ones, drifted by. A single gunshot broke the silence, reverberating through the forest. Several minutes passed. We waited. Danny reappeared.

"I got it. It's a really big one, biggest one I ever saw. We'll have a real feast."

They would wait for the body to surface. The girls and I had seen enough butchery for the day. Just the memory of that putrid odor sent us back up the path back to the VW. Stewart and the boys came with us. The children and I walked across the rickety bridge and Stewart drove across without incident.

Back in camp, we squeezed lemons for lemonade and put together a simple picnic lunch—peanut butter and jelly sandwiches, fruit, and chocolate chip cookies. Mary Beth and Martha and I rested in the shade. A runner came into camp with a note to Diane from Danny. After almost two hours, the second hippo had floated to the surface and the butchers were hard at work. Keith's pickup couldn't carry all the meat. He needed the old flatbed truck. Stewart and one of the African drivers set off to the rescue. Much later that afternoon, close to sundown, the trucks returned, loaded down with a crowd of men and several tons of meat. Stewart was filthy with blood, dirt, and sweat.

They had run out of luck. With the extra weight of all that meat, the hastily constructed bridge gave way. They rebuilt the bridge.

Stewart picked up his towel and trudged toward the river, ready to take his chances with the crocodiles.

"Don't you want to see the distribution of the meat?" Diane asked.

"I've seen enough meat for a while," he said over his shoulder.

The Africans clustered around the truck in hushed expectation. Each one received his allotment gratefully, almost reverently, and expressed deep appreciation for the bounty provided by the missionaries. They piled more wood on the fires and threw great chunks of meat onto the coals for dinner. They cut meat into strips, threaded them onto green sticks, and placed them carefully in the smoke to make jerky. Nothing would be wasted. There was plenty for everyone: no one would go hungry. They gave thanks to God and *Bwana* Danny.

The missionary community dined that evening on a huge roast loin of hippo, with rice and gravy. We, too, gave thanks to God and *Bwana* Danny and fell in line with our plates. I tried not to think about the primal scene on the river, the blood and gore, the flying machetes, the horrendous odor. The roast smelled delicious.

The children went through the line first. Peter watched Keith slice the meat. "Is that hippo? I don't want any of that ol' smelly hippo."

"Maybe you'd rather have some roast beef," Keith said as he deftly carved a couple of juicy slices off the other end of the roast and put them on Peter's plate. "Here you go. Some rice with that?"

"Okay, but don't give me any of that hippo gravy."

It tasted like good roast pork. I went back for seconds, with rice and gravy. More than half of the tenderloin remained. Lucille said, "Tomorrow we'll slice off some steaks, and the next day, pot roast. There'll be some to take home."

But that was not to be. During the night Danny's hound dog broke into the meat locker, ate as much as he could, and dragged the rest of the tenderloin around the compound in the dirt.

Chief Samusamb sent a goat. The cooks killed and roasted it. I found the meat surprisingly tender and tasty.

Early in the morning after the feast, Keith set off with his sons and the Elliott boys for Sakeji School, three hundred miles south, just over the border in Northern Rhodesia. All the little girls cried to see them go. I could hardly bear the thought of the separation. The mothers kept a cheerful countenance until the car was out of sight.

"It's only four months until Christmas vacation," Diane said. Small comfort.

"You know what gets me?" she sniffled and wiped away a tear. "When I strip the beds, I see the impression of their heads on the pillows."

Silently, I resolved once more I would never send my children away to boarding school.

A chastened group gathered around the breakfast table, cheerless without those lively boys. The mothers comforted the little sisters and took all the girls down to the river with tin cans to catch tadpoles. Tim and Peter moped.

"Mom, how come we can't go to Sakeji School? They've got their own swimming hole and everything."

On this last day of Camp Meeting, Stewart preached his final sermon, and we all trooped down to the river for one last swim. As we came out of the trees, Stewart, in the lead, shouted back to us. "There's somebody in the water, above the falls."

Sure enough, a head bobbed in the water. A body drifted rapidly toward a tiny island on the brink of the falls, just a patch of grass around which the river poured over the cliff. I could see the boy clearly now. I held my breath. He managed to snatch handfuls of the watergrass on the very edge. He clung there, frozen with fear as the swift water tugged at him. How long could he keep that precarious hold? How could we save him? Stewart's shout brought several Africans to the river. As the news spread more and more people came until there was a great crowd. A few shouted encouragements to the boy. Most stood quietly, murmuring to each other, overwhelmed by the tragedy developing before their eyes. Perhaps the old malevolent spirits of the region were not banished after all.

"It's Luka," Diane said. "He's an orphan, a friend of Stevie's. He worked for one of the missionary families. They sort of adopted him. They'll be devastated." I remembered seeing Luka in the kitchen. Nice kid. Danny walked over to where we stood.

"Luka. Just what you'd expect. He and Stevie were always up to stuff. If Stevie were here, he'd probably be out there in the river too."

Chief Samusamb and his retinue joined us and stared wordlessly at the scene. Danny approached the chief. A strong swimmer, he proposed to swim across below the falls, climb up on the rocks and reach the boy. Before the Chief could stop him, Danny shucked off his shoes and stripped down to his swimming trunks. The Chief forbade him to attempt a rescue. Danny didn't argue. He put his pants back on. He was sure he could do it, but the chief wouldn't let him risk his life. The chief didn't think it was possible to save the boy anyway, and the Belgian authorities would hold him responsible if something happened to a white man in his territory.

Danny paced back and forth in frustration. Some men threw an old rope into the water again and again, and watched the rope drift back to the bank each time.

Someone fired an ancient rifle in an attempt to keep the crocodiles away. I couldn't bear it. It could have been Peter or Tim out there. They were always doing risky stunts.

During the years I was in high school and college, I worked summers as a lifeguard at the municipal pool in my hometown in Kansas. I might be able to save this boy, I thought. If he survived being swept over the falls, I might be able to pull him from the current in the river below. I was ready; I had my swimsuit on underneath my clothes. I knew what to do. I slipped away and walked downstream. I stepped out of my skirt and waded into the water, searching for a secure spot where I could stand to catch him. No thought now of crocodiles. The chief saw me and shouted at me. The noise of the falls drowned out his words, which I couldn't have understood anyway, but there was no mistaking his gesticulations. I was to get out of the water. Danny joined me.

"The chief says to tell that woman to get out of the water and put on her clothes. He says it's a disgrace. Sorry." Danny gave me a wry smile. "I see what you had in mind, it's a great idea, but there's no way the chief will let you do it."

I was mortified, standing there in my bathing suit, exposed to all those eyes, yelled at by the chief. I was trying to save the boy's life, and he thought I just wanted to attract attention. I couldn't seem to get anything right. I fastened my skirt, put on my sneakers, and followed Danny. The chief glared at me. I ducked my head, looked away. Stewart grimaced. And still the boy clung to his precarious perch. He could lose his grip any minute.

Three men approached the chief. Danny translated for us. These men had fished above the falls and knew the water. It wasn't very deep. They could wade to the boy and bring him ashore. The chief agreed to let them try.

Danny helped them attach themselves to a frayed rope. He held the end of the rope as the men waded into the water a short distance above the brink. I held my breath. Slowly, carefully, they worked their way to where Luka clung to life. It seemed they would be swept to their deaths, but they found footholds, resisted the water's force, and reached the boy. They showed him he could stand up in the water. He was paralyzed with fright. In vain they gestured their intention to walk him to shore. Still another group of men stepped up with another rope. At least there were lots of ropes available. The men took turns, threw ropes to the little group in the middle of the falls. Again and again, they missed. The crowd groaned as the end of the rope drifted away. Finally, the rope drifted close. One of the men lunged out and caught it. The crowd cheered. The men fastened the end of the rope to the boy's wrist, surrounded him, hung on to the rope, supported him in their arms, towed him away from the tiny island of grass. They moved cautiously, held his head above water. Men on the shore pulled them all to safety. They stepped onto dry land, and the crowd whooped and clapped and danced for joy. Women ululated, "*Yee yee yee yee yee.*"

Now we could help. Luka lay on the ground, crying, in shock. Too weak to stand, he shivered uncontrollably. He'd been in the cold water for more than an hour. Diane had blankets ready. She wrapped him up and comforted him as though he were her own son. She sent men back to camp to build a fire to warm him.

When Luka was able to stand, Danny supported him and we all walked slowly back to camp. Chief Samusamb led the way. Luka sat close to the campfire, swathed in blankets, shivering, embarrassed to be the center of so much attention. The rescue team lingered nearby. The chief spoke his gratitude to them and admonished Luka for the trouble he caused. Luka hung his head in shame. The kitchen crews swung into dinner preparations. Gradually the excitement ebbed. Everyone talked of the wonders they had seen that day.

"You know," Danny said, "we started coming here to show that God can overcome Satan. If Luka had gone over the falls, that would have been the end of Samusamb." He sat there for a minute, lost in thought. Then he gestured to Keith and Stewart. "Would you guys come with me for a few minutes?"

Diane knew him well. "What are you up to, Danny?" she asked. "Where are you guys going?"

"I just want to go back to the river for a minute. Don't worry, I won't do anything crazy."

In a few minutes, they came back, laughing. "You should've seen ol' Danny," Keith said. "He wanted to prove he could swim across the river. He was miffed when the chief wouldn't let him try it. He dived in and swam across all right, but he came up without his shorts. That current is swift, that's for sure."

"Danny, you are terrible," Diane said. "You would have ended up standing there in front of everybody in your birthday suit. I hope you're satisfied. What are you going to do when the chief hears about this?"

"I guess I'll have to apologize."

At the campfire that evening, songs of praise and thanksgiving rose to the heavens. Chief Samusamb spoke first, for a long time, and Keith translated for us. No babies cried. The chief recalled the history of the place, once known as the Place of the Dead, the home of evil spirits, where none of his people dared to go. A murmur of assent went through the crowd. The chief continued. Then the *wazungu* came, bringing with them *Mungu Baba Wetu*, God our Father, more powerful than the evil spirits. Today *Mungu* had shown his power, saved this careless, unworthy orphan boy from certain death.

And so it was that a new legend was born that day, confirming for all time the power of God to triumph over death and Satan. The people responded, shouted and ululated, and praised God. Then it was Danny's turn. As the successful hunter, he had the honor to present the tusks of the dead hippos. The heads of the two beasts lay on the ground near the campfire. The tusks had not yet been extracted from the enormous jaws. As was the custom, the first head belonged to Chief Samusamb. The chief accepted the tribute.

Danny turned to Stewart. He thanked him for the fine sermons he had preached. He recalled the many people who had confessed their sins and accepted Jesus as their Savior. He awarded the second set of tusks, not to Stewart, but to Tim and Peter. He declared them the "sons of the great preacher." It was a tremendous honor for the boys, totally unexpected. They were speechless, in awe of their sudden fame and fortune. I stared at their gruesome trophy and wondered how on earth we would carry it back to Jadotville. Stewart expressed thanks to the chief, and to the crowd. He told them what an honor it was for us to have been a part of their Camp Meeting.

The chief ordered the big drums brought out to celebrate the power of God, even greater than his own power as chief. The drummers took their places, and the "March of the Paramount Chief" boomed through the clearing. All my disappointments and frustrations disappeared into this thunderous sound, a primeval celebration of life in the heart of Africa. I can hear it still, and I am back there under the African stars. I smell the fragrant campfire and feel the ground shake with the reverberations of the great drum.

Our last night in the grass hut. Reality came early with the light of morning. Bright red insect bites covered my arms and legs, and Mary Beth's scraped knee was aflame with infection. The boys coughed and complained of headaches and runny noses. Martha looked pale and peaked. Time to leave this place. As we packed the car, four men carried the head of the hippo on a wooden plank. We lashed the trophy of the hunt onto the luggage carrier on top of the metal footlocker, flanked by the shovels and the ax.

We forget how small those Volkswagens are. The top of the car came to my shoulder, the hippo head at eye level. What a sight we must have been as we drove away, followed by a cloud of flies intent on overtaking us. People whooped and hollered as we drove through their villages, gave homage to the great hunter. We acknowledged their cheers with regal waves, as though we were the ones who had slain the hippo. Whenever we slowed or stopped, the ripe smell caught up with us, and a zillion flies enveloped us. Nobody suggested we abandon our prize along the road. By the time we drove into Jadotville several days later, the smell was unbearable. People gathered on the sidewalks to stare at the little car with the rotten hippo head on top. Baba Samuel stood in the driveway, flabbergasted at the sight. Not only would there be loads of dirty laundry, but he would be expected to deal with this hippo carcass. Stewart promised to help him.

They built a fire in the backyard and filled our biggest barrel. They boiled the head for several days to loosen and remove the rotting flesh. When they pried the teeth out of the jawbone, they broke one of the tusks in two. We have them still, a basketful of fist-size worn-down molars and the four tusks, heavy arcs of ivory a yard long, one broken. I used to take the teeth with me when I went to churches and schools in America to tell my tales of Africa. I stopped after a fifth grader in New Haven pocketed a couple of the teeth.

Chapter Eight

Profound changes swept through Sub-Saharan Africa in the late 1950s. The long-suffering Africans, no longer satisfied with empty promises, demanded freedom from their European oppressors. The Congolese were on the move, leaving their villages to seek work in the cities, bringing with them their own languages, loyalties, and traditions. The Belgians had used these differences to fragment and isolate the tribes, to discourage them from making common cause against their oppressors, and they remained confident of their ability to maintain control.

The First All African People's Conference, in Accra, Ghana, in December 1958, brought determined seekers of independence together from all over the continent. Patrice Lumumba, head of the Movement National Congolais, led the Congolese delegation. On his return home, he delivered an impassioned speech to a disorderly crowd in Stanleyville, his hometown. His eloquence sparked a riot in which several people were killed. He served six months in jail, in Jadotville, for inciting crowds to mayhem.

Despite early warning signs, I was caught off guard when violence erupted in 1959 in Léopoldville, a thousand miles north of us. The Belgians summarily canceled a political meeting, and several thousand Africans protested, marched through the streets, threw rocks at the police, and looted stores. Soldiers stormed in with machine guns and killed at least fifteen Africans. Twenty Europeans and a hundred Africans were reported injured. Hundreds more Africans died in the repression following the riots. The Belgians accused them of ingratitude. Joseph Kasavubu, President of the ABAKO political alliance, was held responsible for the insurrection in the capital. The charges against him were eventually withdrawn. He continued to press for independence, "in order and in legality." He would become the first president of the Independent Congo.

Fear took root in my soul. Stewart scoffed. When his parents expressed concern, he assured them that there was nothing to worry about. "If the Europeans would just use their heads and shut their mouths, they'd be better off," he wrote in a letter to his father. "The Congolese have the best deal in Africa. Why shoot Santa Claus? It was quiet here this morning. They won't try anything with a branch of the army right here. It makes life more interesting to have some excitement, a good topic of conversation."

The dry, uninflected voice of BBC News was a presence at our table at breakfast, dinner, and supper. My preferred news source was *Time*, the breezy, slangy American magazine that showed up every Tuesday in *Boîte Postale* 450. *Time* introduced Lumumba as "Kasavubu's chief rival … who wants independence without bothering with elections until later…. Fiery Lumumba, a thirty-three-year-old postal clerk and convicted embezzler, cried NOW NOW NOW at a Stanleyville meeting of his followers, many of them armed and painted as if for battle."

Lumumba was released from jail in January 1960, when MNC party leaders demanded his presence at the Belgo-Congolese Round Table Conference in Brussels. In a widely reproduced copy of a photograph in *Time* magazine of February 22, 1960, he defiantly raises his slender arms, fists clenched to expose his bandaged wrists damaged by too-tight handcuffs. *Time* magazine captioned the photo "Bedlam in Brussels." They described the meeting as "…a mad mélange of inflammatory speeches, door-slamming walkouts, rival press conferences and angry communiques…" The Congolese delegates to the Conference were described as petulant children, the Belgians as long-suffering parents.

I marvel at the journalists at *Time* whose purple prose portrayed the leaders of the emerging nation as buffoons, clowns in a circus. Some missionaries ridiculed Kasavubu as "Joe Palooka the strong man of the Congo," from a comic book character popular at the time. I joined in the derisive laughter. One of the most effective tools of the oppressor is to make fun of those who would be free. Indignant British journalists must have gleefully pounced on the American peasants who dumped tea in Boston Harbor.

Unlike our illustrious Founding Fathers, the Congolese were not well educated. There were said to be only twelve African college graduates in 1960.

King Baudouin sought to calm the situation. He sent word that he favored *Independance* for the Congo "without harmful procrastination, but without ill-considered haste." In December 1959, he paid a royal visit to Léopoldville. Polite cries of "*Vive le roi*" were drowned out by boisterous bellows of "*Independance*." For the first time, the young king experienced rowdy insubordination.

A tsunami of frenzied yearning swept across the Congo. The Belgians abruptly capitulated. Independence would be granted on June 30, 1960. The Congolese would elect a Parliament on May 22.

I've never visited Pompeii. I imagine I would have been right at home there, oblivious, on the slopes of Mount Vesuvius, observing my daily routines, glancing, perhaps, from time to time, at the landmark peak, an occasional rumble, a bit of steam. The citizens of Pompeii, however, didn't know their due date. In the Congo, we were aware of the date for Independence. In six months, our own volcano would erupt.

Just in time, some unexpected good news arrived. New neighbors. Lois and Maurice Persons, veteran missionaries, beloved and admired by everyone, moved into the house where Jim and June and their children had lived. I couldn't have imagined the trials and dangers to come, and I don't know how I could have survived without the steady guidance and support of these two dear people.

Tribal conflict erupted and spread through the colony. Hundreds of Congolese were killed and wounded, and, as I feared, violence came to where we lived. A weekend melee rocked Jadotville. Eleven Africans were reported killed and many more were badly wounded. From our veranda, we watched, incredulous, as a parade disintegrated into a riot. Police clubbed men and women to the ground, beat them mercilessly, threw them into trucks, and hauled them away. Tim and Peter stared wide-eyed at the mayhem. Mary Beth and Martha put their fingers in their ears and hid their faces in my wide skirt. I turned away, unable to watch, but I could still hear the crack of batons on heads and limbs, the screams of the injured, the thunder of running feet. I led the girls into the house and tried to comfort them.

"How can they do that to each other?" Mary Beth sobbed. Tears poured down her face. I had no answers for her, then or now. Had I been so naive as to think freedom could come without conflict? Our only exposure to mayhem had been through the tiny black-and-white television, the bam! and pow! of shivery cartoon characters.

The riot ran its course and the crowds dispersed. I found a sense of order in household chores. Stewart went with the African pastors to comfort the wounded in the hospital across the street from the mission. He returned several hours later, more shaken than I had ever seen him— pale, stunned, and sickened by what he had seen. I started toward him to comfort him, but he shook his head and waved me away. I retreated into the kitchen, made a pot of tea, and carried it into the study. He seemed more composed.

"Maybe it would help to talk about it," I said.

"I don't think you want to hear this. All the beds in the hospital were full. I mean full, more than one person in every bed. Casualties are much worse than they reported. People badly wounded, lying on the floor and in the corridors, moaning, screaming, calling for the doctor." His mug of tea cooled, untouched. "I never want to see anything like that in my life again. Thank God you and the children didn't have to see it." After a moment, he seemed to pull himself together. "I shouldn't have told you these things. You're upset." He turned away. "I can't talk about it any-more."

He was right. I didn't want to hear it. As hard as I tried to put it out of my mind, in my always-too-active imagination I put flesh on the bones, heard the shrieks and moans of the dying, saw the bodies slashed by machetes, piled in the corridors, the floors slippery with blood, the men holding their gaping wounds together as they waited for help which would not come in time.

Stewart seemed to put it behind him. He recovered his equilibrium, but his usual cheeriness felt forced. He must have realized, even more than I, that this was only the beginning.

The African pastors asked Stewart to take them to check on casualties in the nearby villages where fighting had been reported. I was in the kitchen, peeling potatoes, when he came home. He was excited. I detected an air of bravado. Had he developed a taste for danger? I hated danger. I still do. I was afraid I wouldn't be able to protect my children.

"What's it like out there?" I asked. "Have things calmed down?"

He sat on the kitchen stool, alert, eager to tell me about it. "People are still jumpy. We heard some noise behind the church, and I walked over to talk with some of the men. I heard gunshots, really close, too close." It was as though he were watching a scenario in his head, like a movie. "People were hiding in houses all around. Four policemen carried a body out of one of the houses. Murder, in broad daylight." He paused, looked to see if I was impressed. "The police were hauling bodies out of there for three days."

My heart sank. "That is not a safe place to be driving around," I said.

He raised his eyebrows, took a more paternal tone. "We were careful," he said, deliberately. "People across the schoolyard were watching us, and I felt compelled to go over there and not favor one side. I saw burned-out huts, some knocked down. The village leader was in a house when they demolished it, and the roof fell on him, but it didn't kill him. He said God was with him."

That sounded like a rather capricious God, but theology was his field, not mine. "I wish you wouldn't put yourself in such danger." It sounded banal, even to me.

"It wasn't that dangerous. Nothing happened. I'm here."

"What about next time?" I put potatoes on to boil.

I took refuge in books. They can take me away to another place. Deep into the pages of *The Agony and the Ecstasy*, I roamed the crooked streets of Florence with Michelangelo. My children's voices brought me back to the present. What on earth could the girls be screaming about? I set my book aside and followed the noise down the hall to the boys' room. Peter and Tim sat on the top bunk, dangling their skinny legs over the edge. They were pale. Their eyes were huge. Mary Beth and Martha crouched on the floor, each holding a kitten. Between them, another kitten lay motionless on the concrete floor.

"Mom," Mary Beth sobbed, "they killed the kitten. I told them not to do it, but they wouldn't listen. Now the kitty's dead."

I picked up the tiny kitten. It was dead, all right. I looked up at the boys' frightened faces.

"We didn't mean to kill it, Mom," Tim said. "Honest."

"What were you doing? How did this happen?"

"We were just teaching the kittens to parachute," Peter said. "We used one of Dad's handkerchiefs, fastened on with rubber bands. The kitty jumped off the top bunk and the parachute didn't work."

"It didn't jump," Mary Beth wailed. "You *threw* it."

I read confirmation on their anguished faces.

We all cried. Tim and Peter were miserable with their guilt. Punishment seemed like too much. We wrapped the broken little body in the parachute and placed it gently in a shoebox. Peter and Tim dug a hole in the yard and buried the box. Peter said a prayer. He asked God to forgive him.

Mary Beth wouldn't let up. "You boys are wicked."

As they recovered from the shock of it, the boys struck back.

"Oh, Mary, will you please just shut up?"

"Mom, Tim told me to shut up."

"I want all of you to shut up," I yelled.

They stared at me, mouths agape.

The death of this tiny, innocent creature sobered us. All around us, people lived in danger of death or mutilation. The accidental death of a kitten might have seemed insignificant, but the kitten died because the boys had been careless. Life seemed tenuous as death crept into my sanctuary.

And then one morning, the repercussions of independence appeared at my doorstep. Peter came into the office. I was writing letters. "Mom, there's a man at the door."

I finished my sentence and turned away from the typewriter. "Who is it?"

He shrugged. "I dunno. Not one of the pastors."

Probably someone selling something, I thought. I put the cover on the typewriter and walked through the house to the back door. I didn't recognize the man. His shirt was torn, and his dusty dark toes stuck out of his ragged sneakers. Even through the screen, he smelled like he could use a bath. I stepped outside to talk to him. The screen swung shut behind me.

"*Hiyambo,*" I said. "*Habari gani?* [What is it?]"

"*Hiyambo, Mama,*" he said. "*Habari ya nyumba* [It's about the house]."

"What about the house?"

"I have bought the house," he announced. I tried not to stare at his rotten teeth. "After *Independance*, this house will be mine. And you will be my wife."

I stepped back, shocked and repelled by the idea I would have any connection with this smelly, filthy man. I swallowed and said firmly, "You are mistaken. The house belongs to the mission, and we are not leaving like the other *wazungu*. My husband and I will continue to live here after *Independance*. And the children."

Surely that would settle it, the husband and children.

He dug in the pocket of his derelict pants and pulled out a paper. He held it in his grimy hand for me to see. It looked like a form from an old-fashioned receipt book.

"This paper, look at it. I bought the house. I paid money. It will be mine."

I glanced at the form. I didn't want to attach any importance to it.

"Whoever sold you that piece of paper cheated you. Nobody can sell this house. This is my house."

He stared at me, head tilted to one side, appraising me. He peered past me into the screened porch. I waited. Did he expect me to give him a tour of the house? Finally, he took a step back.

"We'll see whose house this is, mama. *Bakia vizuri.*"

"*Kwenda vizuri*," I said automatically, although I did not wish him well. I watched him shuffle down the path. I went inside and closed the screen door. I was frightened. What if he came back with some of his friends? Who had sold him that piece of paper?

"Who was that, Mom?" Peter asked. "What did he want?"

"Oh, just some guy. Nothing important."

But it was important. That awful man. I went into the kitchen. Although I hadn't touched the man or his piece of paper, I scrubbed my hands under running water. When Stewart came home, I met him at the door. "You won't believe what happened today."

He grinned. "Try me. I'll believe most anything these days." I followed him into the study and told him the story of the prospective new owner of the house.

He sighed. "I wondered how long it would be before somebody turned up here. They're all over town with those phony papers, selling them to gullible souls. How can they take advantage of their own people like that?"

"But what about me?" I said, indignantly. "You can't make light of this. What if that man shows up with a bunch of his friends and demands the house?"

Stewart laughed. "Your imagination is running away with you again. Nothing like that will happen. You can't let this stuff get to you." He took some papers out of his briefcase. The conversation was over.

"That's easy enough for you to say," I said, stung by his casual attitude. "You won't be here if they come. You'll be out in the bush somewhere."

I said, "if they come," but I meant "when they come."

He gave me a long look. "I can't stay home and protect you. I'm needed out there. Try to see this for what it is, just foolishness. You don't want to get the children all upset, do you?"

That was the last thing I wanted, to upset the children. My fear had taken root. This was more than I had bargained for. My home, my sanctuary, no longer seemed inviolate. I began to dread those calls at the door.

"*Hodi, mama, bwana iko?*"

"*Hapana* [No, come back later]," I called from the kitchen.

When Stewart was away, I kept the screen door latched. I felt guilty. None of the other missionaries latched their doors during the day.

When the school year ended at the Teacher Training Institute at Mulungwishi, the students who failed their examinations broke all the windows and trashed the dormitory. Those who passed their exams declared their solidarity with their failed classmates and refused to participate in the graduation exercises. This was unprecedented, an indication of what we might expect in the future. In the past, the graduates had staffed not only the mission primary schools but found places in government schools in every part of the country.

The teachers at the *athénée* flew home to Belgium for their annual home leave. They took with them everything of value. They did not intend to return. Hundreds of Union Minière employees left with their wives and children. They sold whatever they could of their goods and furniture and shipped everything of value back to Belgium. I could have bought a piano for twenty dollars. All flights from Elisabethville were completely booked, with additional planes held in reserve.

One Sunday afternoon, we took the children to Elisabethville to witness the first arrival and departure of the impressive new Sabena jet plane. An orderly crowd lined the fence. For most of us, it was the first sighting. I'm sure I wasn't the only one who wished I were leaving on that plane.

The American Ambassador in Léopoldville sent telegrams to all the Americans in the Congo. In the event of trouble, he would advise us. We were to follow his instructions. If an evacuation was necessary, he would contact us by shortwave radio.

"I think he's overdoing it," Stewart said. I wanted to believe him, yet I found comfort in the Ambassador's message. Although we would not be eligible for furlough for two more years, we had some vacation time we hadn't used. A perfect opportunity to explore more of Africa. I sent for visas for Mozambique. We would leave on July first, the day after Independence, and drive to Beira, on the Indian Ocean, for a week on the beach. I hoped the visas would come in time. Surely things would have settled down by the time we came back home.

One evening, Stewart and I sat in the living room, reading. The children were asleep. I closed my book and said his name. "Stewart?"

He looked up, put his finger in his book to mark the place. "What's up?"

"Do you realize we've been married for ten years? Let's celebrate our anniversary, forget all this independence stuff. Let's go out to dinner in a really nice place."

He put his book aside. "There's only one really nice place in town. The Chateaubriand. When would you like to go?"

"On our anniversary, silly. Don't you remember the day we got married?"

"Well, I remember it was hot, and you wore a white dress."

"What about the children?" he asked.

"I already talked to Maurice and Lois. They'll give them dinner."

I had never been to the Chateaubriand, and I planned to make the most of the occasion. I chose my favorite outfit, a paisley circular skirt and a soft pink surplice blouse with cap sleeves. My mother had made it for me several years ago. With her customary meticulous care, she edged the bodice with a narrow binding cut on the bias from the paisley fabric. I eased the skirt over my head and pulled on the zipper. I must have gained weight. Too many cinnamon rolls. I found the panty girdle I hadn't worn for ages, struggled into it, and zipped up my skirt. I whirled around, swirling my dress. I glanced in the mirror. Not bad for a mother of four. I wished we could go dancing. I brushed my hair and put on lipstick and clip earrings.

Stewart looked in. "All set?" He wore his best navy-blue suit, with a white shirt and my favorite silver-grey tie. We sashayed through the living room, putting on a show for the children.

The restaurant wasn't crowded. Seated across the table from each other, separated by an expanse of stiff white linen and heavy silverware and glassware, we exchanged formal, self-conscious smiles.

"Well," said Stewart, "here we are. Happy Anniversary."

The waiter hurried over. "*Bon soir, Monsieur, Madame.* What will you have to drink? *Du vin rouge? Vin blanc? Champagne?*"

"*Pas du vin, merci,*" Stewart said. "Just bring us some water."

"*L'eau minérale ou gassseuse?*" asked the waiter.

"*L'eau ordinaire* will be fine." Stewart glanced at me for confirmation. I rolled my eyes. The waiter removed the wine glasses, frowned slightly with pursed lips.

In this formal setting, in our best clothes, we were stiff with each other. A glass of wine would have helped, but we didn't dare risk it. One of the African teachers had recently lost his job when he was caught in a bar with a bottle of beer. We must set a good example. Stewart didn't care for wine, anyway. The waiter brought two glasses of water and stood, pen poised. Stewart looked at me. "What will you have?"

"The Chateaubriand steak, *s'il vous plaît, avec les pommes frites.* And asparagus."

"*Très bien, Madame. La spécialité de la maison.* The asparagus is flown in from Belgium." It seemed truly decadent to order asparagus flown in from Belgium when the country was going to pieces. But it was, after all, our tenth anniversary.

Stewart said he would have the same as *Madame.* He seemed ill at ease. He fidgeted with his silverware, rearranged the spoons. He looked around the room, nodding at people he seemed to know. I didn't know anybody. The restaurant was popular with mining executives and government officials. I saw only a few black faces.

Memories of our wedding came to me. I remembered clutching my dad's arm as we walked down the aisle of the church to where Stewart waited. He looked solemn, stoic, nervous. I was madly in love, frantic to marry him before he changed his mind, or some other girl snatched him up.

The night he gave me my engagement ring, he showed the ring first to my roommate. I was furious. I pouted. We sat on the couch in the parlor of the women's dormitory, serenaded by the girls who gathered there around the piano in the evening to sing popular songs. Serenaded him. He loved it. He was such a flirt. I thought he would stop flirting with other girls now that we were engaged. He was going to marry me, so why not let it go?

Stewart had wanted to finish seminary before we married. Three more years.

Impossible. I waged a determined campaign. We studied together and I typed his papers. He hated it when I corrected his grammar. And there was that time I beat him at chess. How passive he had been; he let me court him. He finally agreed to set the date. A church wedding, of course, in my hometown in Kansas. My parents were thrilled. A minister! My mother made my dress, clouds of white organdy worn over a chaste white satin slip. She designed the dress to complement the floor-length veil of Brussels lace Stewart bought the previous summer when he traveled to Europe with a group from college. I had nearly lost him to one of the women on the trip. He was reluctant to tell me what he had brought me. His roommate, always my ally, blurted out, "Go ahead; show her the veil." Reluctantly, ever so slowly, he took it out of its wrapping in blue tissue paper and handed it to me. I couldn't believe it was for me. Perhaps it wasn't, but I claimed it—the most beautiful thing I had ever seen—delicate embroidery on the sheerest net, long enough to form a graceful train on the floor behind me.

I carried a nosegay of daisies. My heart pounded when he slipped the wedding ring on my finger. I was afraid his roommate, the best man, would drop the ring and it would roll down into the grating in the floor, irretrievably lost. In the wedding pictures, I look determined, holding onto his arm as we come up the aisle, as though I wanted to make sure he wouldn't get away. I look triumphant. His expression is serious, almost grim, as if he had just received a life sentence. He promised to love me until death did us part.

"You were a million miles away." He smiled. "A penny for your thoughts."

"I was just thinking about our wedding."

"I remember how hot it was."

The waiter arrived and served us with solemn ceremony. The steak was perfection, the *sauce béarnaise* like silk, the asparagus succulent, the *pommes frites* golden brown and crisp as only the Belgians can make them.

"How is your steak?" Stewart asked solicitously.

"It's perfect. I love *sauce béarnaise*. The *frites* are wonderful, aren't they?"

"I'm glad you're enjoying it." When he was in high school, he used to take elderly ladies out for a drive, give the poor things a treat. Perhaps he felt like that now, so pleased with himself. I felt desolate.

"Save room for dessert," he said.

Chapter Nine

Stewart breezed in from his daily trip to the post office. He waved a letter. "Take a look at this." It had been a while since I heard a lilt in his voice.

"I'm kneading a batch of bread. My hands are all sticky. Why don't you read it to me?"

"It's from Bishop Booth. A woman named Louise Morrell is driving around Africa organizing literacy campaigns. The bishop referred her to us. He says this would be a good base of operations for her for a couple of months. Nobody else is willing to take her on. She's funded by the Laubach Foundation, so it won't cost us anything."

I had always wanted to do adult literacy. Before we came to Africa, we had met with Dr. Frank Laubach, who was well known in the international missionary community for his simple method of teaching adults to read. He called it "Each One Teach One." This would be a perfect time. Independence loomed large, two months away. I couldn't think of a better gift for people careening toward self-government. Ninety percent of the Congolese people were illiterate. Every day we heard rumors of communists spreading propaganda up in the bush. Perhaps we could counteract that with some of our own propaganda. We'd give it our best shot.

Ten days later, about five o'clock in the afternoon, a scruffy blue Volkswagen pulled into the driveway. From the kitchen window, I watched a middle-aged woman climb out of the car, stretch her arms over her head and roll her shoulders. Louise had arrived. She wore a wrinkled blue cotton skirt, blue-and-white striped blouse, and tattered sneakers. I hurried out to welcome her. She managed a tired smile.

"I can't believe I'm finally here. I'm hot and dirty and thirsty, and I sure hope you have a bathroom." I liked her immediately. She gulped down a glass of iced tea, and I poured another. I offered a bath. I could hear her singing in the tub. "Jesus, Savior, pilot me/Over life's tempestuous sea...." She came into the kitchen in clean clothes, her short brown hair still wet. "I feel like a new woman. How can I help?"

"Just talk to me while I finish getting dinner ready. Stewart will be home soon."

Mary Beth and Martha came shyly in to be introduced. Louise asked appropriate questions and admired the kittens. Peter set the table. Stewart's car pulled into the yard. Louise turned to watch as he bounded into the kitchen. She offered her hand, and Stewart grasped it in both of his. They took the measure of each other and approved what they saw.

"Dinner's ready," I said. "You must be starving."

"I'm eager to hear about your journey," Stewart said.

Louise said, "I drove alone on primitive roads all the way across Africa, from Nigeria to northern Kenya into the Congo. I passed through areas of tribal uprisings and dreadful contagious diseases, conducting literacy classes whenever and wherever I could."

"You're a brave woman," I said. "I'd be afraid of rebel soldiers."

"Northern Kenya was scary," she conceded. "They're heading for a blowup there, worse than the Mau Mau. But the time I was most in danger wasn't from people. It was elephants. I had a confrontation with an elephant in Kenya that just about scared me to death. I still get the jitters when I think about it."

She had our complete attention. Peter and Tim stared, wide-eyed, eager to hear more.

"I was driving along a dirt road through the open country in the afternoon. I was tired, thinking about stopping to eat something, looking for a shady spot. I came around a corner and almost ran into a herd of elephants standing in the road. I wasn't going fast, but when I put on the brakes, I skidded in the sand. I must have frightened them. There were mamas with babies, so I knew I was in trouble. One big old fellow planted himself right in front of the car and stood there glaring at me, while the others moved off into the bush. He seemed to be thinking it over. He finally decided I wasn't worth his attention. He shuffled slowly away. My heart was beating a mile a minute. I turned off the motor and just sat there for a while before I went on. The road looped around, and a few minutes later I suddenly came upon what looked like the same herd."

She paused. We waited, breathless. She took a sip of water. "I was sure the big elephant in the middle of the road was the same one I had met before. I put the car in reverse and slowly backed up to get away from him. I checked the rear-view mirror, and there was another huge elephant right behind me. I turned off the motor and prayed they wouldn't charge. Either one of them could have smashed the car like a bug. They stood there, swinging their trunks, fanning their ears back and forth. Not a good sign. By this time, it was about five o'clock, not much more than an hour of daylight left, and I had a long way to go. You know how dangerous it is to drive through the bush in the dark. You might come right up on an elephant before you even saw it.

"Even though I was in terrible danger, I couldn't help but notice how majestic those two elephants looked, standing there like a pair of bookends with me in the middle. God must have heard my prayers because they both moved away into the bush and disappeared. I waited as long as I dared, started the car, and drove very slowly and carefully. When I felt I was out of their range I speeded up. I was still shaking when I reached the mission station just as darkness fell."

"That was the scariest thing I ever heard," I said.

"Yes, God delivered me from danger, and I wasn't scared after that. I continued my journey, talked my way through some more roadblocks. Some close calls with gangs of soldiers, but God was with me and His grace is sufficient."

Stewart told me later we had picked a winner for sure. A woman who could survive that trip could do anything.

At morning devotions around the breakfast table, Stewart chose a passage of Scripture prompting us not to eat the bread of idleness. Louise was eager to get this project underway. The pastors and teachers were already gathering at the church, ready for their marching orders. Louise would train them, and they would, in turn, teach others, one by one. Every new reader would become a teacher. With exquisite patience, Louise explained the process. Pastors and teachers listened attentively.

"Illiterate adults have for too long been treated as though they were stupid. They will need encouragement, not ridicule or criticism. As teachers, you must be gentle. Work slowly, help the people gain self-confidence as they learn their letters."

The teachers-in-training spent the morning practicing their technique on each other, one on one, using textbooks and Bibles.

"What about more books?" I asked. "We'll need a ton of books." Surely she had brought books. Perhaps they're still in the car.

"Didn't Stewart tell you? You're going to write the books yourself."

"You always said you wanted to write a book," Stewart chimed in. "Here's your chance." Stewart had recently traded in the old mimeograph machine for a newer electric model, and reams of paper were stacked in the corner of his study. Louise said she'd help me get started. She assured me it was easy to do a simple primer. She showed me prototypes from other campaigns, in other languages.

"Your challenge," she explained, "is to write a simple story, using a very limited vocabulary. It should hold the interest of an adult reader." Swahili, she assured me, was the ideal language to work with, completely phonetic, with relatively simple grammar, no irregular verbs, and no gender. She pulled out a pamphlet she had used in Kenya, a few words on each page, simple drawings. I liked the title, *Kusoma Furaha* (*The Joy of Reading*).

"That's perfect," I said. "And it's already in Swahili. Why don't we just use those?"

"We can't. They're written in East Coast Swahili. The Swahili they use in Kenya is quite different."

I leafed through the little booklet and noticed the illustrations, simply drawn. I protested. "I'm not an artist."

"We will cut and paste pictures and cut a stencil," Louise said, "as they did in Kenya. Let's get started. The new teachers are eager to get to work."

For several days I wrote and rewrote simple stories. I combed through the collection of primers for appropriate drawings, copied them on onionskin paper, and transferred them to the master copy for the mimeograph. Each sheet of standard-size paper made two pages, crossways on the paper. I cut the stencils. The pages were collated as they came off the mimeograph machine and stapled, with a cover of green construction paper.

"My first book! I am an author! We're publishers!"

"Not yet," Stewart cautioned. "First we have to get these books cranked out."

We set up the production line on the screened porch just outside Stewart's office, and soon the presses were rolling. Stewart recruited help. Martin, a lay evangelist who had been converted in prison, supervised the mimeograph machine as it hummed and spat out pages. Ndala David took over at my desk and cut the stencils. He was a former fisherman and self-taught typist, a refugee from tribal warfare. Jacob assembled and stapled the pages. He recruited Peter and Tim and Mary Beth to assist. The crew walked around and around the table collating pages. Everyone wanted a turn with the stapler. Tim had recently put his right arm, up to the elbow, through the wringer of the washing machine. Fortunately, the Maytag had an automatic release and he escaped without serious damage. He banged the stapler with his left hand. We loaded the boxes of books into the battered Volkswagen van, our bookmobile, soon to be a familiar sight around town and in the villages.

We planned a first edition of five thousand copies of *Kusoma Furaha*, for ten cents each. Louise said new readers placed more value on books when they paid for them. Jacob shone as our star salesman. The first edition sold out in a week. Books were snatched up as fast as we could print them. We lavished care on the mimeograph machine and ordered more reams of paper. I started on the first reader, *Tushike Safari* (*Let's Take a Trip*), and planned more advanced self-help books on hygiene and childcare. We talked about publishing a newsletter.

The pastors and teachers fanned out through the neighborhoods and out into the villages. Louise encouraged me to be diligent in my task of writing and assembling the primers. Teachers found students everywhere and encouraged them to sound out the words on the page. Faces came alive as learners recognized the words, realized they could read, and eagerly shared their brand-new ability with others. The movement gained momentum. The joy of the new readers, the light of understanding in young faces, and tired old eyes inspired us to keep the presses rolling.

Louise found time to help me with kitchen chores. She made a special effort to acknowledge my work on the literacy team. I had not yet been included in the special Sunday services in which new readers were honored and presented with a Bible, and Louise gave me a special invitation.

"I want you to be there. You've been working so hard, and you haven't had a chance to see the excitement of the new readers receiving their own Bibles. It's time you saw your own books in action."

The church was packed. The children and I were ushered to a front bench. The new readers scooted even closer together to make room for us, each holding a copy of *Kusoma Furaha*. Stewart and Louise sat with the pastor on the platform. People crowded at the open windows and stood at the back of the church and in the aisles. I hadn't seen this many people in church since Easter. Everyone seemed to be smiling. The metal roof made explosive noises as the sun beat down. Insects buzzed around us, babies cried, children scampered in the aisles, and conversation rose to the rafters. People craned their necks as I doled out coloring books and crayons to my children. Pastor André announced the first hymn, "*Tunasifu Yehova.*" We stood and bawled out the words:

"*Tunasifu Yehova kwa roho ya furaha
Sababu ya nehema, ya milele milele.*
[I praise God with a happy heart
Because He is with us forever and forever.]"

I settled back onto the unyielding bench. The new readers held their primers ostentatiously high, so everyone could see them reading the words. I felt a little shiver of pride. The new readers filed onto the platform, one by one proudly claiming their Bibles. Pastor André shushed the crowd. Babies continued to howl. He shouted to the mamas to give those babies the breast. Gradually the little ones settled down. The crowd quieted. The most accomplished among the new readers took turns with the Scriptures. An old grandmother took center stage, held up her Bible, and read, slowly and carefully, a brief passage from the ninth chapter of the Gospel of John, the story of the blind man who receives his sight. "One thing I do know, that though I was blind, now I see."

She looked out at the congregation. "That's how it is for me," she said, in Swahili. "I could not read. The power of the love of Jesus healed me and now I see."

Tears sprang to my eyes. I hadn't thought what it would be like to not read. I had learned to read when I was four years old, and over my lifetime, I had devoured hundreds of books. How bleak my life would have been without reading. It occurred to me I might spend more time reading the Bible. One by one the new readers came forward, raised their Bibles for all to see, and read their favorite verses. An old man read John 8:12 slowly, sounding out each syllable:

"I am the Light of the World. He who follows me will not walk in darkness but have the light of life."

Pastor André expressed thanks for Stewart and Mama Louise and the pastors and teachers and all the crew. He asked me to stand and share the applause. Startled, the children looked up. "What's going on, Mom?" Tim asked.

"It's for making the books. You kids helped, you can stand up, too."

"But, Mom," Peter protested, "Martha didn't help."

"It's okay. She would have helped: she's just too little." Through Pastor André's interminable sermon, I sat quietly, dazed by joy to have been a part of life-changing work. I had helped to make the books that brought these people out of darkness into the light. God had used me to open their eyes. If I accomplished nothing else in Africa, I had done this.

The excitement of reading continued to spread far and wide through the cities and the countryside.

Louise took leave of us in mid-June, determined to get out of the Congo before Independence. She expressed her concern for our safety. It was quiet here now, but she sensed trouble ahead. She had seen a good bit of violence on her journey through Africa. Stewart assured her we'd be fine. He didn't anticipate any trouble.

"Nevertheless," she said, "I will keep you in my prayers."

I hated to see her go. *"Kwenda vizuri,"* I said as she climbed into her blue Volkswagen.

"Bakia vizuri," she called, as she drove away to Nairobi in a cloud of red dust.

I never saw her again.

After Independence, the African teachers and new readers were targeted by the rebels as agents of the colonial powers. So many of them were killed. How could we—well-intentioned, teaching them to read—not have anticipated this?

They say no good deed goes unpunished.

Chapter Ten

In preparation for Independence Day, Union Minière shut down the smelting plants. This was unprecedented. The old-timers couldn't recall such an event. The familiar background noise of our lives—the hum and rumble of machinery, the whistle signals, the composite round-the-clock din—evaporated into ominous silence. A departing Belgian engineer confided to Stewart the plan to destroy vital parts of the dynamos or carry them off to Belgium. "Let's see them run their own mines now." In the quiet nights, the drums reminded us who would soon be in charge. The unrest was palpable.

The government-operated brewery promised free beer to the Africans. Armed guards patrolled the streets. Two of them stood at the end of our driveway, the entrance to the mission. Greek and Indian shop-keepers, who planned to stay, hoped their status as non-Belgians would protect them. For months they hadn't ordered new merchandise. They spread their wares around on the shelves to simulate a full inventory.

Most of the missionaries continued to deny violence was inevitable. The African teachers and pastors sent their families to safety in the bush. Yet they insisted the missionaries must stay. Didn't we owe it to them? Hadn't they given up their old ways, left their own beliefs to adopt ours? They put their children in mission schools, taught in those schools, and preached in the mission churches. We had encouraged them to lead as the white man leads, to organize a congregation, supervise a classroom or school, follow an agenda. How could we desert them now?

Ultimately the matter rested, not on doctrine or leadership, on faith or lack of it, but on property. Over the years, American congregations had sent money to build and equip churches and schools. The simple buildings and furnishings symbolized the far-reaching power of the American church that paid their salaries, and ours. All of us were obligated to protect the property, to be good stewards.

The end of June was always a busy time at the mission with regional committee meetings and preparation for graduation. The flow of missionaries through our house was even greater than usual. Everyone seemed to be going somewhere, and they all stopped at our place for lunch. Famous for our hospitality, I fed them all. Duvon and Phyllis and their children spent several days with us on their way home from a vacation in South Africa. We persuaded them to delay the 500-hundred-mile drive to Kapanga until after Independence.

Duvon was one of the few missionaries who expected trouble after Independence. He had been threatened at several roadblocks. "Soldiers everywhere," he said, without his usual bravado. "Out of control, most of them drunk. More roadblocks than I've ever seen. Trees, really big trees, dragged across the road." His eloquent hands, surgeon's hands, indicated the size of the felled trees. "They searched the car, looking for guns, and I didn't remember until I drove into your yard I had a bunch of shotgun shells in my medical bag. I stuck them in there when I went hunting last month and forgot all about them. Good thing they didn't look in there."

Duvon and Stewart laughed about this. For Phyllis and me, wives and mothers, it wasn't funny. I was relieved to hear her reprimand him. "Duvon, you've got to be more careful." He brushed aside her reproof.

On the morning of June 30, the four of us sat around the table and listened on the shortwave radio to the Independence Day ceremony in Léopoldville, 1,000 miles away. My inadequate French made it difficult to follow the events. Duvon translated for me. I felt rather detached from it all, looking forward to a week on the beach in Mozambique. Our suitcases were packed for vacation. Surely our visas would come soon.

In the ornate Palais de la Nation in Léopoldville, Baudouin, the pleasant young King of the Belgians, filled with shy goodwill, paid tribute to the "genius" of his great-uncle Leopold II. He didn't mention that Leopold, personal owner of the vast Congo, had conducted a reign of terror that brought years of slavery and conscription, torture and mutilation, unspeakable atrocities and starvation, and the death of uncountable thousands. He cautioned the Congolese against hasty reforms, as though he were handing the car keys to too-eager adolescents.

The new president, Joseph Kasavubu, spoke briefly of the new order, in which the Africans would live in mansions and drive big cars. Patrice Lumumba, the newly elected premier, was not scheduled to speak that day. His African rivals considered him dangerous, a loose cannon, and feared the power of his rhetoric. Suddenly, we heard his unmistakable voice, speaking directly to the people:

> Congolese men and women, fighters for independence, who are today victorious ... no Congolese worthy of the name can ever forget that it is by struggle that we have won, a struggle that was each and every day, a passionate idealistic struggle, a struggle in which no effort, privation, suffering or drop of our blood was spared.
>
> ...
>
> We have known insults, endured blows, morning, noon and night, because we were "niggers." Who will forget that a black was addressed in the familiar *"tu"* not as a friend, but because the polite *"vous"* was reserved for Whites only? We have seen our lands despoiled under the terms of what was supposedly the law of the land, but which only recognized the rights of the strongest. We have seen that this law was quite different for a white than for a black, accommodating the former, cruel and inhuman for the latter.
>
> We have seen the terrible suffering of those banished to remote regions because of their political opinions or religious beliefs; exiled within their own country, their fate was truly worse than death itself.

...

And finally, who can forget the volleys of gunfire in which so many of our brothers perished, the cells where the authorities threw those who would not submit to a rule where justice meant oppression and exploitation.

I could imagine the Belgians, shifting in their chairs, stunned to see their flag pulled down forever and the new Republic of the Congo flag raised, a brilliant gold star on a field of deep blue. The crowd, out of control, screamed and ululated. The Belgians were powerless. The revolution they dreaded was upon them.

Stewart turned off the radio. "That went well, didn't it?" he said.

Duvon seemed perplexed. "What Lumumba said is certainly true about the way the Belgians treated the Congolese. But you have to wonder if this was the time and place to say it."

"I don't think we need to worry," Stewart said. "Our troubles are behind us. Tshombe can take care of the Katanga. There's too much at stake here with Union Minière. The Belgians will see to it that nothing happens."

"I don't know," Duvon mused. "It feels different somehow. I say give it a week, and we'll see. It's that second wave that gets you." He called that one right. The troubles, *les événements*, exploded in exactly a week.

General Janssens, Belgian commander-in-chief of the Congolese Army, made it clear there would be no African officers. He wrote on a blackboard: *"Avant l'independance = Après l'independance* [Before independence = After independence]." It had long been the policy of the army to send men from their native areas into alien territory. This made it easier for the Belgian officers to control them. The soldiers, in charge of people whom they considered enemies, became brutal enforcers.

Time magazine (July 11, 1960 issue) took a provocative slant on the events in Léopoldville on June 30:

... New Premier Patrice Lumumba, jealous of the limelight everyone else was enjoying, took the opportunity to launch a vicious attack on the departing Belgian rulers. "Slavery was imposed on us by force!" he cried, as the King sat shocked and pale.

...

Moïse Tshombe, premier of rich Katanga province ... still threatened to secede rather than hand the province's revenues over to a powerful central government. "The Katanga cow will not be milked by Lumumba's serpents!" cried the secessionist.... In reply, Léopoldville officials sent jets roaring low over the region in an obvious show of force.

By the time those jets roared over Jadotville at rooftop level, I had left the Congo. The children and I were not sunning ourselves on the beach in Beira.

Sometimes I find myself transported back to the Congo I left more than fifty years ago, I see flying red dust, the brilliant red of flame trees, tin-roofed houses, run-down shops selling condensed milk, matches, and dried fish. I smell sweat and wood smoke, salty fish. Women walk by, wrapped in Independence cloth dyed orange, bright blue, red, and acid green, printed with the faces of Lumumba or Kasavubu. They balance chipped enamel basins of cassava on their heads. Babies, held in place by wide strips of cloth, bounce on their mamas' backs. Men in ragged trousers, cotton shirts, and tattered sneakers gesticulate, laugh, argue, interrupt each other, their liquid vowels and consonants flowing like water. Patrice Lumumba strides among them, towering over them. He smiles, cajoles, invites them to share his vision of freedom.

Our papers for Mozambique came in the last post before order collapsed. The mass exodus of the *wazungu* began on July eighth, as Duvon, now safely back in Kapanga, predicted. Congolese soldiers were rumored to have raped some European women, and the Belgians who remained in Jadotville left that night for Elisabethville, where planes waited to take them home to Brussels.

In the business district, people began to loot the shops. Unaware, we packed the car and drove to Elisabethville. Stewart remarked on the unusual number of soldiers on the streets when we arrived at the mission. He received a message that the church leaders in Jadotville wanted him to come back. They needed his protection. Order was crumbling and they feared for their lives. The American consul in Elisabethville summoned all American citizens to meet with him that afternoon for instructions for evacuation. I visualized an airplane, American flags painted on the sides, the six of us on board, surrounded by our friends, on our way to safety. Deliverance. Deliver us from E'ville.

We drove through the crowded streets to the vacant mission residence we had reserved for that night when we still thought we were on our way to a vacation. The family who had lived there for four years had left just days before, on furlough in the States. Lucky them, I thought. The house was empty except for the furniture the mission supplied, beds and tables and chairs, kitchen stove, and refrigerator. No dishes, no pots and pans, no lamps. I told Stewart he could represent me at the meeting with the consul. I unrolled the sleeping bags and unpacked the camping gear we had assembled for our trip to Beira on the beach. He was back within the hour. I met him at the door.

"What's the word?"

"The consul says we're to keep in touch, stay alert. He's arranged for a plane to come for us, possibly during the night. And we're invited to join the Elisabethville missionaries for potluck supper. They want to talk it over and decide what to do."

"What do you mean, decide what to do? Isn't it decided? Didn't the consul say we'll leave on the plane?"

"Well, the women and children will, most of them, anyway."

"I don't like the sound of this. You mean you'd send us out and stay here?"

"It's possible." His eyes shifted away. "I really don't know yet. Let's see what the others plan to do."

I didn't care what the others planned to do. I wanted my family out of there, safe. If I wanted to save my children, I might have to leave Stewart behind. I knew the other missionaries well enough to know they would not feel compelled to follow the consul's orders.

In the social hall of the largest church, we joined the group of eight families, several single women missionaries, and half a dozen African pastors. Some brought rice and beans, pots of chili. I donated a canned ham I had saved for our vacation. The men sat together around a big table and made plans while we women served the food and supervised the crowd of children.

"I hope they send a big enough plane," I said.

"You mean you plan to go?" Lois asked in surprise. She and Maurice were the senior members of the group. Was it their years of experience that made them so confident no harm would come to any of us? Or perhaps it blinded them to the possibilities of what might happen.

"Yes, if the consul orders us to go, I'll go," I said, "and take the children."

"I don't believe the American consul can order us to go," she said. "We answer to a higher authority than the American government. And I don't think Tshombe will let us come to any harm. It's just that Lumumba has got them all stirred up."

The missionaries, like Maurice and Lois who had been there for many years, were close friends with the affable Moïse Tshombe. Bishop Springer, the retired patriarch, had baptized Tshombe and vouched for his character. Tshombe had the support of the Belgians. They were deeply concerned over the future of the mining industry that supplied not only sixty percent of the Congolese economy but represented a source of enormous wealth. Tshombe represented stability. He was always close to the missionaries. He briefed us on political events, depended on our support. We trusted him. We never suspected the perfidy of which he proved to be capable.

"We have to pray about this," Lois said. "We can't just run away and leave our people behind. How would that look? The Africans need our help to defend the mission property. If we leave, we'd lose all respect. We must set an example of our Christian faith. We must be strong in the Lord."

I glanced over her shoulder at the sober faces around the men's table. The African pastors gesticulated as they spoke. They could be very persuasive. And they had already sent their wives and children to safety in the bush.

Stewart would never get on that plane. If it came. I would do what I had to do, what was best for the children.

That evening, back in our borrowed house, we had no electricity. The thrifty mission treasurer, not expecting the house to be occupied, had arranged for the power to be turned off. By flashlight, we tucked the children into their sleeping bags. We must be ready to leave for the airport at a moment's notice when the consul called during the night. I checked the phone: it worked, so far. There was an alternate plan. If the plane didn't come, or if the rebels seized the airport, a convoy would leave at first light to drive to the Northern Rhodesia border. Surely Stewart wouldn't expect me to make that drive alone with the children.

Sporadic gunfire punctuated the silence. Fires burned in the distance. Furtive crowds moved through the dark streets. Army trucks thundered by. In the light of a small candle found in the camping gear, I re-packed our things for the plane. I put Stewart's things in a separate suitcase, a tacit acceptance he might not go with us. I could always re-pack in the morning if it was to be a car journey. I couldn't decide what to wear. Would slacks be acceptable if we flew straight home to the States?

I listened to the quiet breathing of the sleeping children and waited for Stewart to come back from his patrol of the property. He came in, closed the door quietly, and locked it. I searched his face, dim in the light of the candle, for confirmation of his intentions, and found no hint of fear or apprehension.

"Everything's quiet out there," he assured me. "Maybe it won't be so bad."

"If we have to leave, are you coming with us?"

He raised his eyebrows in surprise. "You know I can't do that. Too many people depend on me here. I'll go back to Jadotville in the morning if I can get through. You and the kids go ahead if you want to. I'll join you as soon as I can."

I bit down on my lower lip. We depended on him, too. This might be the last time I would see him. I didn't want to make a scene. He had never promised to go with us. We would go and he would stay. His duty lay with the church, and my duty lay with the children. I was sick of duty. Duty left no room for love, fear, or sorrow. I felt torn in two. I couldn't imagine life without Stewart. He watched my face. He hoped I wouldn't get emotional, make a scene. I shook my head, blinked back the tears. We didn't touch each other. It was as though we were already worlds apart. We stared at each other. The phone rang.

"At least they didn't disconnect the phone," he said as he picked up the receiver. It was not the expected summons to the plane. It was Maurice. The rebels had captured the airport. My fantasy flag-painted plane of deliverance evaporated. Stewart talked on, arranged details for the children and me to join the convoy to Northern Rhodesia. I fell asleep, exhausted.

I woke to daylight. Stewart was up and dressed. "The water's hot," he said, "if you want a cup of Nescafé. The convoy to Rhodesia will leave about ten. Marlene will pick you up. She's going to drive you and the kids in the *wamama* VW bus." Marlene was one of the unmarried women who taught at Mulungwishi. Everyone called the single women the *wa-mamas*.

"Well, you've been busy," I said, irritated. "When did you arrange all this?" I had not been consulted. Were we parcels to be delivered?

"I didn't want to disturb you. You needed to get your sleep; it's going to be a long day. I have to get back to Jadotville right away, before they close the road." Clearly, I was not in control of my own destiny.

Tim came into the kitchen in his baseball pajamas. "Did the plane come for us?"

"The plane couldn't land. The soldiers took over the airport," I explained. "We're going to Kitwe, with Marlene in her car."

"That's great," he said. "If we're not going to America, I'm glad we're going to Kitwe. We can get ice cream." Northern Rhodesia meant ice cream cones and movies in English, toy stores, and sweet shops. "I'll get dressed."

We were packed and ready when Marlene came. We loaded our stuff into the back of her VW bus, small suitcases, camping gear, and boxes of food. Stewart had already put his things in our VW bug, unable to conceal his eagerness to get going, to send us on our way. The children hopped into Marlene's car and began to squabble about the seating arrangements.

"Aren't you going to say goodbye to your dad?" I asked.

They bounced out of the car and hugged him, briefly, in turn. "Bye, Dad."

It seemed like a comedy. For me it was tragic. I knew how much he disliked public affection, but I put my arms around him. I tried not to cry. "Take care of yourself," I said. "Don't do anything foolish."

He patted me on the back, as though I were a child. "I'll be all right. Don't worry, I'll just stay in the house and take care of things and, as soon as I can, I'll come on down to Kitwe."

I kissed him on the cheek and climbed onto the front bench seat with Marlene. As we drove out of the yard, I looked back to see him fold himself into our little blue car, eager, as always, to get underway. I sniffled, searched for a tissue, and blew my nose. Marlene reached over and patted my arm. "Cheer up. He'll be fine."

While Stewart headed up the road north to Jadotville, every other car, van, truck, minibus, and mobylette went southeast toward the border with Northern Rhodesia. Marlene maneuvered her khaki-colored VW bus into the frantic stream of traffic. She ignored the blasts of horns and shouts of drivers.

"Where will we meet the others?" I asked.

She looked blank. "The others?"

"The other missionaries. Aren't any of them going?"

"I told them not to wait for us. This bus is the slowest thing on four wheels. They wanted to get on down to Kitwe and make arrangements for all of us to stay at Mindolo." The World Council of Churches had just established the Mindolo Ecumenical Foundation near Kitwe for the training of church leaders. We called it the Ecumenical Center. We hoped to stay in the dormitories for a few nights until we could return to the Congo—or go home to the States.

"We'll be fine," Marlene said, as breezy and casual as Stewart. "I've done this drive dozens of times. What could happen?"

I swallowed my panic. I mustn't alarm the children. Frenzied drivers jostled for position as they compressed into the two-lane highway. A gleaming black Mercedes sedan swept by. Had they just washed it this morning? For the trip? Dusty American station wagons, pickup trucks loaded with cardboard boxes and furniture, panel trucks, compact European sedans passed each other recklessly. Drivers stared straight ahead, accelerated up the hills, blasted their horns, every man for himself. Frightened faces stared at us from car windows. A pretty little girl held up a kitten.

"I'm hungry, Mom," Peter said. "What's for lunch?"

I looked at my watch, surprised to see it was already past noon. I climbed over the bench seats to rummage through the food box in the back. "I know I've got a can of tuna fish in here somewhere." I found the loaf of bread, the can of tuna fish, but no can opener. "How about peanut butter sandwiches?" I passed them around with cups of lemonade and admonitions to be careful, not to spill anything. Appetites appeased, the children, dusted with crumbs, sticky with peanut butter and lemonade, quarreled listlessly over the division of their territory.

"Mom, make him move. I had that place by the window."

"Mom, I get carsick if I don't sit by the window."

"How come Tim gets to sit up front with Aunt Marlene?"

"I don't have any room at all, Mom."

"Mom, he hit me."

"Oh, shut up. I didn't touch you."

"Listen to me, all of you," I said. "You've got to stop this. I won't have this fussing and fighting. We'll be in the car all afternoon. You've got books to read. Get as comfortable as you can and settle down. Take a nap. We'll be in Kitwe by suppertime."

"Can we go get ice cream cones when we get to Kitwe?" Mary Beth asked.

"We'll see," I said.

"Sure," said Marlene. "We'll go for ice cream."

Before long, the children fell asleep. If only all strife could be settled with ice cream cones. I yearned for the oblivion of sleep, but, exhausted as I was, it wouldn't come. When I closed my eyes, I saw trees down across the road, and visions of crazed soldiers waving guns and machetes, ordering us out of the car. I saw the boys, brave in their terror, look to me for guidance, and the girls clinging to me. Better to stay awake.

The Volkswagen bus was notoriously underpowered, built to carry a load of people and their belongings, but slow. We couldn't hold our own in the stream of traffic. We crawled up every hill as cars accelerated around us. We met no oncoming traffic. Before long southbound cars took over both lanes. Cars passed us on the verge, bucked along through the grass on the rough shoulder. Through the long afternoon, we fell farther and farther behind.

The landscape was monotonous, no long vistas, just endless scrubby trees beyond the margin of the road. No villages, no people, no landmarks. No soldiers. "Talk to me," Marlene said after a long silence. "I'm getting sleepy."

What could we talk about? I suggested, "Let's sing." That always works with a sleepy driver. We sang softly, campfire songs, "This Little Light of Mine," "Jacob's Ladder." The children woke up.

"Are we there yet?" Mary Beth asked, rubbing her eyes.

"I'm thirsty," Martha said. Everyone was thirsty. I passed the paper cups of water around and then everybody had to go to the bathroom. Marlene pulled well off the road and the children scattered into the tall grass.

"Go find an anthill to hide behind," Marlene suggested.

"Don't go too far," I cautioned them, "and watch out for snakes."

Marlene stretched and rolled her shoulders. The traffic streamed by. "How much farther do you think it is to the border?" I asked.

"I'm not sure. It can't be more than a couple of hours, but these hills really slow us down. Don't worry, we'll be there before dark. Doesn't it seem like we've seen mostly white faces all day? I wonder why so few of the Africans are leaving."

"They can always hide in the bush. We can't."

In the late afternoon, as the long shadows stretched across the road, we came around a curve and Marlene braked sharply. Cars blocked both lanes of the road ahead. Brakes squealed as cars pulled up behind us.

Others careened around us and came to rest in the tall grass along the road.

"I wonder what's going on," Marlene said.

I climbed down from the car and walked ahead to a man and woman who stood at the side of the road. "Do you know why everyone has stopped?" I asked in my hesitant French.

"Holdup at the border," he said, in English. "They say those damned border guards won't open the barrier. They're processing every car, just like they always do, taking forever, letting one car through at a time. If the people have their exit permits, that is. Everyone else has to wait."

"How far ahead is the border?"

"Not sure. Miles, I think. I walked ahead for a ways. People have been there for hours, all afternoon. They're starting to panic."

Close to panic myself, I felt my heart pounding. In another hour it would be dark. I took deep breaths to calm down as I returned to the car. I couldn't let my emotions get the better of me now.

"They're waiting to cross the border. With this many cars, it takes a while. You kids can get out of the car, if you want to, but stay close, don't wander away. When it's our turn, we'll go."

They stayed in the car. They must have been frightened. They didn't even quarrel. Stewart should have come with us, taken some responsibility for his family. I was furious with him and felt guilty for my fury. Suppose something happened to him? Suppose he was killed?

Marlene said, "Why don't I walk ahead a bit and see how big this traffic jam is?" She gave me the keys. "Just in case things get underway before I get back." She disappeared through the cars. The shadows lengthened. The forest was already dark.

"Mom, when will we get there?"

"Will we have to sleep in the car?"

"I'm hungry, Mom."

If we could just get through the border, we would have only about thirty miles to the Ecumenical Center. I couldn't admit, even to myself, I had no idea when we'd get there. I blamed myself for bringing the children into danger. I was the one who had wanted to come to Africa.

"We'll probably be there for supper," I said, trying to impart confidence I did not feel. Stewart used to tease me about sounding like Miss

Frances, a saccharine personality on a children's TV program. I encouraged the children to watch her when we lived in West Hartford. The kids liked the puppets. "I wonder what they are fixing for us. What would you like for supper?"

Tim said, "A baked potato with lots of butter."

Peter said, "A hamburger and French fries, with lots of ketchup."

"Yeah, me too," said Martha.

"What about you, Mary Beth? You're being awfully quiet."

"My throat hurts. I just want some orange jello." She had complained of a sore throat. I planned to take her to the doctor in Kitwe. Duvon thought her tonsils needed to come out. Mary Beth's tense face told me she was as frightened as I was and just as stoic. My reassurance and false cheer never fooled her. It was as though we had a silent agreement never to voice our fright.

The sun sank behind the trees and twilight faded abruptly. Marlene appeared out of the gloom. "It's a real mess up there. The guards on this side refuse to open the barrier without checking everyone's papers and the crowd is about ready to riot. There's no way to get out of this so we might as well make the best of it. We could be here all night."

I dreaded being trapped among all these cars in the dark. Rebel soldiers might attack the convoy if they knew we were immobilized. What if the border guards let the rebels know they had the *wazungu* trapped? We sat in the dark car, all of us unusually silent.

"Listen," Marlene said. "I hear cars starting up." Headlights snapped on and people were running to their cars. Car doors slammed. Slowly, the mass of cars and trucks began to move forward. We crept along in the double line, hoping the engine wouldn't stall, holding our own on the hills. At the border, a sullen guard stood beside the open barrier, rifle at the ready as cars full of *wazungu* crawled past.

"Is he going to shoot us?" Mary Beth asked.

"Oh, shut up, Mary Beth," Tim said. He was scared, too.

The guard glared at us and brusquely motioned us past. We crept across a no-man's-land between the border stations. At the Rhodesian border post a hundred yards farther on, a cheery British fellow waved us through to safe territory.

Marlene drove onto the shoulder and shut off the motor. "I want to find out what happened."

The official walked briskly up to the car, clean and neat in his uniform. He saluted and removed his cap. "Evening, ladies. Welcome to Rhodesia."

"You don't know how happy we are to be here," I said.

"Glad to oblige. You can do the same for us when our chaps get their independence and we come up to the Congo for refuge."

"What happened back there?" Marlene asked. "Did the Belgians rush the guards?"

"Just about. They were ready to. The guards finally came out and opened the barrier." He put on his hat, touched the brim in a salute, and moved on. Before Marlene could start the car, another white face appeared at the window.

"Say, ladies, I'm a correspondent with an American newspaper. I see you just came from the Congo. Is it true the Belgians rushed the border back there, staged a riot, and tore down the barrier?"

"No, that's not the way it happened," Marlene said, happy to set the record straight. "The guards finally opened the gate and we drove through with everyone else."

He frowned, turned away, disappointed. He intercepted a passing car. We heard him say, "Is it true the Belgians rioted at the border and rushed the guards?"

Marlene and I looked at each other. "Eventually someone will say yes, that's what happened, and he'll have his story," I said. I shrugged my shoulders. "Let's go."

So that's how history is made.

An hour later, we pulled into the parking lot of the Ecumenical Center. Marlene and I scanned the row of cars and trucks.

"Looks like the Elisabethville contingent made it," Marlene said.

"I hope they saved a place for us."

Lights blazed in the dining hall as we trudged in, exhausted, disheveled, unsure of our welcome. Familiar figures were gathered around chrome tables.

"So, you finally made it. We've been here for hours. We were getting worried."

"We had to wait forever to get through the border," Marlene said. "Did you have any trouble at the border?"

"Just the usual delay."

The African waiter brought British-style sandwiches, thin slices of ham between two pieces of white bread, and pots of tea. The director of the foundation welcomed us and assigned us a room in the concrete-block dormitory. Too tired to talk, the children and I dragged our belongings to the long, narrow room. Two sets of triple-decker bunks. The boys chose the top bunks. I cautioned them not to fall out of bed onto that unforgiving concrete floor. Down the hall in the communal bathroom, we washed our sticky hands and faces, brushed our teeth. The children climbed into bed, murmured their prayers, "… and God bless Daddy," and fell asleep. I lay there looking at the empty bunk. I wondered if Stewart would ever sleep there.

On July 10, the day we left Elisabethville, Tshombe declared the Katanga to be an independent nation, separate from the new Republic of the Congo. This news was crowded off the front page of newspapers by the more sensational news of rebellion in other provinces. A daily briefing of the local newspaper kept us informed of events north of the border.

On July 12, officials at the United Nations received a telegram from the Congolese government requesting "military aid … against the present external aggression." On July 14, the Security Council voted to send military aid to the Congo until the Congolese were able to "fulfill their tasks properly."

Although the children and I were technically refugees, our life in Kitwe was comparatively easy. We had arrived safely with our gear. We met up with our friends, found food on the table and the beds made up. But we were far from home, not knowing if we would ever see Stewart again.

The place was a catch-basin for missionaries. Women from the remote mission stations had driven with their children through the bush over little-used tracks, guided by courageous Africans who hid them and helped them escape to safety. Of the twenty families at the Ecumenical Center, only one, the Sinclair family, was complete—with a dad. He had a good excuse. They were on their way back from a vacation in Southern Rhodesia and were not able to get to Elisabethville. Leonard Sinclair helped all of us, advised on car problems, took a station wagon full of children for ice cream, monitored the shortwave radio.

We gravitated to the dining hall for afternoon tea, mugs of strong black tea, lukewarm, laced with canned milk, and too much sugar. African tea. The children gulped theirs, grabbed handfuls of cookies, and ran back outside. They adapted easily to communal meals in the dining hall. The mothers and Leonard Sinclair compared rumors, hungry for news.

"What have you heard from Kapanga?" I asked Leonard.

"Everyone got out in time, thanks to the new airstrip. They're at Kamina, I think. Some of them should be turning up here before long."

At least the children were happy. The noise of their play drifted in the open window as they pushed their Dinky Toys around. "Vroom, vroom. Watch out, here comes my Mercedes."

A middle-aged African man in well-pressed khaki cotton pants and shirt marched into the dining room and stood by our table. "*Madame*," he said indignantly, "your children are destroying the flower beds." We trooped outside. The boys had torn up a corner of rough grass to make a racetrack under the Bougainville bushes. A minor infraction to us, but the gardener was incensed. "You see, *Madame*, what your children have done," he said to me. "Please do not allow them to play here."

We watched him stalk away. His shoulders twitched. The boys turned their eyes from him to us. "Does he mean we can't play cars anymore?" Peter asked.

"I'm afraid so," I said. "Not here, anyway. Let's go look for another spot. Bring your cars."

The next day they were reprimanded for making noise outside the library. Then, for shooting frogs in the pond with a pellet gun. We were wearing out our welcome.

I gathered up the dirty clothes and carried them to the laundry room. Diane Elliott was already there, elbow-deep in suds. I filled the other galvanized sink, dumped in some soap powder. We stood shoulder to shoulder, scrubbing our son's socks.

"I wish I'd brought Baba Samuel along, and the Maytag," I said.

"Oh, you city folks. You're so spoiled, with your washing machines and electric stoves. We don't have those luxuries in the bush." Of course, she had a servant to heat the water in a barrel over a wood fire and wash the clothes. I kept my thoughts to myself. At least Baba Samuel had an easier time, as long as the water heater worked. He just fed the clothes into the wringer after the agitator beat out the dirt and hung them on the line. And ironed everything.

"Look at these socks," she said. "I just can't get them clean. Those boys are so hard on their clothes."

I stopped rubbing the heels of the socks together and looked over at her. "What does it matter if the socks are white? Why are we worrying about that when the whole country has gone to pieces?"

She couldn't have looked more shocked if I'd said I no longer accepted Jesus as my Personal Savior. "Don't say that," she said with vehemence. "Cleanliness is next to Godliness. God expects us to set an example. We can't let our standards down just because we're not in the Congo."

I smarted a bit under her sharp criticism. When I hung my clean clothes on the clothesline, I noticed her white socks were immaculate, while the red dust had not been completely eradicated from mine. I couldn't accept clean laundry as a test of character. Or faith.

On Sunday, the entire missionary contingent drove into town to church in clean clothes, hands and faces scrubbed, hair combed. After all those Sundays crowded on hard benches, enduring endless hard-to-follow sermons, here were hard-backed hymnals with familiar words to familiar tunes, comfortable benches with backs, windows of colored glass, a sermon in English, an organ. The minister welcomed the missionary refugees from the Congo, asked us to stand, prayed for those left behind. Tears gathered in my eyes.

In the evening after dinner, we gathered in the dining hall for prayers. I couldn't pray. I wanted only one selfish thing: for Stewart to be alive. Either he was alive, at that moment, or not, and I didn't see how my prayers could change anything. As for the future, "Lord keep him safe," was too scary to contemplate. And what about all the Africans in mortal danger? Better just to sit there with hands clasped, head bowed, eyes shut.

Dr. Fred Sadler, professor of linguistics, was one of the few faculty members in residence. In his quiet way, he welcomed us and opened his home. Most of the missionaries ignored his invitation and avoided him. He was a student of languages, not a saver of souls, and suspected of being an intellectual. I warmed to him. After evening prayers, I put the children to bed and walked over to the Sadlers. They were readers and invited me to help myself to the books on their shelves.

Mrs. Sadler made a pot of tea. "Shall we listen to the news? It's almost ten o'clock."

The news from the Congo was horrendous. Belgian paratroopers had arrived in Jadotville to subdue the rioting. Street fighting, the downtown district in ruins. Hospitals overwhelmed with casualties—dead and wounded.

"How are you bearing up under all this?" Dr. Sadler asked.

"I find I can't pray," I confessed.

"I'm not surprised. In your situation, I couldn't either."

Tears welled up. "I can't talk to the other missionaries about this."

"I understand. They have a different concept of the Will of God. Sometimes I wish I believed that way. It would make it easier, I think. But we are who we are. We can't force ourselves to believe what we don't believe."

"I heard an unconfirmed report," I said and swallowed hard to regain my composure. "I heard an American missionary was killed in Jadotville."

He gazed at me with compassion. "I heard that rumor. Several of your friends came to talk to me about it. They felt it best not to tell you until we know more."

"They think he's dead, don't they?"

"Some of them do, yes."

"I thought they were being awfully nice to me."

"But we don't know anything for certain. Try to hope for the best."

He didn't tell me to have faith; I was glad of that. "Do you think anyone has said anything to the children?"

"I don't think so. I hope not."

He walked back to the bleak dormitory with me. We said goodnight and he disappeared down the path, going home to his wife and children. I tiptoed into the dark room and passed the unoccupied bunk where Stewart might, or might not, sleep. For the sake of the children, I would be strong.

We went on as though nothing had happened, trips to the swimming pool, the Dairy Queen, to the movies to see *Snow White*. The other moms offered to look after my children. "They're no problem; we'll keep an eye on them. Why don't you get some rest?"

I wondered what they knew that I didn't. I didn't ask.

I took Mary Beth to the doctor. If I were to be head of the household, I'd better practice.

She opened wide for the doctor and stood patiently while he moved the wooden tongue depressor in her mouth.

"Yes," he said at last, "those tonsils will have to come out. The sooner the better."

"I'd like to wait until my husband is here. He's still up in the Congo, in Jadotville."

He grimaced. I winced. He said, "Not a good place to be just now, is it? Let me know when he comes out, and I'll schedule the surgery. She'll only be in the hospital a couple of days."

Mary Beth put her hand in mine as we walked down the hall. "What's surgery? Is that like an operation?"

"Yes, that's exactly what it is. You remember when I went up to Kapanga for an operation?"

"Yes. Dad burned the meatloaf, and I had to get my hair cut. Will I have to get my hair cut to have an operation?"

"I don't think so. But your hair grows fast."

She tossed her blonde braids. "I like it better when you comb my hair. Dad pulls too hard on the tangles."

"How long have we been here, Mom?" Peter asked the next morning during breakfast.

"I'm not sure. Has it been a week yet?" It seemed like a year.

"Can we go outside and play now?" Tim asked.

"Yes. Carry out your dirty dishes first."

Dr. Sadler came into the dining hall and stood just inside the door, looking around. My heart sank. I could feel its sudden heaviness in my breast. Was he looking for me? He saw me and smiled. Not bad news, then. He hurried over.

"I have good news for you. I just had a phone call, relaying a message. The missionaries from Jadotville and Mulungwishi are on their way here. They're driving down, should be here by noon." He waited for my response.

"Do you know who's coming? Is Stewart in the group?"

He looked puzzled. "I forgot to ask for names; I was so eager to bring you the news. I'm sure he's part of the group, or they would have said." A shadow crossed his face.

I must continue to hope, then, and not give in to doubt. If I doubted Stewart was coming, maybe he wouldn't come. I willed him to be alive and on his way to us. I would know soon enough. Dr. Sadler looked disappointed. I had let him down. I forced a smile.

"I'm sorry, Dr. Sadler, to be so slow. It's wonderful news. I'll tell the children. Thanks so much for letting us know, and for all your support. I couldn't have gotten through this week without your help."

"Glad I could help. Let me know when your husband gets here. I want to meet him." He stopped at several other tables on his way out, spreading the good news. Leonard and Joyce Sinclair came over to my table. They both hugged me. "Just heard the good news. Stewart's on his way," Leonard said. Others came over.

I went outside to find the children. Mary Beth and Martha sat under the mango tree with the other little girls, playing "house" with their dolls.

They looked up when they saw me. "Do we have to stop now?" Mary Beth asked. "We're just getting started."

"Oh, no, my dears. I just wanted to tell you your dad's coming today. He'll probably be here by lunchtime."

"Okay," Martha said. "Can we play till he gets here?"

"Of course. It will be a while. I'll let you know." Already, they were back in the safe world of their imagination, taking care of the doll children.

Peter and Tim looked up from an elaborate racetrack they had created in a pile of gravel. "What's up, Mom?" Tim asked.

"Your dad's coming today, about noon."

"Okay, let me know when he gets here."

I straightened up the depressing narrow dormitory room. We tended to let down our standards when Stewart was away, so we had been sloppy during the week: clothes strewn everywhere, toys under the beds. I tossed the dirty clothes into a basket, folded the clean clothes, put them away in the flimsy bureau drawers, made up the bunks. I looked at the bunk where Stewart would sleep. If he came. When he came.

The hours passed. Noon, and nobody arrived. The children ate lunch with their friends, as usual. I'd eat with Stewart when he arrived. Maybe they had been held up at the border. I tried not to watch the place where cars turned in from the main road. And then, at last, the blue Volkswagen drove in with Stewart at the wheel. He saw me and waved. Thank God, he was alive. I could feel my heart beating. He parked, climbed out, and stretched as I walked over. I stared at him as though I couldn't believe it was him. "I was so worried," I said in a weak voice.

"Why were you worried?" he asked, jauntily. "We weren't in any danger. I don't know why you left. You could have stayed."

I slapped him, hard, across the face. "How can you say that?" I sobbed. "I thought you'd been killed."

I stepped back, horrified I had hit him. The red print of my hand stood out on his cheek. I put the offending hand behind me. "I'm sorry," I wailed. "I didn't mean to do that. I've been so afraid for you."

He stood there, angry, confused, embarrassed, not saying anything. Struggling to put this behind us, I asked, "Have you had lunch? I waited for you."

"I stopped at the Dairy Queen," he said sheepishly. I had been counting the minutes until he came. He picked up his canvas bag and put it over his shoulder. He always traveled light. "Do you want to show me where we're staying?" He still hadn't touched me. We walked to the dormitory in silence, and I opened the door to our room. He closed the door and locked it. We grabbed each other, tore at each other's clothes, fell onto his bunk frantically grappling and then moving hungrily together.

The children banged on the door. "Mom! Dad! Are you in there? We saw Dad's car. Are you there?"

We didn't answer and they finally went away.

Chapter Eleven

S tewart's appearance in Kitwe was the precursor of a change in the atmosphere at the Ecumenical Center. Other dads drifted in, and entire families from the far reaches of the upper Congo brought hair-raising tales of deliverance. The dining room became a family room, the new normal. Under the watchful eyes of their fathers, the children behaved themselves. The waiters and workmen respected the *bwanas*.

Everyone wanted to hear Stewart's story of *les événements*. He tended to make light of the danger.

I couldn't bear to think what might have happened. "What were you thinking? You could have been killed."

"I had to protect the mission property. I wasn't in any danger." He described the events of that week in Jadotville in a letter to our supporters in the States:

> When the order came to evacuate on Sunday, July 8, we were packed for a vacation. This simplified our preparations, and we left almost immediately for Elisabethville. From there, Rosemary and the children went to Northern Rhodesia, where they spent five weeks at the Ecumenical Center in Kitwe. On the afternoon of the eighth, I returned to Jadotville to find tension mounting. The next morning the mutiny exploded in the military camp, and several days of chaos

ensued. Most of the white population left that night, escorted by Belgian troops.

In the absence of authority, fighting, looting, and rape went on as we stood helpless. My colleague, Maurice, remained with me, and together we ducked as bullets whizzed over the house. Almost every store in town was completely cleaned out of goods, wall to wall, and in many cases the living quarters of the proprietor as well. Belgian troops attempted to come in on Tuesday but were forced to retreat again. The next day they were successful, and the mutinous troops laid down their arms, but not until the mayor, a splendid man, had been shot just across the street from the mission.

The destruction in the shopping district rivaled anything a bombing raid might have done. The amount of goods carried off by the mob ran close to five million dollars, and the streets were full of rubbish and junk and broken glass.

On Monday evening we discovered a family wandering in the streets, homeless. Their store and home had been looted and ruined and they had barely escaped with their lives. They stayed at the mission for several days until they could go to friends in Elisabethville. They were not strangers to tragedy. She bore on her arm the tattooed number from a concentration camp in Poland.

As the endless parade of looters passed by the mission, carrying all sorts of goods, many of our church members tried to intervene, but it was impossible to stem the tide. As always in a crisis, many stood heroically in the face of difficulty. The report got out that I had been killed, and a delegation came to our house at once. This same rumor went by shortwave radio to Rhodesia and, fortunately, Rosemary did not hear about it until after I rejoined the family on the sixteenth. Slowly, Jadotville is regaining its equilibrium and wears a semblance of normality, though most of the stores have been boarded up and will not be re-opened. Only a fraction of the white population remains, and everyone is a bit jumpy.

Maurice told me more about that week in Jadotville. "I moved into your house with Stewart. It's farther from the street, and we felt the long driveway would give us more of a warning in case the army or the looters came into the mission. We had people staying with us most of the time, people who had lost their homes or felt safer with us. The Jewish couple—the concentration camp survivors—wouldn't leave the back bedroom. They slept together in the bottom bunk. They wouldn't be separated from one another. They were just terrified. Friday morning, Stewart was in the kitchen cooking his famous oatmeal for the household when an army tank turned into the driveway and drove toward the house. Stewart grabbed a stack of cereal bowls, those bright-colored plastic ones, and ran out the door hollering at the soldiers to get off the property. They backed out of the driveway and didn't bother us again. Africans have great respect for crazy people, you know, and I'm sure they thought he was *fou*, a lunatic. They left and didn't come back."

A correspondent from the *New York Times* reported every window broken in the commercial district, the streets curb-deep in broken glass. When the July 18 issue of *Time* magazine arrived in Kitwe, I learned more about what we had missed:

Violence exploded in mineral-rich Katanga, whose political leader, Moïse Tshombe, has been advocating secession from the Congo. During a night of terror, mutinous Congolese troops roamed the streets of Elisabethville, the provincial capital, screaming war cries and firing machine guns and rifles. Four automobiles returning to the city after evacuating women and children to Rhodesia were stopped at a railroad crossing. Six of the ten European occupants, including Italian Vice Consul Tito Spoglia, were shot

dead, and the others seriously wounded. Cavalcades of cars bearing panicky Europeans streamed eastward to the North Rhodesian border; 3,000 crossed in a single night, and Salisbury hotel lobbies were packed with women comforting whimpering children. The U.S., British and French consuls in Elisabethville called for help. Three hundred paratroopers were rushed by air from the Belgian airbase at Kamina, and for the first time the Congolese mutineers were engaged in battle by white troops. The paratroopers stormed the Elisabethville barracks and routed the mutinous Congolese troops, with some 100 dead.
…

At week's end the Belgian government decided upon armed intervention to rescue and evacuate its citizens in the Congo, who are estimated to number 80,000. Two Belgian officials left Brussels for Léopoldville to put an ultimatum to Lumumba. He was given the choice of inviting Belgian troops to restore order. Should he refuse, the Belgians would intervene on their own initiative. … Either the Congolese government would restore law and order or the Belgian paratroops would do it for them.

Months later, my parents told me they called The Board that week for reassurance. My dad was never comfortable with the telephone. He seldom initiated a call, never a call to an office in New York. Mother prevailed and placed the call, overcoming her reluctance to bother important people.

My dad spoke to the Africa Secretary, who claimed to be in daily communication with the missionaries on site. He assured my parents everything was fine, all quiet in Jadotville. Their small television screen showed a different story, the destruction of the city. Their confidence in church leaders began to erode.

None of the missionaries were allowed to return to the Congo without permission of the American Consul. He allowed only the men to cross the border to attend meetings with the African church leaders. "President Tshombe joined us at a church service," Stewart wrote, "in great pomp and circumstance."

A fresh crop of missionaries from the States joined us at the Ecumenical Center. They had just completed their language studies and orientation and were eager to cross the border and get to work. They were full of themselves and not slow to tell us where we had gone wrong. Hadn't we just been expelled from the country? It wasn't easy to listen to them, so sure of themselves, so disdainful of us, who had allowed things to fall into chaos.

For a time, it seemed certain we would all be sent back to the States. That would have been my preference. I had never intended to raise my children in the path of opposing armies. These catastrophic events, and those that followed, would have been unimaginable when we first arrived in the Belgian Congo.

My priority was Mary Beth's tonsillectomy. I delivered her to the hospital and immediately became aware of the sharp geometry of the Rhodesian color bar. Prominent signage reminded me we were entering a hospital for the white race only. People of color mopped floors or carried trays.

The admitting desk was unattended. Murmurs of conversations and the rattling of teacups drifted down the hall. Except for those restrictive signs, the place looked like an American hospital, with wide corridors, shiny floors, and an air of cold efficiency.

Mary Beth tugged at my arm. "Let's go home. There's nobody here."

"But Mary, your dad took the car."

"That's okay. We can walk."

As if on cue, the admitting nurse appeared. She nodded at us, took Mary Beth's hand, and led her away down the hall. I had expected to take my daughter to her room, help her undress and tuck her into bed. She looked back over her shoulder in panic. She began to cry. My heart ached for her, taken from her mother by officious strangers.

Stewart and I came during visiting hours the next day. Mary Beth was pale and listless. "My throat hurts," she rasped. We brought ice cream. By the next afternoon, she had made friends with the other children in the ward. In a couple more days, the doctor released her to our care.

We couldn't stay forever in our narrow dormitory room. There was more talk that we would all be sent stateside soon. I proposed we go on safari. This might be our only chance to see more of Africa, to visit the game parks of Northern Rhodesia, to see Victoria Falls. Stewart agreed and we packed our bags. On August 15, we drove away from the Ecumenical Center, stopped at the doctor's office for Mary Beth's final check-up, and headed south for a long drive across the dusty plains to Victoria Falls.

We heard it before we saw it. The roar of the falls shook the ground. The great Zambezi River plunged three hundred and fifty-five feet into the gorge. This was not a Niagara-like panorama, where one viewed the falls from below. We stood at the level of the brink of the falls, looking across a narrow canyon at "The Smoke that Thunders." Far below, shrouded in mist, the water churned away toward the narrow outlet of the canyon, where a suspension bridge spanned the chasm. Facing us at eye level, the mighty Zambezi hurtled toward us and plunged over the brink. The ground opened at our feet, wet, uneven. There were no railings.

Mary Beth clung to me, in tears. She begged me to take her back to the car. Martha tugged at my hand. We trudged along the slippery mile-long path parallel to the cataract, through a rain forest perpetually green from the spray and festooned with a myriad of rainbows. We were soon as damp as the forest, our clothes soaked. I was terrified. Peter and Tim scampered along the path, climbed into the trees, threw rocks into the depths. I shouted to them to get back from the edge. The cacophony of the river drowned my cries. Stewart, oblivious of the danger, stared at the magnificent panorama. We finally walked back to the car. I was faint with relief.

The government rest camps were full. We had not thought to make reservations. A primitive campground offered a tent and a cot. A nearby bathhouse provided hot showers. Stewart bought some sandwiches and built a campfire. I was given the place of honor on the cot. Toward morning I woke, shivering. The omnipresent booming of the falls made me wonder if I had slept at all. We packed up and drove over the bridge, arched high over the gorge. Far below, the Zambezi thundered on. I turned away. We went in search of breakfast.

A hundred miles down the road, we entered the Wankie National Park, five thousand square miles set aside for native wild animals, roaming free. All afternoon we drove, slowly, on unimproved roads, alert for sightings of exotic beasts: all varieties of antelope, gemsbok, and kudu. A herd of impalas floated through the bush. Giraffes, well camouflaged, remained invisible until they moved. A huge herd of water buffalo stood motionless and menacing in the tall grass. Warthogs ran by, so ugly they were cute, their stiff flywhisk tails straight up as they trotted along. Stripes flickered as zebras changed formation. A clan of baboons draped themselves in the branches of a tree, with a tiny baboon baby so cunning, Martha begged to take it with us. She cried when we left the baby there with its mama.

The rest camp was fenced in, a sort of zoo in reverse where the animals roamed free. We feasted on canned spaghetti heated on a camp stove. We planned an early start the next morning, hoping to see lions, but the car rebelled. Perhaps it was too cold. We shivered in our light sweaters. The entire staff of Africans joined us, and we pushed the car until the engine caught. On our way over the hundred-mile circuit through the reserve to the main camp, we followed the tracks of a lion, but never caught sight of it.

Mary Beth demonstrated a talent for finding giraffes. The ungainly creatures stared wistfully as they munched the leafy treetops, their soft brown eyes framed by luxurious lashes, like ancient glamour queens. They moved away on stalky legs, their rocking gait taking them into invisibility in the forest.

We rounded a bend and braked for a herd of elephants in a water hole beside the road. The ranger had warned us not to annoy the animals, and to stay in the car at all times. The elephants towered over our little Volkswagen. They stretched their sinuous trunks, tore large branches off the trees, and slowly munched them. They waved their enormous delicate ears to catch the slightest sounds. I was scared. The young ones were as big as our car. Stewart got out of the car with his camera.

"Stewart," I hissed, "get back in the car."

"Aw, you're just a bunch of sissies," he said. But he got back in.

We ate our sandwiches at the midway camp, a small fenced-in area in the middle of the wilderness. Stewart said, "You know, those elephants reminded me of a story Keith told me about one of the Baptist missionaries up in the bush. He drove a VW like ours, and he met a herd of elephants. He stopped to take pictures, and just as he had his camera ready, they started walking toward him. He got nervous and got back in the car and blew the horn to frighten them away. They got upset, and a huge elephant charged the car, with him in it. He ducked under the dashboard, and that elephant split open the car like a can opener. The guy said the elephant tried to get his trunk around him. He curled up as tight as he could and the elephant finally gave up, but it didn't leave. He spent the whole night on the floor of the car. The next morning, someone came along and rescued him."

"Dad," Peter asked, "is that a true story?"

"Sure it is. Uncle Keith told me. You can ask him."

A few kilometers down the road, we had a flat tire. Stewart broke all speed records as he put on the spare. We kept a sharp lookout for elephants. A herd of impala grazed in a salt pan. A band of baboons played in and around a full-grown acacia tree while the baby baboons romped in a tiny bush. Ostriches trotted by in the distance, kicking up puffs of dust.

Later, we came to a pool where the elephants bathed in the heat of the afternoon. One old fellow stood almost submerged. He hooked his trunk around a reluctant brother, dragged him into the water, and sprayed the others. They snorted and splashed like kids. On an impulse, Stewart drove closer to the little ones and their chaperones. Just behind us the biggest elephant of all came out of the bush and crossed the road where we had been a minute ago. I held my breath, hoping he wouldn't challenge us for the right-of-way. Stewart eased the car into gear, and we crept away. I thought of Louise Morrell and her narrow escape in Kenya.

The main camp had lots of cabins and a small grocery store. The children, restless after a long day in the car, ran around the camp. They invented a complicated game with bottle tops and ran races with each other. I arranged our things in the cabin, relieved they were entertaining themselves. Sudden screams shattered my reverie. Martha came running, pursued by a great ugly bird as tall as she was. The bird had a huge heavy beak. The other children ran after the bird, trying to divert it. I opened the screen door, Martha dashed in, and I slammed the door in the face of the bird. The ranger caught up with the children and wrestled the bird into submission.

"Sorry. Didn't mean to scare you. It's a pet, you see, he just loves to chase little children. He's not dangerous. He just wanted to play. Sorry he frightened your little girl." He tucked the bird under his arm.

I held Martha in my arms. She stared wide-eyed at the scene. Peter and Tim gathered around the ranger.

"What in the world is that thing?" I asked.

The ranger laughed. "It's a hornbill. He's harmless, an orphan. We like to keep him around; he amuses the tourists. I'll put him back in his pen now." The boys followed the ranger. Mary Beth came into the house.

"That bird scared me, Mom." She and Martha stayed close to me the rest of the day.

We planned another early morning search for the elusive lions. At first light, we bundled into sweaters for the dash to the bathhouse. The stars faded, and the moon flickered through the trees. The car started, reluctantly, after a posse of young men pushed us around the parking lot. We piled in and drove through the gate. A herd of ungainly animals streamed across the road.

"Look at all those wild animals," Mary Beth said.

"Look again, Mary," Tim said. "Those aren't wild animals. They're cattle."

But Mary Beth was right. We had come across the legendary migration of the wildebeest. Wild-looking hairy creatures, they surged like a river across the road and thundered into the scrub. We stopped counting at a hundred.

By the time we reached the waterhole, the animals had left for the day. We packed up and drove out of the reserve, headed for Bulawayo.

We drove south for hours on the narrow road—parallel tarred ribbons of pavement on the sandy soil.

"Why can't they build some decent roads?" Stewart grumped. "I hate these strip roads." When we met a car, we were never sure if it would swerve to the right or left. If we got caught in the sand, we'd be stuck. The children invented a monotonous chant, "Bulawayo, Bulawayo."

Bulawayo, the city, was a disappointment. I had imagined a fabled romantic town, something like Samarkand, but with streets wide enough to turn a team of oxen. I was a hundred years too late. Cars were parked in a double line down the middle of the fabled street.

Stewart left me with duffels of dirty clothes at the self-serve laundry and took the children with him in search of an auto mechanic. He reserved a bungalow in the Matopos Hills, twenty-five miles south of town.

Neat, thatched cottages with lawns and gardens nestled among the boulders. I sat on a bench by the small lake and watched the children climb the rocks. Hundreds of bunny-like creatures hopped around, hyraxes, known here as rock rabbits. Martha called them "wock wabbits." She loved those shy furry creatures, sunning themselves outside their caves. They disappeared into the rocks when the children approached.

Toward evening the ranger came by. "I noticed your children chasing the hyraxes. Those rocks are full of deadly snakes. You shouldn't let your children play there." Couldn't he have mentioned it sooner? Martha continued to slip away and squat by their burrows in the rocks, heedless of my dire warnings.

These rocky hills had for centuries been the domain of the people now known as Bushmen. Small in stature, they had long ago mastered the art of living in the desert. Their enemies, black and white, had hunted them almost to extinction. My interest in the small people was piqued by reading *The Lost World of the Kalahari*, by Laurens van der Post.

The ranger offered an escort for us up into the hills to visit a cave in which the Bushmen had created wall paintings, thought to be thousands of years old. We followed the guide, a taciturn elderly African, up a rough path only he could discern. We would never have found the wide shallow cave by ourselves.

Red, brown, and black figures covered the walls. There were stories here if we could only read them. The most primitive paintings, which I assumed to be the most ancient, were partially defaced by abstract shapes in harsh colors. Had vandals done this? The guide explained that as the lives of the Bushmen became more precarious, they began to cover their early work with angular globs of paint, to obliterate the mystical figures depicting happier times. I can't tell you how this grieved me. I can't forget the mystery of those hidden paintings high in the hills, and the awful sadness at the loss of the clever, peaceful Bushmen, with their astonishing language of clicks, pops, and glottal stops, heard no more.

The next day we made an easier climb to the tomb of Cecil Rhodes on a barren summit with a panoramic view. Rhodes, who stopped at nothing in his conquest of southern Africa, named it "View of the World." It was, indeed, a spectacular view, but, for me, his arrogance and rapacity tarnished the magnificent landscape.

We couldn't be tourists forever. Time to head north. We drove to Lusaka, a beautiful little city, clean and modern, and stayed in a small motel. Bishop Booth was in town, and he gave us the "all clear" to return home to Jadotville. I wondered if it would still feel like home.

West Hartford 1957

Open house at the
parsonage, West Hartford
Christmas 1956

Bishop and Mrs. Booth

Leaving Brussels for Africa

"The dress"
Elizabethville, 1958

Dinnertime
Jadotville

Homeschooling

Jadotville church, Mary Beth

Martha, Ngoi, Mary Beth

Tim, Greg, Peter

Martha, Mary Beth, Peter, Tim
and friends with hulahoop

Stewart and Gaston

Swimming pool Jadotville
Tim, Mary Beth, Peter

Jadotville downtown

Stewart and pastors

Jadotville church

Thirty-foot metal barrel cross
at Mulungwishi

Mulungwishi church service

Halloween

Bishop Springer with Tim
and Peter

Stewart and teachers

Pastor Joab and Mama
Lena with teachers

Literacy campaign with
Doris Bartlett

Literacy campaign
with Stewart

Ecumenical Easter Service
1960 Elisabethville

Camp meeting at Samusamb

Hippo hunt at Lulua River, Samusamb

Rescued boy (2nd from right)
with his rescuers, Samusamb

Mission plane

Loading the station
wagon onto the boat

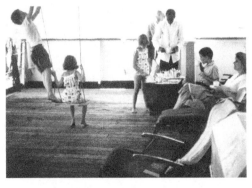

Martha on board on the
swing

Christmas Jadotville 1962

Railroad bridge near
Mulungwishi after attack

River crossing near
Mulungwishi

Crossing
at the Lufira River

1962 New Haven

At home in America
with a new friend

Back in America 1963

Chapter Twelve

The Republic of the Congo commanded the attention of the world that summer. Two protagonists emerged: Patrice Lumumba, Premier of the Congo, and Dag Hammarskjöld, Secretary-General of the United Nations. Each sought, in his own way, to preserve the integrity of the new nation. Hammarskjöld argued for the intervention of the United Nations, while Lumumba fought to hold his own fragile coalition together. Both men would forfeit their lives.

Lumumba was a natural leader and a compelling orator. Neither he nor his small staff had experience in implementing policy. His shaky coalition remained vulnerable as the balance of power shifted among the tribal groups. Although Lumumba was branded a communist, his first appeal was to the United States. He asked President Eisenhower to send a peacekeeping force to help him hold the new nation together. Ike declined and referred Lumumba to the United Nations, providing that body an unprecedented opportunity to rescue an emerging nation from chaos. In response to Lumumba's request for help, Hammarskjöld asked Dr. Ralph Bunche, Under-Secretary-General for Special Political Affairs, who was in Léopoldville, to do what he could to assist Lumumba. The powerful Africa contingent in the Security Council opposed the move, but the Council was able to fend off Cold War politics. They forced an agreement from the Western powers and the Soviet Bloc to send in UN troops to restore order. Five African countries volunteered soldiers to serve under the UN flag, and by July 18, there were four thousand of them in Léopoldville.

Hammarskjöld put his prestige on the line and threw his support to Lumumba. He found the besieged premier extremely difficult to work with. Lumumba insisted that the Belgian troops leave the Congo, including the Katanga, immediately, and that Tshombe's self-declared independent state be forced to re-join the Republic of the Congo. Tshombe ignored the UN and threw in his lot with the Belgians. Belgian soldiers, ordered out of the Congo, went directly to the Katanga. Tshombe welcomed them into his own army, ensuring the alliance of Belgium and the Katanga, a guarantee that the wealth of the Katanga would continue to flow to Belgium, rather than be diverted to Léopoldville.

Tshombe's intransigence caused dissension within the Africa bloc in the UN. Several African nations threatened to break ranks and send their own troops to remove the Belgians from the Katanga.

The Soviet bloc offered supplies and personnel to Lumumba, no strings attached. He accepted the offer. Dr. Ralph Bunche went in person to Elisabethville to inform Tshombe that the UN forces would enter Katanga. Tshombe defied him. Bunche returned to Léopoldville to report to the Secretary-General. Hammarskjöld argued that armed intervention was against the mandate of the UN. Then he modified his position and no longer opposed the use of force to replace the Belgians with UN troops.

The fragile coalition between Lumumba and Hammarskjöld was short-lived. Within the Security Council, the African nations and India united to block the Soviet Union. The Council warned Belgium to withdraw its troops from the Katanga immediately and to allow the UN troops into the Katanga to implement the Security Council resolutions. The UN troops were to remain neutral to internal conflict. When the UN forces entered the Katanga on August 12, the wily Tshombe denied he had ever opposed UN intervention. His only concern, he said, was for the UN not to be a tool for the central government. His archenemy, Lumumba, planned to accompany the UN troops into Katanga. Hammarskjöld adhered to the Security Council resolution and refused to include Lumumba or any representative of the Central Government in the UN operation.

Furious to be denied a triumphal entry into the Katanga, Lumumba accused Hammarskjöld of betrayal. Once again, the Security Council supported Hammarskjöld, though not without strong dissension, and approved his proposal for an advisory council of representatives of all countries that sent troops to the Congo. For the moment, this satisfied Lumumba. Albert Kalonji, Lumumba's former chief lieutenant, followed the example of Tshombe and declared the independence of his own tribal area, the diamond-rich Kasai province, on the northern border of the Katanga.

Lumumba ordered a contingent of the Belgian Force Publique, under the command of Colonel Joseph Mobutu, to put down the rebellion in the Kasai and the Katanga. This strategy reawakened ancient tribal antagonisms. Mobutu's soldiers brought devastation throughout the Kasai and killed at least a thousand civilians. Hammarskjöld denounced the action as genocide and blamed Lumumba. Mobutu would become the despot who ruled Zaire for thirty years.

We came home to Jadotville on August 30, 1960, the second anniversary of our first arrival, by permission of the American consul on a day-to-day basis. The Jacaranda trees that lined the streets were in bloom, as they were in 1958 when I first delighted in those clouds of blue blossoms. How naive I was then, full of hope. I thought I was prepared to be a missionary.

The shops were closed; plywood covered broken windows. Metal awnings over the sidewalks were torn and twisted. Burnt-out wrecks of cars littered the streets. White Jeeps, filled with dark-skinned United Nations soldiers in light blue helmets, sped recklessly by. *Les Casques Bleu.* The soldiers glared at me and fingered their rifles.

"At least they cleaned up the broken glass," Stewart said. "It's a good thing you didn't see the place during the fighting. I sure hope our house is okay." Stewart had contracted with Baba Samuel to come every day until we returned, but anything might have happened. We turned onto the mission property, drove down the long driveway with the hedge of thornbush. Baba Samuel stood at the door, smiling.

"*Hiyambo, mama. Habari gani?*"

I could have hugged him; I was so happy to see him. We shook hands in the European manner. Baba Samuel walked through the house with me, proud to show me everything in place and very clean. The children scooted to their rooms while Stewart and Baba Samuel unpacked the car. Baba raised his eyebrows as he carried in bag after bag of dirty laundry and muttered to himself as he filled the washing machine and sorted the clothes. I reclaimed the kitchen, my domain, and put away the groceries we had brought from Northern Rhodesia. I found cans of food in the cupboard, twelve cans of pumpkin bought months ago from a departing missionary.

"Mama, someone at the back door," Baba Samuel said. An image flashed through my mind, the ragged stranger who had come to the back door with his receipt of ownership of the house. And me. Had he come to collect?

The man who sold strawberries greeted me. I bought all he had, ten boxes, twenty cents a box. It seemed a good omen, an incredible luxury, to have an unexpected abundance of strawberries.

"What are you going to do with all those strawberries?" Peter asked.

"How does strawberry shortcake sound?"

"Oh, boy! Hey, Tim, Mom's making strawberry shortcake!"

"With whipped cream?" Tim called.

"Sorry, no whipped cream," I said. "We could whip some powdered milk."

"Ugh, no thanks. That stuff tastes terrible."

It seemed as though we had never been away, never been forced to flee to safety in another country.

Baba Samuel washed and ironed our traveling clothes. I packed suitcases, one for each of us, and stashed them in the hall closet where I wouldn't have to see them. I gathered my treasures, baby pictures, photographs, the children's drawings, souvenirs, a few favorite books, into a sturdy footlocker, ready to ship to the States.

Stewart checked the post office and found a few letters. All airmail came via Léopoldville, and the postal workers there threw away mail for the Katanga. How would I know what was happening without *Time* magazine?

Stewart went to the *athénée* to enroll Tim, Peter, and Mary Beth. I checked out the grocery shops. The blue-helmeted Moroccans met my tentative smiles with hostile stares and startled me with their snarled unintelligible utterances. Weren't the United Nations supposed to be the good guys?

The shops opened for two hours in the morning and the afternoon. I didn't find much on the shelves. The baker said to come back tomorrow; he might have bread. My purchases didn't fill one basket: a couple of cans of evaporated milk, a few eggs, a handful of potatoes, tins of pilchards in tomato sauce.

"People seemed awfully glad to see me," I told Stewart. "Shopkeepers came out to stare at me. What's going on?"

"I was afraid of that. I didn't want to tell you, but you're the first white woman to come back to town. Everyone says it's a good sign and that others will come back now."

"What about the *athénée*? Will they have classes?"

"Oh, yes, no question. They'll have some kind of classes. It's called the International School now. Very few of the Belgian teachers have come back. They told me there are a hundred European children in town, but I don't believe it. Of course, this gives African kids a chance at the government schools, but I'm concerned about the teachers." This was not good news. Our children needed to keep up with their peers when we went home to America. "The best thing is for you all to go to the States," Stewart said, as though he read my mind. "That way the kids won't get behind in school and you can all be safe."

"You can't send us home," I said. "You can take us home, but you can't send us. We're a family and we're going to stick together. If it's not safe for us, it's not safe for you. Why don't we all just get out of here?"

He sighed. "You just don't get it. I can't leave my work. The teachers depend on me to get the schools up and running again, and the pastors need a lot of supervision and encouragement. And I don't have permission to go."

It would depend on the International School, formerly the *athénée*. Just in case, we ordered books for the Calvert Homeschool study course.

How different our lives would have been if I had used common sense and returned to the States with the children. The Board would have paid transport and given us some financial support for six months, but then what? And where would we have gone? How would we have lived? Despite my fears, I still felt a strong sense of duty, a commitment. To what, I wonder now? Was I just stubborn and didn't want to leave Stewart?

A week later the coalition in Léopoldville fell apart. President Kasavubu, coached by the Western powers who feared the intervention of the Soviets, dismissed Lumumba, the premier. Lumumba dismissed President Kasavubu. Civil war seemed inevitable. In the Congolese parliament, Lumumba's eloquence won the day, and he re-instated Kasavubu. Lumumba continued to ridicule him and undercut his authority. Kasavubu vowed revenge.

Waiting in the wings was twenty-eight-year-old Colonel Joseph Mobutu, now in command of the Force Publique in Léopoldville. He had been in charge of the army that laid waste to the rebellious Kasai Province. On Kasavubu's orders, he shut down the parliament, put the university students in charge, and ordered the Soviets out. He closed the airports and the radio stations and arrested Lumumba and his lieutenants. The men escaped and returned to Lumumba's residence. The UN put a cordon of security around the house. Kasavubu had access to the powerful radio station in Congo Brazzaville, just across the river. He silenced Lumumba's eloquent voice. In spite of the ban on air traffic, planes continued to bring weapons into Elisabethville for Tshombe, who crowed there was no dissension in the Katanga, *his* republic.

No wonder we embraced Tshombe and independence for the Katanga, the only section of the country not in complete chaos. Thanks to the mining interests of the powerful Belgians, the infrastructure of the Katanga was intact, the roads open, phone service uninterrupted. The mines and processing plants operated at full capacity.

On the opening day of school, I thought of the excitement of my own first days of school when I was a child. A new dress, new shoes and socks, a new tablet and pencil, the commemorative snapshot. A bit of ceremony. Not here, not now. Only Mary Beth, eager to learn to read, was excited. Peter and Tim fussed and dawdled, tried to extend the vacation as long as possible. I refused to use my pitiful French and risk the scorn of the African teachers. I left it to Stewart to deliver them to school. Martha went along, although there would be no kindergarten for her. For the first time in months, I had an hour to myself. I'd just settled down with a cup of Nescafé and a book when Stewart and Martha returned.

"That was quick," I said.

"Well, it's not good news. There are only two teachers so far. Rumor is the French teacher wasn't allowed to get on the plane to come back because he is a Protestant. None of the kids' friends from last year have shown up. All those European children they talked about are mulattos and none of them have any French. The boys just got in line with the African kids and marched into class, Mary Beth wouldn't let go of me."

"What happened?"

"She just sobbed and sobbed. You know how she does. She said how could she go to school, she was only five years old, and she didn't even know one plus one. She wanted to go back to kindergarten. Of course, there isn't any kindergarten."

"How did you get her to stay?"

"I just told her she had to go to school if she wanted to learn to read and she finally went into the class and I left in a hurry before she changed her mind."

My heart ached for Mary Beth. I would never forget her first day of school in Brussels when she thought I had given her away.

A few days later, Tim's teacher demoted him to third grade. He said my son couldn't do arithmetic. Maybe the teacher had trouble with arithmetic, but Tim was a whiz at it. We took him out of school. He moped around the house, chagrined at his failure. Good thing I had a rush order on that home study course.

Martha sat on the floor in a patch of sunshine. She paged through *Life* magazine's *Picture History of Western Man*. Tim wandered in. "There's nothing to do," he complained.

"Why don't you play with Martha?" I suggested.

"Come look at this, Dim," Martha said. "They got no clothes."

"Any clothes, Martha," he said. "They don't have any clothes. That's Adam and Eve."

I looked over his shoulder at a reproduction of Michelangelo's painting of the Fall. Before and After. Tim sat beside Martha and interpreted.

"God told them not to eat the apple, but the serpent told Eve it was okay. God wouldn't mind. And she gave it to Adam, and he ate it, and God got really mad and told them they'd have to leave the garden."

Martha stared at the painting. She turned to the previous page—she read books backward—to the head of Flora from Botticelli's *Primavera*. "Dat man is wearing flowers because he's going to a party," she said.

"Oh, Martha, you don't know anything," Tim said. "That's not a man; it's a woman. It's a painting about Spring."

Martha turned back a few more pages to Giotto. I thought she was looking at the *Adoration of the Magi*, her attention caught by the golden haloes of the Holy Family and the angels and the Wise Men as the mother shyly held out her swaddled baby for the adoration of the kneeling king.

"What happened to all dose dead babies?"

"Dead babies? Where do you see dead babies?" Tim challenged.

She pointed to the smaller picture across the page, Giotto's *Massacre of the Innocents*. Sure enough, a pile of dead babies. "Mom, why does dat man want to kill dat baby?" she asked.

I bit my lip as I looked over Tim's shoulder at the picture, at the mother who struggled to prevent the murder of her child, the one baby left alive in the picture. How could I possibly explain about Herod the King? It would have been a simple story back home in West Hartford, safe in suburban America, isolated from such atrocities by time and distance. I had chosen to bring her to a place where Western colonists had for more than a hundred years inflicted mutilation and slavery and death on the Africans, and now the Africans were slaughtering each other. Martha, at four, might have been more aware than I realized of the events of the past few months, her attention caught by cruel violence.

Tim looked up at me. "It's just a story, isn't it, Mom?"

I took the resolution he offered. "Yes, it's a story in the Bible. King Herod was afraid when he heard Jesus was born to be King of the Jews, and he did some terrible things." Eager to change the subject, I looked at my watch. "Mary Beth and Peter will be coming home for lunch before we know it," I said with phony brightness. "Tim, will you set the table? Martha, pick up your toys."

I put the book away on a high shelf, but the picture was imprinted on my mind. A pile of dead babies.

After we put the children to bed, I told Stewart what had happened.

"Obviously, Tim needs to be in school," Stewart said. "I think we should send him home to the States."

"How can you even think such a thing? He's only eight years old. Where would he go? You know our parents can't take him in. Aren't you concerned about Martha and the dead babies? I think we all need to go home."

Stewart sighed. "Not that again."

"Besides, we ordered all those expensive books for home study."

"You're a good teacher, no question about that."

I felt my cheeks flush. I warmed to his unexpected praise. "I'd love to teach Tim. He's so bright and quick."

"He needs to be with other kids in a classroom situation."

"I know, but what else can we do?"

We dragged ourselves through this argument every evening. We went round and round. Theme and variations. We couldn't seem to resolve it. We made ourselves miserable, picked at the components, moved the pieces around on the board, and got nowhere.

A solution to our quandary presented itself. Leonard and Joyce phoned with an invitation for Tim to live with them in Elisabethville for the school year. "I'm already teaching David fourth grade, and I can add Tim to the class," Joyce said.

"It's a very generous offer, Joyce," Stewart said. "I appreciate what you and Leonard are willing to do. Can you give us a little time to think it over?"

"Of course. Take your time and let me know."

"It *is* very generous of them," I said, "and it would certainly solve the problem. Let's think about it. Leonard seems a bit stern. Joyce would be a good teacher for Tim. But it breaks my heart to think of sending him away."

"People drive back and forth to E'ville all the time. He could probably get a ride home on weekends. And it's certainly better than shipping him to the States."

And so we agreed Tim would be sent away. I don't remember if we asked Tim how he felt about it. With a heavy heart, I re-packed his suitcase and we delivered him to E'ville.

The mission schools got off to a rocky start. Jules Samuel, our former Swahili teacher, had just completed his two years of training as a school administrator. Stewart taught him to drive and assigned him a mission car. Jules was well qualified to be a supervisor. He was fluent in French and several tribal languages, and he could get along in English. He had a mixed racial background. His European father had never acknowledged him, and no tribal group would claim him.

He hired teachers and opened all the schools. Three teachers from the Baluba tribe, the dominant local tribe, claimed *they* had been appointed school directors. No place for Jules.

Stewart refused to concede to their demand. He asked for a meeting with the minister of education of the province. He came home from that meeting in a terrible temper. He threw his briefcase on the dining room table. "The minister of education says Jules is unacceptable because he's from a foreign tribe. The minister of security has a file on him. Can you believe this? So much for independence. I'm going to ask the pastors to intervene for Jules. After all, the church still has jurisdiction over the mission schools."

The pastors proposed a compromise, the appointment of another teacher to the post, bypassing Jules and the three locals. The minister of education refused to confirm their choice and the schools remained without a director. The powerful cabal of evangelical missionaries called Stewart on the carpet. I heard him shouting on the phone. I went into the study as he slammed down the receiver.

"They told me to be in Elisabethville at nine o'clock Monday morning," he said.

"I'm going with you."

"What about school?"

"Not a big deal. The kids aren't learning anything anyway."

I left Stewart at the mission headquarters in E'ville to face the wrath of his colleagues. The children and I spent the morning at the swimming pool. I asked Joyce if Tim could join us, but she preferred we not interrupt his schedule. "He's working hard to catch up."

We picked Stewart up at noon. "Those guys told me not to rock the boat," he fumed. "They said we live and work in this country, so we must go along with the government. They all said they agreed with me *en principe*. It just makes my blood boil. I told them if Jules goes, I go. Last year, this same crowd met with me at that conference to plan for the schools, and they all agreed that when the day came when we could not appoint our own directors and control and discipline our teachers, we would close the schools. Well, at least we won't have those three hotheaded locals in charge. That would split the church wide open. They'll appoint someone else."

"What about Jules?" I asked. He was my favorite of all the teachers. He never made fun of me when I struggled to learn Swahili or smirked when I spoke French.

"It's all arranged. Jules and Rose and the children will go to Kitwe so he can work on his English and then go to the States to study. I was supposed to work with him last year, but he couldn't find the time. He told me somebody turned him in to the director of security as a Lumumba supporter."

So now we lived in a police state. The Africans had, of course, lived in a police state since Leopold II took over the Congo. "How can we stand up for our principles when they cave in like this?" I asked.

Stewart shrugged. "Guess we'll find out. Well, what did you and the kids do all morning?"

"We had a great time. That Union Minière pool is the nicest one around. United Nations soldiers came, Swedes, so young, great looking, wholesome, far from home. They didn't waste a glance on me, of course. There were beautiful young Belgian gals there in bikinis—secretaries,

I suppose. The soldiers are under orders not to fraternize, so they just looked. Most of them probably don't speak French, anyway."

"They do look awfully young," he agreed. "The guys told me one of them couldn't get his gun together yesterday at the airport during the drill, and everyone laughed, including the officer in charge."

I could believe it. When they paraded by in uniform, they looked like the cast for the school operetta. "I wish we had them in Jadotville instead of Moroccans. Those guys are so tough I don't dare look at any of them. I'm sure none of them have trouble with their guns. If they did, they'd probably be shot."

The home-study course arrived. Eighty dollars for postage for that rush order was worth every penny. I had already arranged to teach Peter at home as soon as the materials came. He wasn't learning anything at the International School. Mary Beth had settled in and made friends, as she usually did. She called them "my girls." She continued there each morning in French while I taught third grade to Peter. In the afternoon I taught Mary Beth first grade in English.

The transition from French to English complicated Peter's lessons, especially in spelling. I drilled him relentlessly. I asked him to spell sheep.

"C - H - I - P," he said, and waited expectantly for the next word.

"That's the way it sounds in French—you got that right—but not in English."

I was content to stay at home, glad to have a task to fill my days.

UN planes flew over the town almost every day at a low altitude, dropping leaflets, terrorizing all of us. They looked as though they were no more than a hundred feet above. In spite of this intimidation, the tension among the tribes increased until it overflowed in skirmishes and neighborhood battles. The casualties were hushed up, but the pastors knew and told Stewart about the wounded. He came home from the hospital pale and shaken and wouldn't talk about it.

He tried to put the terrible sights out of his mind and put his energy into the new church under construction in Kambove. He always enjoyed building projects. He put in long days working alongside the African construction crew, stacking the mud bricks and putting in windows and doorframes. "It's satisfying work," he said. "I'm actually accomplishing something for a change."

After the completion and dedication of the Kambove church, Stewart was at loose ends again. He tried to ignore the disintegration of the mission schools, which were now out of his hands. At the time of Independence, Pastor Joab had replaced Stewart as District Superintendent of churches. Stewart described himself as Joab's chauffeur. Joab was a wise and capable leader, but his style was permissive. Stewart had to watch his own hard-gained order and discipline fall apart. The older pastors saved his sanity when they asked him to conduct weekly classes for them one day a week in theology, church history, and church administration. This was exactly what Stewart had wanted to do since we came here. These older pastors hadn't had much formal training, and now they asked Stewart to teach them.

"I think I'll do two series of classes: one on the life of John Wesley and the other on effective evangelism. How does that sound? Oh, and by the way, remember those teachers, the ones who wanted to get rid of Jules? They want me to set up a school for their wives to learn to cook European style."

He must have seen the look on my face. He quickly added he didn't expect me to teach them. "I'm thinking of hiring some of the men who used to cook for the Belgians. A lot of them are looking for work. We could set up a model kitchen in the social center."

I hadn't seen this much enthusiasm for months. He was happiest when he was busiest, as he was again with grateful pastors gathered around the dining room table, learning about John Wesley, the founder of Methodism.

Chapter Thirteen

On Sunday, November 27, 1960, Joseph Kasavubu was officially recognized by the United Nations as the legal representative of the Republic of the Congo. Resplendent in a gold-and-white uniform, he celebrated his triumphal entry into Léopoldville.

On that same day, Patrice Lumumba escaped from house arrest during a torrential rainstorm. He concealed himself under a blanket in the back seat of the Chevrolet that transported his household staff. He slipped through a cordon of ANC soldiers and set off for Stanleyville, his base of support. Had he been successful, the country would have plunged into a bloody civil war.

Hammarskjöld ordered the UN troops to withdraw their protection of Lumumba, and Mobutu's soldiers caught up with him at the Lufira River. Lumumba had crossed on the makeshift ferry and looked back across the water to see his wife and child, who were waiting to cross, captured by the soldiers. He came back and delivered himself into the hands of his enemies.

His driver attempted, in vain, to persuade the detachment of Ghanaian UN soldiers to rescue Lumumba. They had their orders not to intervene. The Congolese soldiers beat Lumumba and his two aides with their rifle butts and carried them to the Thysville prison. For them, it was the beginning of the end.

Unaware of the grave events, we celebrated Thanksgiving.

Seen in retrospect, the failure of Lumumba and Hammarskjöld to bring an independent Congo into being seemed inevitable. Both men were idealists. Lumumba wanted freedom for the Congolese people and Hammarskjöld wanted peace for the world. Lumumba had no experienced advisors. Hammarskjöld had too many. Subject to the Security Council, he couldn't act on his own. Both men were surrounded by powerful enemies eager to seize power. The Congo would kill them both.

Months later, I learned that Lumumba died on January 17, 1961. That day had been, for me, a day like any other. I stirred the oatmeal while the children got dressed. I had once again set a place for Tim at the breakfast table. I forgot he was in Elisabethville with the Sinclairs. I just couldn't seem to reconcile myself to his absence. We gathered around the table.

"Mom," Martha said, "I can't find my other shoe."

"Mom," Mary Beth said, "I want to wear my pink dress and ruffly petticoat."

"Daddy," Peter said, "there's a man at the door."

"Pipe down, everybody," Stewart said. "I want to hear the news."

The BBC newscaster spoke with impeccable British diction. He made no mention of Patrice Lumumba. The world had yet to learn that on this day he and his two aides were no longer in the prison in Thysville, near Léopoldville. They were prisoners on a plane, on the way to Elisabethville. Deliver us from E'ville. Before the day ended, they would be delivered, more dead than alive, into the hands of Moïse Tshombe, president of the Katanga, and his chief of security, Godefroid Munongo.

In our morning prayers, we failed to mention either Patrice Lumumba or Moïse Tshombe.

"Mom," Mary Beth said, "Peter didn't close his eyes during prayers. He made faces at me."

Peter sneered. "How did you know unless you peeked, too?"

"Stop it, you two," I said. "Mary Beth, let's do your hair."

"I can't find my hair ribbons."

"Where is your homework?"

"I forgot to do it." In the scramble for supper and baths after last night's late-leaving guests, she had forgotten.

"Hop in the car, girls, you'll be late for school."

A half-dozen African pastors occupied the dining room chairs, deep in Bible study with Stewart. They looked up and smiled as Peter and I trooped through on our way to the schoolroom. Martha followed, wheeling her kittens in the doll carriage.

"*Hiyambo, mama. Hiyambo, Watoto. Habari gani?*" they said.

"*Hiyambo yenu. Habari njema, asante,*" I responded.

Our makeshift classroom had originally been a storage shed, then a primitive guest room. We'd cleaned it out, whitewashed the walls, hung up posters and a bulletin board. I'd sewed curtains and a local carpenter made kid-sized desks. As we did every morning, Peter and I saluted the flag and sang "My country, 'tis of thee/Sweet land of liberty." He started on his spelling words.

Unexpected visitors drove in mid-morning. Two American women, experts in the organization of social centers, accompanied eight young Africans in training. They had come to see our own social center, the former bar across the street from the big church. Not even time for coffee. Stewart took the delegation on a quick tour and rushed them on to their luncheon appointment at Mulungwishi.

I scrubbed potatoes and put them in the oven with meatloaf. Martha dressed squirming kittens in doll clothes. Peter finished his arithmetic assignment. We turned to *Silver Pennies*, a lovely little book of poems that took me back to my childhood. My parents had given me the same collection of verses, and I had learned many of them by heart. Peter and I recited them together. He memorized them as easily as I had. Then it was time to pick up Mary Beth at school.

At the headquarters of the United Nations troops, surly soldiers in blue uniforms loaded trucks for another trip up-country. More trouble. I pushed those thoughts aside. Sufficient unto the day. We stopped at the post office for the weekly mail. Letters from family in the States today, and *Time* magazine.

The pastors gathered up their books and lingered at the front door to talk to Stewart.

It was Peter's turn to set the table.

"Martha, take off those muddy shoes and put on your slippers. Mary Beth, we'll do your lessons after lunch." I scraped a handful of carrots and called the family to the table.

"I hate meatloaf," Peter said. "How come we never have steak?"

"No complaints," I told him. "We're lucky to have anything at all."

"Quiet," Stewart said. "Time for the news." He turned on the radio. The BBC announcer said, "The situation in the Congo remains tense."

"Wasn't that the same thing the guy said yesterday?" I asked.

The real news of that day, the fate of Patrice Lumumba, went unreported. He and two of his aides were on the plane, bound with heavy ropes. Hour after hour, the Force Publique soldiers beat them with rifle butts and kicked them with their heavy boots. They smashed Lumumba's glasses.

Baba Samuel washed the dishes and cleaned up the kitchen. It was time for Mary Beth's lessons from the home study course. French in the morning at the *athénée*, English in the afternoon with Mom. Peter helped her with her lessons. He was good that way. "Mom, I showed her how to do the arithmetic, just like you showed me. And there are a couple of places where her reading needs a little attention." Children can break your heart when they show unexpected kindness to their siblings. I gave him a hug.

"Time for a swim," I said.

Armed guards waved us through the gate at the Union Minière club and pool, our favorite oasis, a well-kept place. Brilliant branches of bright red bougainvillea covered the chain-link fence. We had the place to ourselves. The Belgian families were still in Europe. I wondered if they would ever come back.

I had offered to teach the African children to swim. The church leaders considered my conservative one-piece bathing suit immodest, even obscene. Good Christian women didn't expose their bare legs to public view.

"Watch this, Mom," Peter said. He cannon-balled into the deep end of the pool.

"Mom, he got me all wet," Mary Beth complained. "Make him stop."

Later in the afternoon, the plane carrying Lumumba and his

companions landed in a remote corner of the airport in Elisabethville. In spite of the tight security, Katanga soldiers and United Nations soldiers, and some Africans and Europeans, saw the Force Publique soldiers heave three prisoners, tied together with heavy ropes, onto the tarmac. They recognized Lumumba and the others, bloody from six hours of beating and torture on the plane, barely able to walk. Lumumba was blind without his glasses, and tufts of his hair had been torn from his scalp. The three were shoved into a car and driven away, supposedly on their way to prison. Word of the sighting was dismissed as rumor. Tshombe kept out of sight, but he couldn't resist a triumphant visit to gloat over the captives. He had much to gain from the death of Lumumba.

Stewart came home late. He slammed his books down on the desk as he came through the office. "These new missionaries!" he stormed. "One of them made a speech at the staff meeting. I wish you could have heard him. He's an idiot. He claimed to be a new type of missionary, here to be their friend, not like us old-fashioned authoritarians, who exploited them and kept them down. I wanted to choke him. And I had to translate for him. His Swahili isn't even good enough to explain he is their true friend. I was tempted to forget the translation and make up something. But Joab was there, and I couldn't risk it."

His fury alarmed me. This wasn't like him. I was afraid he might have a stroke. I reached out to him, put my hand on his arm.

"You don't think the Africans fell for all that stuff, do you?" I kept my voice as level as I could. His eyes focused. He looked at me. "We didn't sound like that when we first came, did we?" I asked.

"We certainly did not," Stewart said, cooling down after his tirade. He took a deep breath, and then another, almost a sigh. "We kept our mouths shut until we learned the ropes." He looked around the room at the desks and the books and filing cabinets, orienting himself.

"Well, cheer up," I said. "It's your night for a sauna." Stewart's friend Werner, the proprietor of the local sawmill and woodworking shop, fired up his sauna every week and Stewart had a standing invitation to join him. Tonight, Peter had been included in the invitation, and, after the sauna, Werner would come home with them for a late dinner. He liked my cooking. He found American food interesting. He urged me not to go to any trouble, just fix something simple. What could be simpler than tuna fish and noodles? Stewart grimaced. He recalled our first few months of marriage when we lived in a crummy basement apartment in Emporia.

Mary Beth and Martha had a treat, too, a bubble bath. The electric water heater on the wall in the bathroom had taken a direct hit from a bolt of lightning and the replacement part had not yet arrived. Late in the afternoon, Baba Samuel built a fire in the back yard under a truncated steel barrel, carried buckets of warm water into the house, and filled the bathtub. The girls enjoyed a long soak with bubbles. Peter had gone to the sauna and wasn't there to torment them by dropping spiders through the window into their bathwater.

Rosy pink from the tub, dressed in clean cotton pajamas, they perched on high stools in the kitchen, chatting contentedly as they ate scrambled eggs and toast, while I prepared the infamous tuna casserole and mixed biscuit dough. Werner loved hot biscuits. I set the table and arranged a bowl of frangipani blossoms for a centerpiece.

Stewart, Werner, and Peter arrived, glowing from the sauna, and smelling of eucalyptus oil. Werner brought a box of chocolates from Germany. It had been months since I had seen chocolates. He praised the tuna casserole and helped himself to biscuits, which he called "those little hot breads." I basked in his admiration. We talked about books we had read, movies we had read about. Politics, not so much. Nobody mentioned Patrice Lumumba. His suffering was almost over. Nearly dead from the vicious beating, he and his two companions were driven to a remote location in the swamps east of Jadotville. Someone shot them. Their bodies were hastily buried, then dug up, hacked to pieces, and burned.

Twenty miles away, we slept, unaware.

For several weeks, Lumumba was rumored to be in prison some-where in the Katanga. On February 10th, the prisoners were said to have escaped. On February 13th, they were reported killed by villagers, who, it was alleged, tore the bodies to pieces. The Belgians protested they had no control over the savage Africans, who were enraged by the atrocities Lumumba's troops had enacted in the invasion of the Kasai.

We accepted this explanation of the death of Lumumba. I wasn't sorry to learn of his demise. It seemed inevitable. I was inured to death and destruction. He'd represented a threat to the security of the Katanga, and we considered ourselves Katangaise through and through, grateful to Tshombe for law and order. I was not sufficiently sensitive, then, to the editorial bias of *Time* magazine. I concurred with those writers who seized every opportunity to heap scorn on Lumumba and praise on Tshombe.

Over the years, we heard rumors the CIA had been involved in his death, and Tshombe had a hand in it. The records were sealed. The Congo had troubles enough without digging into history. The truth of the tragedy finally emerged, as truth will, when the archives were opened at the Royal Museum for Central Africa in Brussels, fifty years after *les événements*. Lumumba had been betrayed by everyone: the Belgians, the United Nations, the United States, the CIA, and by his African enemies: Joseph Kasavubu, Joseph Mobutu, and Moïse Tshombe. Mobutu had begun his climb to power, rewarded for his participation in the downfall and death of Lumumba by an appointment as head of the Force Publique. He parlayed this into his reign as absolute ruler of Zaire, as much a despot as Leopold II.

Unaware of the true story of Lumumba's death, we followed our customary routines. The Secretary for Women's Work in Africa came through on a tour of inspection while Stewart was in Kolwezi for a week of meetings. While safe in her office in New York, convinced we exaggerated the peril of our situation, she had chided us missionaries for our complaints and unease, our lack of faith.

She arrived at our house for lunch, pale and shaken. On the road from Elisabethville, a gang of armed youths had flagged down her car and stuck a gun in her face. The driver had protested she was with the mission. There were no weapons in the car. She was not harmed but was understandably nervous. I proposed a cup of tea and put the kettle on.

We sat on the sofa in front of the window. A plane, a DC-3, buzzed the house, flying at about a hundred feet, right over the mission, right over the house. I knew the plane was dropping leaflets; it flew over every day about this time. But she didn't know that. She looked at me in alarm as the noise increased to a deafening roar. I gave her a tight little smile and sipped my tea. The plane thundered away. I hoped it would make another run.

She took a deep breath, put down her teacup. She patted me on the knee. "You're a brave girl," she said, "to stay here all alone."

Chapter Fourteen

Newspaper clippings from the first few months of 1961 reveal the extent to which the unconfirmed death of Lumumba and the subsequent turmoil in the Katanga held the attention of the American press. Lumumba was said to have fled into the bush. Sightings were reported for weeks, amid speculation the Katanga would not be able to maintain its integrity, independent of the rest of the Congo. To the extent Jadotville enjoyed any stability at all, let alone order, we depended on the United Nation soldiers in residence. Troops from various nations cycled through from Sweden, Ghana, Morocco, Ireland. The European troops behaved with order and discipline, while African soldiers tended to be hostile and surly. I came out of the grocery store with a basket of vegetables, and Moroccan soldiers wearing the ubiquitous Blue Helmets of the United Nations, cursed me and the children, and shoved us off the sidewalk into the street.

Stewart went to the post office. When he attempted to turn the car around in the parking area, the soldiers shouted at him and ordered him off the property. Other soldiers fired at a car in which several *wazungu* ladies were passengers. No one was hit. The Moroccans finally left, and Irish troops moved in, dressed in kilts and playing bagpipes.

Several hundred miles northeast of us, in the Stanleyville area, a group of missionaries was flying home to Lodja from Usumbura, in Ruanda-Urundi (now Burundi), where they had taken refuge after

Independence. They were unaware that among their fellow passengers were African rebel soldiers disguised as civilians. As the passengers deplaned, the rebels were discovered to be smugglers of arms and uniforms. Local authorities attempted to defend the missionaries, but the talking drums had already spread the word that the church supported the rebels. The missionaries were harassed, threatened, and roughed up. The eldest man was taken hostage. Two doctors, part of the mission group, stepped forward. If anyone was detained, they volunteered, they must also be taken. The soldiers, unwilling to jeopardize the medical work, released everyone.

After this narrow escape, Bishop Booth conferred by cable with his people. All missionaries, for their own safety and that of their followers, were to leave the Stanleyville area until the situation stabilized. Most of them found temporary work on mission stations in other parts of Africa. Others defied the bishop and remained at their posts. The area continued to be a hotbed of conflict. Everyone was suspect.

I stayed close to home with the children. Every weekday morning, after Mary Beth went off to school, Peter and Martha and I trooped out to our own makeshift schoolroom. A lesson a day, sometimes two. We'd have to hustle to finish by the end of May. We might be granted an early furlough.

In the afternoon, while I worked with Mary Beth, Peter played soccer with the African boys. He tried in vain to teach them softball. He needed more comradeship and competition, I thought. He talked constantly about going to the States.

He missed Tim. For a while, he refused to sleep in the room he and Tim had shared. Mary Beth traded places with him. She always preferred to have a room to herself. Tim's absence unbalanced our family. It didn't occur to me the other children might wonder if they, too, would be sent away. Stewart and I found comfort in assuring one another Tim's education must not be interrupted, and the Sinclair's invitation was an answer to unspoken prayers.

I found refuge in books. In stories. Some literate and considerate souls had left books behind in our house, and I had long since read and re-read them all. *For Whom the Bell Tolls, Gone with the Wind, Moby Dick,* and *My Antonia.* We had a few books about Africa, *The Flame Trees of Thika* and *Out of Africa, Cry the Beloved Country, The Nun's Story.* Tim and Peter shared a copy of *Tintin in the Congo,* in French. *Peyton Place,* a sex-drenched shocker of the time, surreptitiously made the rounds among the missionaries.

I browsed the shelves in Stewart's study. On his recommendation, I plowed through the works of the Niebuhr brothers, Richard and Reinhold. Bishop Springer gave us a copy of his late wife's account of their early days, *I Love the Trail, a Sketch of the Life of Helen Emily Springer.*

Once in a while, new books arrived in the mail, gifts from family and friends. I was thrilled to receive a copy of a recently published novel, *To Kill a Mockingbird* by Harper Lee. I devoured book reviews in *Time* magazine and longed for access to a public library.

Starved for classical music, I grew bored with our pitiful collection of well-worn phonograph records, *Swan Lake, Organ Works of J. S. Bach, Christmas in Europe.* One morning, I spotted a broadside on the wall at the post office. Philippa Schuyler, an African American pianist and journalist, would perform in Jadotville. I wondered if there was a decent piano left in town. Many of the Belgians had absconded in haste, leaving their furniture behind, and the tropical climate was deadly for pianos.

About fifty people, mostly Europeans, few Africans, sat on folding chairs around the Union Minière pool. An upright piano graced the concrete deck. Miss Schuyler, young, black, beautiful, and self-assured, wore a lovely gown. A black lace shawl slipped from her shoulders during the most dramatic passages. The piano was hopelessly out of tune, with at least one dead key. A mosquito buzzed her relentlessly. Undaunted, she played works by Ravel and Chopin, and some modern composers unfamiliar to me. The audience was attentive and respectful. Transported by the beauty of her music, I forgot the daily tribulations of my life. How brave of her to bring such beauty into our remote and troubled city. She stood by the piano, graciously acknowledging the applause. I smiled at her, and she raised her eyebrows as though inviting a conversation. I could have talked with her, thanked her for her music, learned more about her odyssey in Africa, but I was constrained by the shyness which paralyzes me when I am in the presence of such talent. I'm afraid I'll say something foolish. How foolish is that? And so, I missed the opportunity to tell her what her music meant to me.

Stewart planned a visit one Sunday to four villages in a remote area of his district. The children and I agreed to go with him. The road, reinforced in swampy areas with sticks and small logs, was little better than a bicycle path. Tall grass on both sides dwarfed our Volkswagen. Ominous clouds added to my unease at the chance we might be marooned if the rains descended. The few people we met on the road could not have been more astonished if a spaceship had landed in their midst. I trusted they were unaware of the uproar in the countryside over the death of Lumumba and that the armed men we met on the road were after game no bigger than a partridge.

The chapel in the first village was dark and dank. The next was a sort of A-frame: a roof of grass extending to the ground on both sides, with an unobstructed view at both ends and low rough board benches. The ultimate destination, a primitive village of the old days seventy miles from home, seemed untouched by current political events. These people had not seen a missionary since Bishop and Mrs. Springer made their last trip through there forty years ago. They had not been neglected. The vanguard of the literacy project had reached them, and they pleaded for more books. Their welcome made me glad we had ventured on. The tiny chapel was freshly plastered with mud and decorated with flowers. The crowd spilled into the yard. Everyone, inside and out, participated in the service. Stewart baptized so many children and adults I lost count. Everyone took communion, passing around little aluminum cups of grenadine. The villagers pleaded for more visits and sang us on our way, following the little car down the narrow path until the forest closed in on us.

"Now, that wasn't so bad, was it?" Stewart said.

We saw village life as it must have been in the early days, just like in Mrs. Springer's book, *I Love The Trail*, recounting when the Springers first arrived. "And wasn't that a great welcome?" Stewart said, wistfully, "At least somebody was glad to see us."

"Good news," Stewart said. "Joyce just called. She's declaring a week off from lessons. They're going to Mulungwishi on Friday afternoon and they'll drop Tim off."

It was as though a great weight had lifted, one I hadn't realized I carried. I took special care to make up Tim's bed. Peter helped me clean up their room. The girls planned special treats for Tim. I inspected the larder, hoping for hidden treasures. I found a can of cherries. I could make his favorite dessert, Creeping Crust Cobbler, with ice cream from our hand-cranked freezer. The ratio of one cup powdered whole milk to one cup of water made a rich and delicious ice cream.

The Sinclair's car drove up. I ran out to hug Tim. He seemed subdued, unsure of himself. I carried his little suitcase to his bedroom. The Sinclair family—Leonard, Joyce, and their three children, Eddie, David, and Sally—came in for tea and cookies. Joyce told us what we longed to hear. "He's doing so well. He and David get along just fine, and he works so hard on his lessons. I'm really pleased with his progress." They didn't stay long. Tim offered a polite goodbye, some stiff hugs, and they were on their way.

Perhaps Tim would be more comfortable, now that it was just us, I thought. He answered our eager questions with reluctance. I should have realized how difficult it was for him. The Sinclair household rules were far more rigid than ours. He must have felt forlorn and rejected, sent away to live with people he hardly knew. Yet Joyce had assured me he fit well into the family.

Peter, Mary Beth, and Martha followed Tim into his room.

Stewart said to me, "I think he needs some time."

I agreed. I started dinner preparations: fried chicken and potato salad. And Creeping Crust Cobbler a la mode. I set the table for six. Tim seemed to relax a bit, be more like himself. The cobbler, his favorite, was a big hit. After the children were in bed, Stewart and I talked about Tim, and what we could do. "Let's see how it goes tomorrow," he said. I went out to the kitchen to straighten things up for Baba Samuel.

Stewart turned on the shortwave radio for the late news.

"Come quick. You've got to hear this."

"What now?"

"The new Katanga money. Issued today. The old currency will be worthless after tomorrow. There were rumors, but nobody expected it to be so sudden. What can we spend it on this time of night?"

"Maybe the gas station is still open," I suggested.

"It's going to be a mess tomorrow. Can you imagine the line at the bank?"

Tim was a bit more cheerful at breakfast. "Sometimes Aunt Joyce lets me make pancakes. I miss our house." I put my arm around him, hugged him to me. His sad eyes haunted me. I hated to think of sending him back to Elisabethville.

Stewart was gone for several hours, searching for a place to exchange the old money for the new. "Just what you'd expect," he reported. "Lines around the block, no organization, not enough small bills, an incredible mess. Some days this country just seems hopeless."

The boys were eager to see the new money. Stewart opened his briefcase.

"It looks just like Monopoly money," Tim said. "What's it worth?"

"Good question," Stewart said. "I just hope it's worth something. The old Congo money is no good anymore."

"Can I have it then?" Peter asked.

"Not yet. We have to keep trying to exchange it for money we can use. The new government wants to show we're a separate country now," Stewart explained, "with our own stamps and money. And license plates will be next. The soldiers get really mad if you say anything, so be careful. We've got to walk a fine line here."

No one was ready when the time came for Tim to go back to Elisabethville. He didn't want to go, and none of us wanted him to go, either. Peter brooded about losing his partner-in-adventure.

"What in the world are we doing that's important enough to justify breaking up the family?" I asked Stewart.

"Beats me. Let's hope it's just a few more months."

Tim was stoic when they drove away.

Several weeks later, I made another odyssey to church, this time to Northern Rhodesia for the seventy-fifth annual observance of the World Day of Prayer. This international, interdenominational service for women holds a special meaning for me. To commemorate the occasion, church women from all parts of Africa came together for three days of study, discussion, and prayer. I would be a thread in a great tapestry.

Sarah and Marlene, two of the unmarried missionaries, invited me to travel with them. Everybody called them the *wamamas*. *Wa* formed the plural of the ubiquitous *mama*, the designation by which all adult females, black and white, were known. Marlene and I had made the hazardous evacuation together at the time of Independence, and I looked forward to getting to know Sarah. Oblivious of my rudeness, I questioned her.

"Why is it that women as attractive and intelligent as you and Marlene aren't married?" I thought she would be flattered by my supposed compliment. She stared at me as though I were a stranger from another planet.

"I'm single by choice," she said, rather stiffly. "We're all single by choice. I've turned down more than one offer to be a wife."

A revelation to me. Single by choice. How could I have been so naive?

"We're supported by the Methodist Women in America, you know. We have our own houses, our own cars." She didn't have to say, "Better than yours." We all knew the American churchwomen were known for their generosity to their representatives abroad. I eyed the *wamamas* with new respect.

In the past five years, I had celebrated World Day of Prayer in three different countries: The United States, Belgium, the Congo. None was more meaningful than this one, the fourth, in Northern Rhodesia. In a "real" church, we sat in comfortable pews, with backs. The organ music brought tears of joy. The mid-afternoon sun highlighted details of the stained-glass windows. Why were these amenities so important to my worship? Was I worshipping the amenities? Could that be why I found it so difficult to find sisterhood with the Kipendano women? I admonished myself silently for my attachment to beauty and comfort. Among these outstanding women from all over Africa—teachers, preachers, nurses, YWCA secretaries, church workers, mothers, and homemakers—I saw hope for the future.

Sarah, Marlene, and I stopped in Elisabethville on our way home. In the shower, I discovered a lump in my breast. Oh, no, not again. I decided not to say anything until I got home the next day.

We drove into Jadotville mid-morning. Stewart came out to greet us, Martha and Peter trailing behind. Mary Beth arrived from school, and the five of us sat down for lunch. If only Tim were with us. If only cancer weren't on my mind. I waited for evening, after the children had gone to bed, to tell Stewart my news.

"Where is it?" he asked.

"Same place as the other one, the one Duvon took out. I don't know if that's good news or bad news. I need to go back to Kitwe and see Dr. Fisher as soon as possible. Can you drive me down? We could probably stay at the guest house."

He hesitated. "It's a really bad time for me to be away, and I hate to take Mary Beth out of school. How long do you think you might be there?"

"I don't know. I thought I'd have Dr. Fisher examine me and see what he says. I don't want to do this all by myself again, without you there." I started to cry.

He patted my shoulder. "Don't worry, I'm sure you'll be all right." He was quiet for a minute or two. "Bishop Booth is in Elisabethville, just back from New York. He's driving down to Salisbury tomorrow. You could get a ride as far as Kitwe. I'll call him in the morning."

"How would I get back?"

"There's always somebody coming and going. Let's take this a step at a time. You need to have this looked at right away."

The next evening, as I tucked Mary Beth, Martha, and Peter into bed, I put on a brave face for them. "I have to go to Kitwe tomorrow to see the doctor."

Peter said, "You'll bring us something from Kitwe, won't you?"

"Sure. Shall I bring ice cream?"

Mary Beth looked puzzled. "I don't think you can do that."

I smiled at her. "Well, anyway, I won't be gone long. I want you to work hard on your lessons and help your dad all you can." They nodded, soberly.

They said their prayers. "God bless Mom and make her all right."

I tried to hide my tears.

In the morning Stewart drove me to Elisabethville. The bishop was ready to go. "Once we get to Kitwe, I won't need my car," he said. "I'm going to fly to Salisbury. Would you mind driving my car back to E'ville?"

"I'd be glad to. And I'll drive now, if you like, so I can get used to your car."

We were comfortable with each other. "I'm concerned about you," he said, "I'm glad you're seeing Dr. Fisher. He's a good man." The bishop was exhausted. He dozed for a while. I loved driving his little Volkswagen. It took the hills without slowing to a crawl. We crossed the border without any trouble. I dropped him at the Ecumenical Center.

"Be sure to let me know what the doctor says," he said, "I'll keep you in my prayers."

Dr. Fisher greeted me gravely. "How is your daughter?"

"She's fine. Still mad at you, I'm afraid. She says you gave her a sore throat. She's so much healthier after the tonsillectomy."

He probed gently and thoroughly. I watched his face for clues. "What do you think?"

"Yes, I feel an anomaly there, all right, very near the scar from the previous surgery. I don't believe it merits immediate attention. Let's wait for a couple of months. It may disappear. These things often do. I expect you are under considerable stress up there in the Congo, and that affects your health. Do you have any idea when you will return to the States?"

"Probably this summer. We'll know soon. It's a year earlier than we'd planned."

He smiled. "If you go home this spring, you can have it taken care of there if it persists. You might prefer that. In the meantime, I want you to continue to examine yourself carefully. Let me know if there are any changes. Or if it disappears."

On my way back to E'ville, alone this time, I replayed our conversation over and over, relieved there would be no immediate surgery, but aware of the Sword of Damocles hanging over me. If only a doctor could say I did not have cancer and never would. But at least I had a reprieve.

I stopped to see Maurice and Lois. "Don't think we're going to let you go right back to Jadotville," Lois said. "Maurice and I will have you all to ourselves. We'll get caught up. I'll call Stewart and tell him to bring the kids tomorrow. We'll have a picnic," she said, in her brisk way. "I'll invite the Sinclairs, so you can see Tim."

I almost didn't recognize Mary Beth without her ponytail. She looked up at me shyly through her bangs. The new short cut bounced as she turned her head.

"Mary, what happened to your hair?" I blurted. Her face puckered up.

"Dad took me to the beauty shot." I always loved it when the children misspoke. A beauty shot, indeed. Charming! "He couldn't brush my hair like you do."

"Those tangles at the back of her neck," Stewart said. "I just couldn't do it. She screamed."

"Never mind," I said. "Mary, it looks really nice. You look so grown up."

She looked relieved. "You're not mad?"

"Of course not. You just surprised me. For a moment, I didn't recognize you."

"The kids at school didn't recognize me either." She hunched her shoulders and put her hands over her bare neck. Stewart sat down beside me. He balanced a plate of spaghetti on his knees and bit into a chunk of fresh-baked bread.

"I hope you're not upset," he said. "I think she looks kind of cute."

"I just wish you'd talked with me first."

"I didn't know how long you'd be gone. I didn't think you'd be back so soon."

Lucky for him, we were in a roomful of people.

I sighed. "Well, it's done now." I didn't want to make a scene.

"It'll grow back," he said.

Tim shrugged off my attempt to hug him. He mumbled something and went across the room to join Peter.

The mission treasurer resigned, accused by a member of a rival tribe of embezzlement. Glad for an opportunity to be useful, I volunteered for the unenviable job of bookkeeper. How hard could it be? With a great deal of help from Lois, I prepared a report for the upcoming meeting in Kolwezi of the regional administrative body, the Field Committee. Bishop Booth chaired the committee, which was composed of a mix of Africans and *wazungu*. Their decisions set the course for all the work of the district, and for how funds would be allocated.

I was more interested in Easter plans than trial balances. I accumulated enough eggs to color and made fancy cookies and hot cross buns. We entertained lots of guests. Ten children sat around the picnic table in the yard. We had angel food cake, a freezer full of hand-cranked ice cream, and a hunt for the hidden decorated eggs. No time for a heart-to-heart talk with Tim.

So many people stopped by on their way to Field Committee in Kolwezi that we ran out of clean cups. Baba Samuel chuckled as he boiled water for Nescafé, and restocked the plate of cookies, proud to be part of the family's reputation for hospitality.

Stewart was in Kolwezi all week. Marlene moved into the guesthouse and spent her days out in the villages, supervising the literacy work and delivering more of our homemade books. One day she stayed around to help me entertain three home economists, two of them displaced from the Central Congo. United Nations soldiers from Nigeria had looted their mission, stolen all their belongings, and demolished the Girls School. "They even ripped out the toilets and carried them away," one of the ladies confided.

The guest of honor was a distinguished professor from Howard University. I was uneasy serving lunch to professional home economists.

We sat down to lunch and hadn't even said grace when Werner drove up. He rushed in without pausing to knock.

"Are you all right?"

"As far as I know," I answered, rather flippantly. "What's up? And may I introduce our guests?"

"I can't stay. There are riots in Elisabethville against the United Nations, and I just wanted to make sure you were all right. I promised Stewart I'd keep an eye on things while he's in Kolwezi." He turned to the guests. "Everybody confuses the United Nations with the United States," he explained. "I was afraid someone might start something here."

"I wonder if we should send our guests on to Mulungwishi," I said to Marlene. "until things settle down in Elisabethville."

"Let me see what I can find out," Werner said. "Did you know your phone's not working?"

As he eased out the door, his sister drove up. "Stewart called me. He couldn't reach you or Werner. He asked me to let you know the mission plane will land at the Jadotville airstrip in thirty minutes, and would we make all the arrangements."

"I'll go to the Army commandant and tell him the plane is coming," Werner said. "I'll tell the soldiers not to shoot, and to move the obstructions off the runway." He nodded to the ladies and rushed out the door, followed by his sister.

"Who do you suppose is coming?" Marlene asked.

"It must be the bishop," I said. "I can't think who else it might be. I'll bet the Elisabethville airport is closed."

Our guests had remained calm through all this. I suggested they go ahead with lunch.

Marlene and I drove out to the airstrip. It was just a clearing in the bush seven miles out of town, surrounded by armed soldiers, who were surprised to see two *wazungu* women. Marlene persuaded them to clear the brush off the grass runway. I was grateful for her courage and her facility with Swahili.

They had barely finished their work when we heard the plane. The soldiers hid in the bush, guns ready. The little Cessna 210 circled the clearing, came in to land, and taxied to a stop. The door opened. After a breathless moment, a little girl popped out of the plane, her white dress fluttering in the breeze like a flag of truce. The soldiers laughed and put down their guns. Marlene went out to the plane. She recognized Cindy, daughter of Danny and Diane. Stewart and Danny called to us from the plane, evidently surprised to see us. And to see the soldiers.

"I thought the whole crowd would be here to see the plane come in," Stewart shouted. "We've brought Cindy."

"So I see," said Marlene. Cindy burrowed into her embrace.

The men stayed on the plane. "Weren't you expecting her?" Stewart yelled. "We tried to call. We thought she'd enjoy being with you. She was bored with Field Committee."

The soldiers murmured and brandished their weapons.

"You guys better get going," Marlene shouted. "We'll take care of Cindy."

The door slammed shut. The pilot hadn't even turned off the motor. The little plane taxied to the end of the runway, took off into the wind, and disappeared. The sound died away. We could hear the soldiers laughing. Those crazy *wazungu*, sending a *mutoto* in a *ndege*.

Cindy was small for five years old. She hadn't stopped crying since she got off the plane.

"What were they thinking?" Marlene asked.

"It's a good thing she recognized you," I said. "Let's get out of here."

The home economists were gone. Baba Samuel brought out the leftovers for us. Cindy wasn't hungry. She huddled on Marlene's lap and sobbed.

"Why is she crying like that?" Mary Beth asked.

"She misses her mommy. She doesn't really know us. Why don't you bring her some of your dolls?"

My girls brought their best dolls. Cindy turned her head away and howled.

Peter made funny faces. "Hey, Cindy, look at this." Cindy peeked at him, hiccupped, watched from the safety of Marlene's lap. She had brothers not much older than Peter. She stopped crying and sniffled. Marlene tried to wipe her nose. Martha went in search of kittens.

"Cindy, you can sleep in my bed," Mary Beth offered.

Cindy shook her head. "I want my mommy," she said in a small voice.

That night she slept on a cot in the guesthouse with Marlene.

It would be a long week.

"Let's take her out to the villages," Marlene suggested the next morning. "She lives on a rural station, after all, not in town with factory noise all day and all night."

"Do you think it's safe?" I asked.

Marlene snorted. "Safer than here. And I really need to get out there with more books."

I made sandwiches and we all piled into the Volkswagen bus. At every village, the children poured out of their mud-brick schoolhouse and ran out to greet us. They shouted and cheered, delighted to interrupt their lessons. They stood in a circle around us, hopped up and down in excitement. The teacher came, smiling in welcome. The mamas left their chores and gathered around, chattered, and clapped their hands together. The men of the village watched and waited to greet us. Cindy seemed to enjoy herself. Marlene was in her element. She introduced me to the crowd. "*Mama aliandika kitabu hiki,*" she said, holding a primer, indicating I was the author.

"*Ah, ah, ah, ah,*" I heard." *Akisanti kabisa* [Many thanks]. *Akisanti, mama.*" The writer of the book had come, in person. Women gathered around me, took my hand, talked rapidly, placed a hand over the heart in respect. One woman presented me with a chipped blue-and-white enamel pan filled with eggs. I placed the palm of my hand over my heart in thanks and respect and regretted I had neglected my Swahili lessons. I managed to ask them to read for me.

Women ran to their huts and brought tattered copies of *Kusoma Furaha*. We sat together on the bare ground under the mango trees, the women in their bright-colored dresses. Babies peering over their shoulders or nestled in the folds of their blouses, contentedly nursed while the mothers struggled with their words. The schoolchildren gathered around and looked over their shoulders at the books, shaped the words along with the mothers. My heart filled with joy. I was part of something worthwhile after all.

Cindy had been content all day. Now she resumed her lament. "Where's my mother? I want my mother. When is my mother coming?"

Mary Beth and Martha gazed at her, in awe to witness such grief. "Why doesn't her mother come and get her?" Mary Beth asked.

"She's in a meeting in Kolwezi," I said. "She'll be here Sunday."

"How many more days is that?"

"Today's Friday, so we're almost there. It's hard for her, you know. She doesn't know us very well, and she's still pretty little."

"She's older than Martha, and Martha doesn't cry like that," Mary Beth said, sternly.

I could have bawled along with Cindy.

On Saturday morning, Peter took over. "You kids run and hide, and I'll come find you." Mary and Martha scattered to their favorite hiding places. Cindy stayed close to Marlene. Peter strolled around, checked the kitchen for cookies, took his time to start the search for the little ones. He let them beat him to home base, and they started all over again.

Peter loved to tease Mary Beth, who was prone to believe everything he said. Whoever had built the old garage had included a grease pit for the guys who liked to do their own tinkering. Leaves and trash accumulated in the excavation over time, and the garage was off-limits to the children. Peter launched the legend that the grease pit contained a monster. Mary Beth was terrified of the very notion of the grease pit. He loved to jump out from behind the car and roar, "I'm a monster and I eat little girls."

Cindy walked cautiously by the garage, and Peter did his monster thing. Emboldened by Cindy's presence, Mary Beth, challenged him.

"You're not a monster. You're Peter."

"Ha!" he roared. "Fooled you! I'm a monster that looks just like Peter. I ate him up."

Mary Beth ran for the back door, shrieking, the Peter-monster close behind.

Cindy laughed. "Do it again," she begged.

Peter tired of the game and went off to play soccer with the African boys.

Early on Sunday morning, all by herself, Cindy put on the frilly white dress in which she'd arrived. Marlene brushed and braided her hair and tied the ribbons. "I have to leave, now, Sweetie, I have things to do at Mulungwishi." Cindy dug deeper into Marlene's lap, glared at me, and sucked her thumb. Marlene handed her to me, got into the car, and drove away.

Cindy moved her little chair just outside the front door, watched the driveway, and sucked her thumb. She rubbed a satin hair ribbon to comfort herself. Mary Beth and Martha gave up on her and went to find the kittens.

Just after noon, the Elliott's station wagon eased down the driveway. Cindy came to life. She screamed "Mommy! Mommy!" She leaped into her mother's arms and sobbed and sobbed.

"My goodness," Diane said, "what's all this? Didn't you have fun?"

"She really didn't," I said. "She missed you terribly."

"I was afraid that might happen," Danny said, "but we thought she'd have a good time with you all. She was so bored in Kolwezi. Nobody to play with. Stewart said you'd be happy to have her."

Stewart clambered out of the back seat and brushed red dust from his shoulders. Danny liked to drive with the windows open. "Come on in," I said. "Lunch is ready."

Later, when they had finally gone, Stewart said, "I have some good news. Bishop approved furlough for us this summer. We're going home." I burst into tears and forgave him for sending Cindy.

"Is it true, Dad?" Peter asked. "Are we really going home to America?"

Stewart laughed. "Yes, it's true. We'll leave in July. We can travel through Europe, as we did before."

"I just want to see my grandma and grandpa," Mary Beth said. "I don't want to see anything else."

"Me too," said Peter. "I don't want to drive around all the time in the car. I want to go to America and eat ice cream whenever I want."

Stewart turned to me. "What would you like to do?"

"I don't mind if we stop for a bit in Europe somewhere, but I need to get home and see the doctor."

Mary Beth leaned against me and sucked her fingers. "Yes, that's right," Stewart said. "Let's get you home."

Chapter Fifteen

August 1962, Brooklyn

Rain thrummed on the roof of the car. The children were quiet, pensive, sad for friends left behind again. Heartsick myself, I couldn't conjure up any cheeriness for them. Stewart steered slowly through the drab streets of Brooklyn. Everything we would need for the trip, for the twenty-one-day voyage to Cape Town and the three-thousand-mile drive to Jadotville, filled the back of the station wagon.

"It's a good thing I ordered extra-heavy shock absorbers," Stewart remarked, as we bounced through potholes, searching for the route to the docks.

"Are we lost?" Mary Beth asked.

I couldn't trust myself to answer, too close to tears. We were lost, all right.

Stewart spoke up. "No, we're not lost. I'm just not sure where we are. Don't worry, we'll find the ship."

And there it was, at the end of the street.

"Are you sure that's the one?" Tim asked.

"That's it, all right, I'm pretty sure," Stewart said.

"I wish we were going on that other one," Tim said, "the one we just saw."

On our way, we'd passed the pier in Manhattan where the *Queen Elizabeth* was about to embark. Hundreds of well-wishers crowded the dock, a send-off for President and Mrs. Eisenhower. My thoughts flashed back to our first departure five years earlier, when we sailed on the *Nieuw Amsterdam*. A festive group of family and friends had gathered to wish us Godspeed. This time it was just the six of us. Visitors were not allowed. It was just as well. I stared at the ship, a dull-grey freighter in need of paint Her name on the bow: *South African Merchant*.

Stewart found his briefcase and ruffled through his papers.

"I'll go find the purser and see when we can go aboard," he said. He splashed through the oily puddles and disappeared up the gangplank.

The voyage was his idea. "It'll be a real vacation for you. Three weeks, no beds to make, no meals to prepare."

"Why this ship?" I'd asked. He knew that apartheid was anathema to me. I wouldn't even buy South African apples. "How could The Board justify using a South African ship?"

"It's the cheapest way to go," he explained, "and we can take the car on board, and drive home to Jadotville, see new country."

No use to remind him I had no wish to see that particular new country. The tickets were purchased.

I'd created a fool's paradise for myself during that furlough year. Stewart's Great-Aunt Mary welcomed us into her comfortable home in New Haven. An eminent cancer specialist examined me and assured me that the anomalies in my breast were gone. It was not unusual, he said, for the problem to disappear when stress was relieved. I remained free of symptoms. He'd advised against a return to the Congo.

A kind and brilliant pediatrician brought our children into his practice. He and his wife remained mentors and my best friends through the years to come.

The public schools were another story. The principal of the local primary school put the children through their paces, and the brusque woman who would decide if Mary Beth was ready for second grade challenged my teaching abilities and asked about my credentials.

"As a matter of fact, I have a minor in education and teaching credentials in Kansas."

"Well," she said, "we're not in Kansas anymore, are we?" She stared at Mary Beth. "Let's see what you can do. Can you write?"

Mary Beth nodded. She glanced up at me, terrified. The teacher handed her a piece of chalk. "Write cat," she commanded.

Mary Beth trembled. She was not accustomed to a chalkboard. Laboriously she wrote, in cursive, CHAT.

"Look at that! She can't even spell CAT." Mary Beth tried to hide her tears.

"She speaks French," I said. "Chat is French for cat."

"We speak English here," the woman barked. "She can't even print!"

The principal finally intervened. Mary Beth would repeat the first grade, and this Gorgon would be her teacher. I was devastated, humiliated. All those hours of drudgery to get her ready for an American school seemed wasted.

Martha loved her mornings in kindergarten. The kids caught the school bus on the corner. The children and I made friends in the neighborhood and in church. The boys joined a Cub Scout troop. Mary Beth was a Brownie. I became an assistant Brownie leader.

We didn't see much of Stewart. On weekends he traveled, preached, and raised money for Congo missions. He spent weekdays at Yale Divinity School, working toward a master's degree in Africa Studies. We would all pay a price for that degree.

On a perfect sunny afternoon in June, Stewart received his degree in an impressive ceremony on the quadrangle of the Yale Divinity School. He brought home travel brochures, planned our return trip to the Congo.

"I got a telegram from Sakeji School," he said one morning. "They're holding places for all four children, starting in the fall quarter."

"Did we talk about this?" I asked, blindsided by the news.

"I'm sure we discussed it," he said. "Don't worry. I know you don't want to send Mary Beth and Martha. That was the headmaster's suggestion. They like to get the kids early, in first grade."

"I know. So they can break them into the system."

"Well, you can't teach all four of them by yourself. They need to know right away."

I stared at him as though he were a stranger. "You mean we're going back?"

"Of course we're going back. We don't have a choice. We owe The Board for my degree. It's a lot of money. We'll be paying for it the rest of our lives."

"We're indentured servants," I said.

"Why do you always exaggerate? We talked about it," he said.

Stewart startled me when he opened the car door. "We can board any time, but the ship won't sail until this evening. They can't finish loading until the rain stops. Our rooms aren't ready. We can stay in the lounge. They'll give us some lunch. We'll just take what we can carry. They'll bring the rest later."

He supervised the workmen as they unloaded the contents of the station wagon onto wooden flats. My dad had given us a set of Oshkosh suitcases. The men covered them with worn tarps. We carried satchels of books, dollies and dolly suitcases, small duffels and briefcases, trudged up the slippery gangplank, not quite a ladder and not quite stairs, and trooped into the lounge.

Wide windows framed a wondrous view of the harbor. The *Queen Elizabeth* sailed majestically past the Statue of Liberty, a bevy of tugboats in attendance. Staten Island ferries scurried back and forth like industrious waterbugs.

A brown-skinned waiter, handsome in his crisp white cotton jacket, brought a tray of sandwiches and a pot of tea. "Those are fine children," he ventured. I wondered if he had fine children at home, and where home was. "My name is David," he said. "I'll be serving you on the voyage."

I stared out at the rain. Peter and Tim finished the comic books their grandfather had given them and set to work on the bag of balsa-wood model airplanes. A fleet of little planes covered the tea table. Oh, dear. I'd planned to give them one at a time, to last for the entire trip.

"This is different than when we sailed on the *Nieuw Amsterdam*," Stewart remarked. "How many people came to see us off then? Twenty? Thirty?"

"I was embarrassed when you asked everyone to pray," I said. "I was afraid you were going to ask us to kneel on the deck."

He laughed. "I might have done it if I'd thought about it. Anyway, I got to preach the Sunday service. I wonder if they have a service on this ship. We seem to be the only passengers."

"Mom, I'm bored," Peter said. "Can I go look for my room?"

"They asked us to stay out of the way until they get everything aboard," I said. "We'll have plenty of time to explore later."

"The brochure mentioned a swimming pool," Stewart said. "I'll ask about that when we're underway."

"Maybe they have to inflate it," I said. I thought that was a joke.

The rain finally stopped, and the longshoremen swarmed onto the pier. The cranes swung loads high into the air at a speed that made me dizzy. A workman slipped and fell hard on the deck. The thick glass muffled any sound, but I could see him screaming, sprawled on the deck, bleeding.

"Is he dead?" Mary Beth asked.

"No, he's not dead," Tim said. "He's yelling."

"He'll be all right," Stewart said, too quickly.

It was dusk when the crane hoisted the white station wagon and swung it high.

"What if they drop it?" Peter said.

"They won't drop it," Stewart said.

The car disappeared into the center hold. Large metal covers clanged down on the hatches. The shore-based crewmen hustled home to dinner. Several of the ship's crew carried our luggage on board, and we followed them to our three adjoining staterooms, private bathroom in each. The prospect of the children in separate rooms made me uneasy. What if they walked in their sleep? They never had, but anything could happen. The railings around the deck, three strands of wire threaded loosely through the stanchions, wouldn't catch them if they slipped. I would need to practice extreme diligence during daylight hours, but what about the nights?

The engines rumbled into action, the gangplank was hauled aboard, rattling and clanking. Every surface was wet from the rain. Lines cast off; the tugs nudged the ship away from the pier. Grey daylight faded to dark, and lights bloomed onshore. Neon signs blinked, lights flashed, the tall buildings of Manhattan glittered, traffic flowed up and down the avenues. I could see all the way up Broadway, like looking between rows of corn. We passed between the giant piers, where the Verrazano Bridge would one day span the entrance to the harbor, and had our last glimpse of Liberty holding high her lighted torch. The ship paused to let the pilot off, the tugs backed away, and the *South African Merchant* moved steadily into the dark. The glow of the city faded behind us. The next port of call would be Cape Town.

The dinner gong sounded. In the dining salon, we joined the captain and the ship's officers, six of them, polite and reserved. The children were seated in an alcove at a separate table set with a crisp white tablecloth, big napkins, heavy china plates, and an array of silverware. Their own waiter, David, presided.

We stood around, waiting for our cues from the captain. A tall, slender man burst into the room; his tanned, weathered face broke into a broad smile. His bright blue eyes sparkled behind little spectacles. He was obviously a seaman, but not in uniform. He was barefoot.

"Hello, sorry to keep you waiting," he said. He nodded to the captain and the officers, took my hand in his. "I'm Captain Theo," he said. "Your fellow passenger."

He shook hands with Stewart, pulled out my chair, and we all sat down to dinner.

"I'm a yachtsman," he said. "A captain without a ship. I'm on my way home from South America, crewing with friends in a trans-oceanic race. We came in third." The men around the table warmed to his enthusiasm. They all seemed to know him.

"I've done a bit of sailing myself," Stewart ventured, "off the coast of Maine. When I was just a lad, I borrowed my grandfather's sloop, without permission, shanghaied my cousins for crew, and sailed to Monhegan Island. Had a bit of trouble finding my way back. Scared the family to death."

Theo beamed. The other men showed a flicker of interest. Maybe this was going to be a good trip after all.

I'm going home to Cape Town," Theo said. "Is that your final destination?"

"We're headed for the Congo," Stewart said. "We have our car on board."

"That's quite a drive," Theo said. "I'm looking forward to meeting your children."

He had lovely manners. He would serve as a sort of interpreter. He explained to us the ship's protocol and the strange customs of the Americans to the seamen.

David was teaching the children to fold napkins into rabbits. They looked up, curious, to see the barefoot stranger.

"This is Captain Theo," I said.

Peter looked puzzled. "I thought the other man was the captain."

Theo smiled. "He's the captain of this ship. I'm a captain without a ship."

Mary Beth wrinkled her brow. "What happened to your ship?" she asked.

"I'll tell you all about that later," he said. "We have a long voyage ahead of us."

"Would you and your husband like bed tea in the morning?" David asked.

"Yes, thank you."

"And the children?"

"Yes, please. Thank you, David, for taking good care of them."

"My pleasure," he murmured.

I helped Mary Beth into her pajamas. "Mom," she said, "what's bed tea?"

"I'm not real sure, but I think they bring you tea while you're still in bed."

"Will David bring it?"

"Yes, I think so."

"But I'll be in my pajamas," she said.

"It's all right," I said. "This is what you do on ships." I fluffed the pillow, tucked her in. "We're right next door. Call if you need anything. I'll see you in the morning."

At 7:30 in the morning, David brought tea with milk and sugar to all of us, and those tasteless little cookies the Brits call "biscuits." A lovely way to start the day.

Breakfast and lunch were informal, buffet style, men coming and going, just the right amount of polite conversation. The children blossomed under David's supervision.

Theo suggested the ship's carpenter put up a swing.

"Good idea," I said, "The kids will love that."

Stewart and Theo sprawled in deck chairs and supervised the children while I unpacked.

Suddenly, shouts. Tim's voice. "Push her higher."

Mary Beth screamed, "Stop! Stop it!"

What in the world? The swing I'd visualized was next to the cabin, its arc parallel to the flimsy railings. The swing I was looking at carried Martha toward the railing. I felt as though I'd been punched in the stomach. I couldn't watch, and I couldn't not watch.

"Hold on tight, Martha," I hollered. "Peter, don't push her so high. Catch her." Crew members gathered, grinning. Peter caught the swing. I grabbed Martha.

"I'm sorry," Captain Theo said. "I wasn't thinking."

The ship's carpenter took down the swing and installed it in a safer place.

"Stewart, what in the world were you thinking?" I asked. "We could have lost her."

"She'll be all right," he said. "You worry too much."

"We'll be careful, Mom," Tim said. "Don't worry."

The carpenter looked to me for approval. I nodded. "That's better."

"I'll have the men set up the ping-pong table," he said.

Martha climbed onto the swing again and moved sedately back and forth. "I like a boat better than a jet," she said, dreamily. "You can't swing on a jet."

The next morning, Stewart and I brought our books on deck and settled into chairs next to Theo. The girls played quietly with their dolls. A formation of flying fish flashed by. A pair of dolphins appeared off the starboard bow in a demonstration of synchronized swimming.

"This is more like it," I murmured. "Peace and quiet, at last."

As if on cue, a sudden harsh metallic, grinding noise blasted the morning calm. A shrill whine with an abrasive undertone penetrated. It was as though a crazed person had decided to destroy some huge thing directly below me. I waited for the racket to stop. It didn't stop. I turned to Theo.

"It's an electric burr," he shouted. "They scrape off the paint, put on a fresh coat. They'll take a break for tea and lunch. You'll get used to it. By the time she comes into port, she'll be shipshape."

"And the Captain told us to keep the children quiet so the crew could sleep," I muttered.

Captain Theo accomplished in five minutes what all of us had been working on for five years. He watched Martha suck her thumb. "I used to do that," he told her, "and look what happened to me." He performed a sleight-of-hand trick, to make it appear as if he could remove the upper half of his thumb. Martha hid her hands behind her back.

"Do that again," Tim said. "Show me how to do that."

That was the last time I saw Martha with her thumb in her mouth.

The air cooled as we left the Gulf Stream. I dug out our sweaters. The sea remained remarkably calm. An albatross flew high above. An enormous marlin leaped up out of the water alongside the ship. I read to the children *Kon-Tiki* and *The Swiss Family Robinson*. We played board games in the long afternoons. At night the crew set up chairs on deck, rolled down a big screen, and showed old movies and TV shows like *Gunsmoke* and *Dragnet*. When the children could no longer keep their eyes open, we carried them off to bed.

Theo called my attention to a long horizontal chart on the wall of the corridor.

A crewman kept the chart updated. I checked it at least once a day.

"When will we cross the equator?" I asked Theo.

"Should be this Sunday," he said. "The captain will let us know."

"It's our first crossing," I said. "I hope there won't be any kind of hazing."

"Ah, you read too many books. Don't worry. It will be a quiet crossing."

"The sailors told us to brace ourselves, to get ready for a big bump," Tim said.

"They're telling you tales," Theo said. "The captain is quite skilled. He'll maneuver the ship so you won't feel a thing."

On Sunday afternoon, July 29th, we gathered on deck and crossed the equator at five o'clock. "Did you feel anything?" Captain Theo asked the children. They shook their heads.

"I can tell we're going downhill now," Tim said.

"Say goodbye to the Big Dipper," Theo told us when the evening grew dark. "Watch for the Southern Cross. You know the Southern Cross, right?"

"Oh yes," Peter assured him. "We see it all the time in Jadotville."

The captain hosted a barbeque that evening to celebrate the equatorial crossing. The crew set up chairs on deck, hung strings of colored lights, and covered the ping-pong table with a sheet. The kitchen crew brought hams and turkeys and baked potatoes. The purser presided at the barbeque pit, half an oil drum propped on logs. He cooked piles of steaks and chops and sausages. Cases of beer appeared, stacked on the deck. We drank tomato juice. One of the engineers got quite drunk. He persisted in trying to explain to me the difference between football and rugby. He pestered me to make a date to play ping-pong. I managed a firm no. Stewart was amused.

"I see you have an admirer," he said.

"Let's get out of here," I said. We thanked the captain, gathered up the children, and retreated to our quarters.

Mary Beth appeared at my bedside the next morning, carrying her mug of tea.

"This tea tastes funny," she said.

"It's the milk," Stewart said. "They've run out of fresh milk and they're using canned milk now."

"What about the cow?" Mary Beth asked.

"What cow?"

"The one that gives the milk. Captain Theo told us there was a cow on board."

"He was teasing you," Stewart said. I'm quite sure there's no cow."

We passed quite close to the island of Saint Helena, twelve hundred miles off the coast of Africa, our first sight of land since leaving Brooklyn.

"That's where Napoleon spent his last days," Stewart said. He offered an impressive history lesson and patiently answered the children's questions. His red baseball cap flew off his head and danced away on the water, far below.

"Can we go back and get it?" Mary Beth asked.

"Not a chance," Stewart said. "It's gone."

She frowned. "But you liked that cap," she protested.

"I can get another one," he said.

Captain Theo joined us. "Dad lost his cap," Mary Beth said.

"So I see," he said, "I've received some bad news myself. Friends have wired me that my name is on a list of people in South Africa who are not to be interviewed or quoted by the press. An unpleasant new interpretation of the infamous Sabotage Act. It's the end of a free press for South Africa."

"What will you do?" I asked.

"It's not unexpected. I'll settle someplace where the weather is warm. Bermuda, perhaps."

Mary Beth heard the sadness he sought to conceal. "You'll miss your friends," she said.

He scooped her up in his arms. "You mustn't worry about me," he said. "I'll be all right. I have my boat. I'll make new friends."

"Will I make new friends?" she asked.

"Yes, I'm sure you will. You'll have fine new friends."

She looked thoughtful.

Stewart's baseball cap was a red dot on the water, far away.

Some subtle change stirred in the atmosphere, a quickening of life, the anticipation of the end of the voyage. The hideous metallic grinding no longer shattered the morning calm. The entire ship shone, from stem to stern, transformed, painted, waxed, and varnished. The swing and ping-pong table disappeared.

During the voyage, the ship's officers had talked a bit about their homeland. Listening to them was quite an education for me. Some mentioned selling their homes and moving, possibly to New Zealand.

"By the way," Theo said, "you may have noticed that your sons have made themselves scarce the last couple of days. The engineers wanted to show them around the engine room, explain how things work. I took the liberty to tell them. I didn't think you'd mind. I hope I didn't overstep."

"Certainly not," Stewart said.

"I hope you aren't in a hurry to head north," Theo said. "I can pick you up in the morning at your hostel. You should see the Cape of Good Hope, where the Atlantic meets the Indian Ocean. It's quite a sight. There's a good restaurant at Lion's Head. Have you ever had rock lobster?"

"That will work out just fine," Stewart said, "We have to wait here a couple of days for the car to be serviced before we start north."

The ocean developed a chop as we neared our destination. Stewart felt a bit queasy and took to his bunk. That wasn't like him. He never got seasick. I wondered if he had some misgivings about returning to Africa. I kept my own misgivings to myself.

On our last night aboard, the captain hosted a celebratory dinner. Stewart sent his regrets. The captain raised his wineglass. "It has been a pleasure to have you and your family on board," he said.

"Hear, hear," seconded Captain Theo.

"The first lighthouse will come into view at 2:30 in the morning," the captain said. "If you plan to see it, be sure to dress warmly."

I missed seeing the lighthouse. We were up and dressed and on deck for sunrise, our first view of Table Mountain looming over the city, the brilliant white tablecloth of cloud draped across the summit.

I have since experienced other remarkable landfalls: Nantucket Harbor at dusk, with its silhouette of three church steeples; St. John's and the tiny settlements that ring the island of Newfoundland; historic Battle Harbor, Labrador; Victoria, British Columbia on a rainy afternoon. Cape Town is the fairest of them all.

We passed close to Robben Island on the port side, site of the infamous prison where Nelson Mandela would spend twenty-seven years of his life. His compatriot, Walter Sisulu, was already incarcerated there. I asked a passing seaman, to be sure it was Robben Island.

"Never heard of it," he said.

The ship slowed, moved deeper into the harbor. Time speeded up. The ship docked; the gangplank clattered down. Lines were secured. Captain Theo, ashore, his seabag over his shoulder, waved and disappeared into the crowd. The dock rolled under my feet. It would take some time to get my shore legs. We loaded our gear into a cab, drove through the city, and checked in to a missionary hostel halfway up the mountain. From that vantage point, the city seemed calm and lovely, the grid of streets, the trees, the parks. I didn't want to think of Jadotville, devastated by the street warfare that followed Independence. A wintry wind chilled me. We put on heavy sweaters and asked for more blankets. Late in the afternoon we walked around the neighborhood, found a park, and sat in a row on a bench.

"Look, there goes our ship," Peter said.

Far below, in the harbor beyond the city, the tiny *South African Merchant* left the pier, sailed past the breakwater, through the outer harbor, out into the open sea.

"When will we get to Africa?" Mary Beth asked.

"What do you mean?" Tim asked. "This is Africa."

"I mean the real Africa," she said.

"We'll get there soon enough," I said.

Chapter Sixteen

Captain Theo came by in the morning, as planned. He drove us around the Cape, past the Lion's Head, to the headland where the Indian Ocean and the Southern Atlantic collide in tremendous surf. We stopped for lunch at a small restaurant that overlooked the turbulent sea. He insisted I try the local rock lobster, and I accepted his invitation to have a glass of the local wine. Theo's future was uncertain since he was on the "watch list" of subversives. Our own prospects were uncertain as well. I wanted to cry when he drove away.

Our spartan accommodations in Cape Town offered the basics, no frills: iron cots with thin mattresses and thin blankets, insufficient for the wintry southern tip of the continent. We missed the comfort of bunks and bed tea on the *South African Merchant*.

For two long days, we traveled north on excellent roads, across the Karoo desert to Johannesburg. We checked into a cheap hotel. The children and I went for a walk, in search of a playground. I have seldom been more uncomfortable. If I made eye contact with white people on the street, I received hostile stares from the icy blue eyes of the *herrenvolk*. They seemed to intuit we were strangers, probably sympathetic to the blacks. If any blacks met my gaze, they looked down and hurried past.

We found a public playground near the hotel. The children raced to climb the monkey bars and took turns on the merry-go-round. I pushed Mary Beth and Martha in the swings, higher and higher, still grateful to be on dry land. We had the park to ourselves. African children watched us, their faces pressed against the fence. I hadn't noticed the signs on the fence. *WHITES ONLY.*

"Why don't those children come in?" Mary Beth asked.

"They can't," I said. "It's not allowed. It's just for white people."

"Well, that doesn't make any sense," she said.

All the pleasure was gone, like air from a balloon. "Let's go," I said. They didn't argue. We walked past the silent ragged children at the fence.

I'm not usually immune to a beautiful landscape, but the mountains and deserts of South Africa made me sad. What a wretched country. We came at last to the Limpopo River, "the great grey-green, greasy Limpopo River, all set about with fever-trees...," as Rudyard Kipling wrote. The children were too hot and too bored to respond.

We crossed the river at Beitbridge into Southern Rhodesia, drove to Salisbury, and stopped for the night at a modest hotel owned by a family originally from India, one of the many entrepreneurial families who have flourished in Africa for generations. Concrete cabins, minimally furnished, surrounded a bathhouse and an outdoor kitchen. I organized preparations for supper. Mary Beth and Martha trooped into the bathhouse. Stewart supervised filling the deep concrete tub, and in a few minutes, the girls emerged, wrapped in big towels. The sun had just set, and they shivered in the chilly air.

"Let's get you into your pajamas and bathrobes. Where did your brothers disappear to?" Peter and Tim came around the corner. "Get your towels, and pop into the tub. Supper will be ready in a few minutes."

It was our last evening with the boys. Stewart fried sausages. I stirred a pot of cocoa. In the morning we'd meet the pilot of the mission plane at the airport, and he would deliver Peter and Tim to Sakeji School. The remote location had been chosen on purpose to discourage visitations. We wouldn't see them again until December. I was determined to have a cheerful evening. No tears.

The boys were excited about the trip, their first in a small plane. Whoops of joy came from the bathhouse and sounds of splashing water. They wrestled in the tub, hollered, and dunked each other. The concrete floor was awash. The towels were soaked. "What in the world do you think you are doing?" I shouted. "Look at this mess. Get out of that tub right now and mop up this water."

Searching for dry towels, I burst into tears. Their last night with us, and I lost my temper and yelled at them. This was supposed to be a special family evening. Popcorn, maybe. I'd spoiled everything.

Mary Beth and Martha, rosy in their clean pajamas, watched me, concerned.

"What's the matter, Mom?" Mary Beth asked. "Are you sick?"

"Oh, no, honey, I'm just upset about the boys leaving tomorrow." She hugged. "It's all right Mom, you still have me."

The boys came in, chastened, dripping wet. "We're sorry, Mom," Peter said. "We didn't mean to get water all over everything."

"I know. I'm sorry I yelled at you. Get your jammies on and let's have supper."

The sausages were overdone, the rolls stale, the cocoa boiled over. But we were together.

In the morning, a subdued family drove across town to the airport. Nobody jostled for window seats. The boys carried their suitcases and the small aluminum case holding their toys. Stewart asked if they had locked their suitcases. Tim nodded and held up the keys on a string. "Let me hold the keys for you," I said. "You might lose them." I slipped them into the pocket of my skirt.

We waited on the tarmac. We spotted the yellow Cessna 210 as it taxied toward us. Paul, the pilot, jumped out. Everybody called him Paul Pilot. "Ready?" he asked. "We need to get going. There'll be thunderstorms this afternoon out to the West."

Paul often transported missionary children off to school. He knew it was important to not dally. One last hug and Tim and Peter clambered into the little plane. Paul stowed their gear, climbed into the cockpit, slammed the door. They waved, we waved, and they were on their way. The plane looked awfully small as it taxied down the runway. Then they were in the air, looking even smaller, just a little dot, and gone.

Stewart put his arm around me. "I didn't even get to kiss them good-bye," I sniffed. I reached in my pocket for a tissue and pulled out the keys. "And they won't even be able to open their suitcases," I sobbed.

Stewart looked as though he, too, might cry. Mary Beth and Martha watched us, wide-eyed. We walked slowly back to the car. Plenty of room now, just four of us.

"Do you suppose we can find that shop where they sell ice cream?" I asked.

"But Mom," Mary Beth said, "we just had breakfast."

"I think it would be okay," Stewart said, "just this once."

We stopped at the Post Office, put the keys in an envelope, and sent them off to "Peter and Tim Manchester, Sakeji School, Kanene, Northern Rhodesia." By the time the keys arrived, the boys had solved the problem with a hammer. The headmaster reprimanded them for bringing playing cards. He called them "sin cards."

We drove north across Northern Rhodesia, stopped overnight in Kitwe, stocked up on groceries, visited the Dairy Queen, and crossed the border, headed home to Jadotville.

Chapter Seventeen

Our downsized family of four arrived home without fanfare. The house was just as we left it. Pastor Joab and his wife came to greet us. Baba Samuel turned up and took over his familiar duties. The girls and I swept out the schoolroom and started lessons. Our worldly possessions were on the way—by ship to Lobito and eventually by train to Jadotville.

"You set the table for six again," Stewart said. He put his arm around my shoulder and pulled me to him. "I know, it's hard, but the boys will be happy at Sakeji."

Their first letters arrived. Peter wrote on 2-9-62 (see next page for original letter):

Dear Mom, dad, mary & martha,
Yesterday was pinch and hit day. We all the boys were pinching and hitting the girls the girls were dodning the same to us. It was a battle il never forget. Timmy was having a ball. after the bell rang for breakfast we had to (quick) quit. we do that every begining of the monts. I (hope) hope are toy suitcase is on the way. We have movies every week. we saw a cartoon of woody woodpeker. we are studying space in since. Tomorrow is (f) half turm we get a shiling worth of candy and we go swiming twice a day. we built a half turm hut everybody does. ours can fit five people but their is only (to) two of us Billy (mucher) michel (in) and I.
    Love, Peter Manchester

Dear Mom, dad, mary & martha

yesterday was pinch and hit day. We all
the boys were pinching and hitting the girls
the girls were dodning the same to us. It was
a battle it never forget. Jimmy was having
a ball. after the bell rang for breakfast we had
to (quick) quit. we do that every begining of the
monts. I (hope) hope are toy suitcase is on the way
. We have movies every week. we saw a cartoon
of woody woodpeker. we are studying space
in sience. Tomorrow is (f) half turm we get a
shiling worth of candy and we go swiming
twice a day. we built a half turm hut everybody does. ours can fit five people but their
is only (ld two of us Billy (mechers) michel
(in) and I.

                    Love
              Peter Manchester

"Yes, he does sound happy," I said. But pinching and hitting? That can't be right. And his spelling is atrocious."

"Funny, I never learned to spell either," Stewart said. "They must send them just the way the kids write them down."

Tim's letter, written the same day:

Dear Mom & Dad
Hope your fine, I am. Could you send me some white shoe pollish, I need it bad.
We are havind a nice time at the river too it's a very nice place to play making houces. Here is a rough picture of my room.
Your son,
Tim

(see next page for original letter)

"Most of his letter is a diagram of his room," I said. "They said all the children would write home every Sunday."

Those precious Sunday afternoon letters became my lifeline to my sons. I never mentioned their exotic spelling.

Six weeks passed. I wondered if our things were lost, strayed, or stolen. Then, one Saturday morning, a flatbed truck careened up the driveway, closely pursued by Stewart in the station wagon. I recognized the familiar trunks and steel barrels.

"I was driving home when I saw the mission truck tearing around the corner," Stewart said. "Boxes flying off the back, books scattered all over the road. Wait a minute, I thought, those look like *our* books. I flagged the guys down and scooped up the books. What a mess. I hope I got everything." He dumped an armload of battered theology texts onto the table. The workmen rolled the barrels up the sidewalk.

Mary Beth looked over the pile of boxes, trunks, and barrels on the screened porch. She said, "Where's *my* stuff? Can I open a box?" Stewart said he wanted to get organized first.

"I don't see the new Maytag," I said.

Sakajila.
2.9.62

Dear Mom & Dad

Hope your fine, I am. Could
you send me some white shoe
pollish, I need it bad.

We are having a nice time
at the river too it's a very
nice place to play making
houces. Here is a rough picture
of my room.

TOYS →

←PETE
SLEEPS
HERE IN
OTHER
ROOM

MY BED

CUPBOARD

"Oh, that. I have the paperwork. The washing machine will come later." Bad news for Baba Samuel. He'd continue to wash everything in the bathtub. He sighed and shuffled back to the ironing board.

Stewart arranged his books on the new shelves in the office. I set up the sewing machine and hemmed curtains. The girls sorted out their dolls and toys. The plumber finished the installation of the new water heater on the bathroom wall.

The town seemed unnaturally calm. The Blue Helmets of the United Nations patrolled the street in trucks. I felt the usual tension before the relief of the first rains of the season. Political storms were brewing as well.

Joab asked Stewart to drive him to one of the villages and conduct services for a few days before the rains began. Stewart suggested that we all go. "The girls might enjoy it, and you could use a break. It would be good to get out of town." My familiar quandary was whether to stay home and wish I had gone, or go and wish I had stayed home.

I asked him, "How far is it?"

"About a hundred kilometers. We'll be there for three days. Joab says there hasn't been a missionary there since 1934. Think of it! He wants to reach out to some of those remote places."

Joab had grown up in those remote places. When he was just a boy, the pioneer missionaries, Bishop and Mrs. Springer, had come to his village, and he had followed them, gone to school, become a pastor. Those were the days of real missionaries. Mrs. Springer would not have hesitated to go to a remote village. What was the matter with me?

"Mom, let's go," Mary Beth said. "It'll be fun."

Martha joined in, tugged at my skirt. "Yeah, Mom. Let's go."

I thought of the big Camp Meeting at Samusamb, the hippo hunt, the crocodile scare, the young boy rescued from the lip of the waterfall. Peter and Tim had been with us on that trip. I winced at the familiar ache of their absence. Stewart waited, raised his eyebrows. It was up to me. "Okay," I said. It would be a relief to get away from the soldiers.

I plunged into a flurry of preparation: food, water, bedding, first aid kit, camp stove, lanterns, clothes, books. Mrs. Springer would have been astonished. In those days, they traveled light.

The village people came out to meet us, clapping in rhythm, singing, and dancing. The wild, shrill ululations of the women and the primitive passion of their cries never failed to stir and frighten me.

Joab turned to me with a warm smile. "You see, mama, they are glad to see you."

"I'm glad somebody's glad to see me," I said. Joab's smile faded. I had stooped to sarcasm. In the rearview mirror, I saw Stewart's frown of disapproval. "I'm sorry, Joab. That was very rude."

Ever gracious, he said, "I know how hard it must be for you, mama."

We drove slowly through the crowd. Chickens bustled across the path. Mothers snatched their children out of the way. The village chief directed us to the grass hut they had prepared just for us. The hut was smaller than the station wagon. I shivered to think of all the lizards, spiders, and other creatures in that dry grass. We'd sleep in the car, Mary Beth on the front seat, Stewart, Martha, and me on an air mattress in the back. This was the era of big station wagons. Pastor Joab carried his little bag into the hut. He would sleep there.

We woke early to giggles. A dozen village children pressed their faces against the car windows. In our sleeping bags, we struggled out of our flannel pajamas and into our clothes. Stewart built a fire and cooked oatmeal. I mixed powdered milk with some of the water we had brought from home. Mary Beth and Martha arranged their dollies and their accessories on the tailgate. The villagers observed every development and had a lot to say. I wish I could have understood their comments. Mary Beth stayed close to me. The children loved to touch her blonde hair, and she shied away from them. They made a sort of game of it, grabbing at her pigtails. I didn't like to shoo them away, but Mary Beth needed my protection.

Stewart became the center of attention when he lathered his face and shaved. He squatted down to look in the rear-view mirror of the car. The little ones squealed and jumped up and down when he squirted shaving cream from the aerosol can into their hands. They just couldn't get enough of the exotic customs of the *wazungu*. Stewart and Joab went off to conduct the morning preaching service. The children gathered around to watch while Mary Beth, Martha, and I did lessons. We skipped the Pledge of Allegiance and went directly to spelling, reading, and arithmetic. We were onstage. In this village, there was no school, no teacher. Mrs. Springer would have found a teacher, started a school.

The night had been chilly, but the day was fiercely hot. I held out a big towel to give Mary Beth and Martha some privacy to change into their bathing suits, and we walked through the village to the stream. Shy at first, they soon joined the other children and splashed in the shallow water. Some of the children wore their ragged clothes, and some of them were naked. Mary Beth and Martha stared in wonder. I waded into the clear water. All around us, women scrubbed laundry and babies.

Joab and Stewart conducted morning and afternoon services and led literacy classes. They baptized a lot of people and served communion, the first in many years for this village. I wondered what it all meant to the Africans. How did they interpret the rituals of the church, baptisms, the communion service with crumbs of bread and little aluminum cups of grenadine? They watched Joab carefully, held up their hands in a sort of Boy Scout salute, and repeated after him, "*Yesu ni Bwana.*"

We toured their gardens full of carrots, beans, and, of course, manioc. One of the men raised strawberries. I wondered where he found a market for them. I never saw an African eat a strawberry. He filled a large basket, and I gave him the equivalent of ten dollars. His smile told me I had been generous. On the way home, we stopped at Mulungwishi to share our bounty with the missionaries there.

Home looked good to me. Our clothes and bedding smelled like sweat and woodsmoke. Baba Samuel grimaced. Where was that washing machine? At least we had a new water heater. No more heating water in a barrel over a fire in the yard—as long as the electricity worked, anyway. I drew a deep bath for the girls, added bubbles for a treat. They stayed in the tub a long time, playing with their rubber ducks and bickering amicably. I shampooed their hair, wrapped them in fresh towels, and helped them into clean pajamas. As was our custom, I took my turn in the tub, and then Stewart. Clean bodies, clean pajamas, clean sheets. God bless Baba Samuel. And real beds.

"That wasn't so bad, was it?" Stewart asked. He yawned. "I'm exhausted. How about you?"

"I'm okay." I felt churlish. I hadn't worked nearly as hard as he had. He'd driven on that awful road and preached and taught and listened to people all day. And cooked, so good of him. I can't cook over an open fire. I should have paid more attention in Girl Scouts.

"The girls seemed to enjoy themselves."

"Yes. I wish I could have just relaxed and not worried all the time about what might happen. They had such a good time in the stream, and all I could think about was bilharzia. And crocodiles."

"Sometimes you just have to have faith." He yawned again.

"I know. Isn't it funny, I was the one who wanted to come, and you're the one who's good at this. I don't know why I'm here. I'm just not comfortable with most of the Africans, and they know it. I'll get a tutor and work on my Swahili."

I looked over at Stewart. He was asleep. He'd been so happy in the village. Why was it so hard for me? My mother was right, I wasn't cut out to be a missionary. I couldn't even stand to see children with runny noses. And I couldn't seem to get used to being the center of all that attention, every action discussed. And what was the big deal about cleanliness? I thought of that day in Kitwe when Diane and I scrubbed our son's socks. Maybe cleanliness really was next to Godliness. At least I wouldn't wake up in the morning with all those faces pressed against the window, watching me. I didn't want to study more Swahili. I wanted to go home, and the only home I had was right here.

When I look back at that last year in Africa, I marvel at the normality of our days—most of our days, anyway. Every morning, lessons with Mary Beth and Martha. Every week, letters from Peter and Tim. Every day, people dropped in. I served meals, attended meetings.

In anticipation of Mary Beth's eighth birthday, I sewed a new dress for her and planned a party for six little girls. On the day before her big day, I put together a cake with a couple of eggs from our allotment from the flock at Mulungwishi and a bit of margarine. Stewart had stumbled across a case of powdered milk in a rundown shop. I no longer flinched when I sifted the weevils from the flour. We had long since put to rest the lame joke that when we ate the bugs and threw out the flour, it was time to go home. It was long past time to go home. No candles, after all those power failures. How could I have forgotten to bring little birthday candles from the States? I dug out the Advent wreath from the Christmas box, cut the candles in half, and stuck them in the frosted cake. I rationed our supply of matches from Rhodesia. There had been none in the local shops for weeks.

Stewart and Joab drove away early in the morning in the mission truck to visit some remote villages. He promised Mary Beth he'd be back in time to watch her blow out the candles. He missed the party. Evening came, the sudden darkness followed. Mary Beth and Martha were asleep. Hours later, a car drove in. I heard voices outside. The car drove away. Stewart stumbled in, exhausted. Without saying a word, he waved me away, went directly to the kitchen. He filled a glass with water and re-filled it, again and again.

"Are you all right?"

"More or less."

He set down the glass, wiped his face on a dishtowel. "I've never been so thirsty. The truck broke down in a village about fifty miles out. We worked on it for a couple of hours. There wasn't a single car or truck in the village. Not even a bicycle. Finally, a truck came by. Some chiefs had been to a celebration. It was afternoon by the time the men finished off two cases of beer." Stewart drank more water. "The driver offered to give us a lift back. We left the mission truck in the village and got in the car with the drunken chauffeur. The radiator went dry, I gave him half of our drinking water. We jounced along, not saying much. After a while, the driver said this was where he turned off. Joab and I got out and walked. We didn't meet a single soul. No villages, no cars, no bicycles, no shade. The sun was ferocious. We were pretty used up, and so thirsty. After an hour or so a car came along with a bunch of guys who had driven up from Rhodesia on an old route through the bush. I didn't even know the road existed. It wasn't really a road, more of a track. They gave us a ride into town." He gulped another glass of water.

"I thought of going out to look for you, but I didn't know where you were."

"You never would have found us."

"What about the truck?"

"It can wait. I'll take one of the mechanics out there with me. Those old trucks are a disaster waiting to happen. We should have taken the Ford."

He took off his shoes and socks. I winced to see the blisters. "Are the girls asleep?"

"Yes, they tried to wait up for you. They were worn out."

"I'm sorry I missed the party. Was Mary Beth upset?"

"Yes, but she got over it."

Late in October, the General Secretary of African Affairs, from New York, came through on a lightning inspections tour. Pastors, teachers, laymen, and laywomen gathered from all over the district for a big regional meeting in the church in Mulungwishi. Bishop and Mrs. Booth showed up. President Moïse Tshombe dropped by, unannounced, with a delegation from the United Nations. We scurried for more coffee urns and raided our pantries for popcorn and cookies.

I'm quite sure none of the dignitaries had given a thought to Halloween. The missionary children added a note of surrealism to the scene, dressed, as usual, in the same set of costumes, cowboys, pirates, and ghosts in pillowcases. The general secretary, known for his preference for current sociological jargon, discussed the "structured and non-structured" aspects of the work. I couldn't help myself. I giggled, envisioning Tinkertoys, structured and unstructured, scattered all over the floor. I have a low tolerance for pomposity.

The meeting degenerated into a heated argument about automobiles. Why hadn't the people in America sent cars to the Africans? And why didn't the missionaries share their cars? The G.S. meant well. He listened. He may have been surprised or disappointed, perhaps, about the resentment that had built up about the ownership of vehicles. There was so much to be done and so little he could do. He would return to New York and take refuge with the other executives in their comfortable offices in the Interchurch Center on Riverside Drive, high above it all.

The United Nations finally lost patience with Tshombe and issued an ultimatum: Katanga must reunite with the Léopoldville government by

November 15th. Friday morning, the banks didn't open. It was rumored that the government would appropriate 5 percent of every account and 50 percent of rental income: a gift for Independence.

One afternoon, a delegation of Kipendano women appeared at the door. I invited them in, served tea. They made themselves comfortable, shifted the babies from their backs, set the toddlers on the floor. This was not a social visit. They had come to set me straight. They lectured me on what they expected of me, and how I failed to meet their expectations. I didn't take them in the car to the wholesale market and buy fabric and sewing supplies. I should conduct sewing classes, as the other mamas did. I didn't drive them to the villages to conduct evangelistic services. And I didn't send my children away to school, as the other missionaries did.

"Mama, you spend all your time with your children."

"Why did you come here, mama?"

"Don't you love Jesus?"

Martha stood beside me. She glared at the women and watched me carefully, too, not understanding their Swahili, uncertain what was happening, but sure it wasn't good news. Their accusations hurt. I chose my words carefully.

"God gave me these children," I said. My voice shook. I took a deep breath. "God expects me to care for my children, as you care for your children. When you send your children away, you send them to family members. My family is far away, across the ocean."

The women looked around at each other, frowned, shook their heads. They gathered up their children, fastened the babies onto their backs with that graceful flourish I loved. They filed out the door.

"*Kwenda vizuri,*" I said in as firm a voice as I could manage.

"*Bakia vizuri, mama,*" they muttered.

I watched them go. They didn't bother to lower their indignant voices. Martha stood by me, holding on to my skirt. I had a sudden vision of the church ladies back in America, so quick to find fault with me.

I didn't cry until they were well down the path. Martha broke away and ran after the women. She yelled at them. "You mean old ladies; you made my mother cry."

They didn't turn. They probably didn't even hear her. Anyway, they wouldn't have understood her words. We were a long way from understanding each other.

Stewart came home, and Martha met him at the door. He swooped her up into his arms. "What's up?" he said.

"Those ladies made Mom cry. They said she was bad."

"She looks pretty good to me," he said, with a puzzled smile.

"I'll tell you later," I said.

After the girls were tucked into bed, teeth brushed, prayers said, Stewart and I sat side by side on the uncomfortable vinyl-covered couch. The specter of the cranky women hovered in the room. I told Stewart about the visitation. He rested his chin on his hand. I wasn't sure how much sympathy he felt for me. My dilemma made his life more complicated. We didn't agree about sending the children away. He knew how stubborn I could be when I thought I was in the right.

"Why don't you talk to Lois?" he suggested.

Good idea. Everybody loved and respected Lois and Maurice. They had years of experience in Africa—in Liberia and the Congo. In 1924, when he was a young man, Maurice had served as chauffeur for Bishop and Mrs. Springer. Mrs. Springer christened the car, a Model A Ford, "Ophelia Bumps." I loved to hear the old bishop tell of their travels through the bush on overgrown tracks before there were roads.

"Let's have a cup of tea," Lois said, in her brisk manner. "I'll just put on the kettle." Afternoon tea was a ritual for her. Everyone, black and white, came to her for advice, seeking her wisdom and comfort. She found time for all of us. She listened carefully as I poured out my anguish. The African women had already shared with her their displeasure with me.

"Of course you must put your children first," she said. She had taught their sons, David and Jon, in their early years. When the boys were eight and ten, they went away to boarding school.

"Let's find time to work on your Swahili together," she offered. "Perhaps you can help the women with special projects. Go to the meetings when you can, and look for opportunities to get involved, when you feel comfortable."

The Kipendano women and I went forward in a sort of truce, careful of one another. I heard muttering, saw shoulders shrugged. Martha watched them carefully, protective of me. She twitched away when any of the women touched her.

The women looked forward to their annual district meeting at the end of the rainy season, a weekend away from husbands and home duties. Forty delegates would gather at the church in Kambove, sleep on the floor in the church, on grass mats. I helped where I could, drove the women to shops to buy food and supplies. They gloried in the endless planning sessions, debated who would preach and lead worship. I lost patience. I complained to Lois.

"Why does it take them so long to decide?" I whined. "Everybody has to weigh in on everything, and they just go round and round. What a waste of time."

Lois drew her brows together in a frown. It wasn't like her to be cross. "You must realize," she said tartly, "twenty years ago, none of these women would have dared say a word in church. We must never forget what it means to them to have control over something in their lives."

I saw them in a new light and felt a new kinship with them.

On the appointed Friday afternoon, Lois and I loaded the Volkswagen bus with bed rolls, camp stoves, cases of soft drinks, baskets of bread and smelly dried fish, and as many mamas and babies as we could pack in. An hour later we drove up the steep hill to the Kambove church and schoolhouse. A crowd of women surrounded the car, clapping their hands, dancing, and singing, "*Asante kufika, Asante kufika* [Thank you for coming, thank you for coming]." Lois seemed to know everybody, greeted each one by name, asked about their families. I resolved to follow her example, to get to know these women. They were dressed in their best clothes, wrapped in yards and yards of bright patterned cloth in hues of cobalt and turquoise blue, brick red, bright orange and yellow, vivid green. Cloths tied around their heads hid their intricate braids. Another length of printed cotton tied around the body held the baby, on the back for travel, on the front for nursing. Heads jounced as the mothers trotted along. I loved to see the babies' little feet sticking out of the cloth on either side of their mamas. My custom of parking the baby in a stroller seemed perverse. I felt inarticulate and awkward among the crowd of lively African women, drab in my drip-dry skirt and blouse. I pushed myself to be part of the scene, not a bystander. I used my rudimentary Swahili. It was easy to admire those precious babies.

We put our bedrolls on woven straw mats lined up on the floor of the mudbrick, two-room school. Lois and I had brought air mattresses. We entertained the crowd as we huffed and puffed and the mattresses took shape. The women started the camp stove outdoors and made tea for everyone. It grew dark; the campfire blazed. We sat on the ground under the stars and sang hymns in Swahili. The brilliant Southern Cross dominated the heavens. The crescent moon disappeared into the trees before the songs and testimonies ended. The babies were long asleep. By lantern light, we found our pallets in the schoolhouse. The women closed the tiny windows to shut out the last bit of fresh air and sang and talked most of the night.

At dawn, the hostess committee brought warm water for washing and hot water for instant coffee. We ate some chunks of bread and assembled in the mudbrick church for the opening worship service. I found it hard to follow the sermon of the district secretary. Her complicated parables were too much for me. We plunged into the business meeting, heard reports of the year's work in each of the twenty towns and preaching places represented. Women brought forward coins tied up in a cloth, their sacrificial offering accumulated through the year. Altogether, they had raised almost ninety dollars for the girls' scholarship fund at the secondary school. How had they managed to do this, when they had so little? Their generosity and dedication overwhelmed me. They had given so much, and I had been stingy, even with my time. Shame on me.

The election of officers dragged on through the afternoon. A delicate balance of power had to be maintained among the tribal groups represented. The process broke down when the candidate for vice president, under intensive questioning, admitted her husband had taken a second wife. The church had a strong position against polygamy, and she finally withdrew her name. I felt sorry for her. It wasn't her fault her husband had broken the rules.

After the election of officers, a woman wearing a midnight-blue velvet floor-length opera cape swept down the aisle and made an impassioned speech, which I couldn't follow. Had I been wearing such a stunning cape, I'm sure I, too, would have been compelled to show it off. The used-clothing street bazaars in the Third World yield an amazing variety of outmoded garments. Her cloak was outstanding. She wore it well.

Lois woke on Sunday morning to find her air mattress had leaked during the night. "I have a flat," she said, and laughed at her discomfort. Then everybody laughed at me as a dear little baby, curled up on the mat beside his mother, woke up, looked at me, and began to scream. I tried to console the baby, reached out to him. He screamed louder and clung to his mother. African mothers tell their children to be good or the white folks will get them. I knew the history. How could I forget what the Africans suffered at the hands of the white colonialists? How could I explain I wouldn't hurt him for the world?

We walked down to the river. I waded in the clear cold water while others bathed. The babies squealed and tried to catch tadpoles that flashed in the sun as their mothers sudsed and dunked them.

All cleaned up, ready for church, we crowded onto the backless benches for two hours of songs, prayers, Scripture, and long sermons. The sun beat down on the tin roof, causing sudden loud pings as the metal expanded. Flies and mosquitoes and insects I didn't recognize flew in and out the open windows and droned around us. Babies cried, were shushed, and nursed.

For Sunday dinner, the ladies served *bukadi* with fish sauce and stewed greens with *pilipili*. The local pastor's wife prepared rice for Lois and me, a much-appreciated kindness. I never developed a fondness for *bukadi*. We all sat on the ground, our chipped white enamel plates in our laps.

Cars and trucks from Mulungwishi brought more women and girls to the final session. We packed the church as the students sang. They presented a drama based on the Biblical tale of "The Wise and Foolish Virgins." The stoniest critic would have given it a rave review. The five foolish virgins, one toting a baby on her back, admired each other's dresses and hairdos. They rushed off—too late—to buy oil for their lamps as the wise virgins filed smugly into the wedding feast. The foolish virgins begged them to share their oil. In vain, they beat on the door, entreated the bridegroom to let them in. Finally, they trooped away in defeat. They sobbed loudly as the audience applauded.

I joined the circle of women outside, danced in a circle, clapped hands, and sang. I watched to see the pattern of the dance, a shuffle to one side, pause, swing hips, shuffle to the other side. The pattern changed constantly. I did my clumsy best, laughed along with the women who nudged each other and pointed at me.

They supported each other, made the best of what they had. I admired their selflessness, their dedication, their devotion, their faith.

We gathered goods and people into the cars and trucks as the Kambove ladies clapped and sang. Were they singing "*Asante Kwenda?* [Thank you for going?]" I concentrated on driving the bus down the steep, narrow rutted track. Their eerie ululations echoed through the trees.

"*Kwenda vizuri*," they called.

"*Bakia vizuri*," we responded.

My passengers sang all the way home. On this one day, at least, we loved one another.

Chapter Eighteen

I counted the days in December until our trip to Sakeji. I longed to have the boys home again, sleeping in their blue bedroom, filling the empty chairs around the dining room table, teasing the girls. I treasured their weekly letters. The girls and I completed lesson sixty, a hundred more to go. We'd take a break while the boys were home.

The girls packed and re-packed their little suitcases. They chattered about what they'd wear at Sakeji. They watched the kittens at play with a small lizard the mother cat had brought in. Mary Beth was horrified. Martha was enchanted. She put a stick down the back of Mary Beth's sun suit and told her it was the lizard. Mary Beth screamed and ran around the room, trying to shake it off. Martha laughed.

"You'd better not try that when your brothers are home," I told her. "You might find out how it feels to have a real live lizard down your back."

We had specific instructions for the trip. We would arrive no earlier than four o'clock on Monday afternoon. On Tuesday morning there would be a Christmas party, a pick-up lunch, and prompt departure. Stewart took extra care with preparations and make sure to include the usual jerry cans, ax, and shovel. Ed Mathews insisted we borrow his block and tackle. "Just in case," he said. I prepared the picnic basket and filled jugs with water. The girls made final decisions about pajamas, party dresses, and Sunday shoes, coloring books, and dolls. No kittens.

Heavy rains had fallen late in the season. "I hope the station wagon can handle it," Stewart said. He had traveled that road once before in the Volkswagen, in the dry season, searching for the headwaters of the Lualaba River.

On Sunday morning, we stopped in several villages to conduct services. We spent the night in the mission guest house in Kolwezi, got an early start and slogged into Mutshasha, a tiny town on the railroad where another missionary family, also bound for Sakeji, waited for us in their Jeep. We launched in tandem into the forest, fifty miles of deep, sticky mud ahead.

You couldn't really call it a road. It was more like a track, or a primitive trail. The car lurched along for about an hour, then suddenly bucked, and slowed to a stop. Stewart grimaced. "Bad spot for a flat." He stepped out into the mud, shook his head. "It's the tire. I'll put on the spare." He wrestled the tools out of the car and thrashed around in the mud, muttered to himself.

"We won't be able to get that tire fixed until we get to Sakeji," he said, wiping the muck off his shoes with his handkerchief. "We'll have to go on a wing and a prayer."

As it turned out, we couldn't get the tire fixed until we got all the way back to Kolwezi. The Jeep and the station wagon crept along, slid down one slippery hill after another. If we missed the narrow bridge at the bottom of each gully, we'd be deep in the swamp. Other cars had passed this way, and the deep ruts of their passage carried a warning. "You should not be here. Save yourselves. Go back if you can, before it's too late."

The forest seemed uninhabited. Once I thought I saw two men some distance away, but it might have been an illusion. No villagers or children ran out to greet us. No chickens fled in terror. Rain poured down, and the mudholes were even more treacherous. We crossed the Lualaba, just a small stream, no signs posted. Stewart recognized the place, confirmed it on an ancient map of the terrain. Not a roadmap. The same map affirmed we would soon cross the unmarked border into Northern Rhodesia. When we were almost there, the rain stopped. Tendrils of sunlight crept into the forest.

We emerged into a sort of meadow after a mile or two and turned onto a paved road. At ten minutes past four, we pulled up to the entrance to Sakeji School. A crowd of kids lined the road and hung on the gates. Peter came over from the soccer field, uncharacteristically shy. Tim appeared, and we shed some discreet tears together. A cluster of little girls took Mary Beth and Martha in hand and escorted them to the play-house and the sandbox. Peter and Tim gave us a guided tour of their classrooms, their dormitory, the playing fields, the infirmary, and the dispensary. I couldn't help but be impressed and pleased with all that went on inside the simple brick buildings.

The librarian introduced herself. "We have over four thousand books in the collection. The reading average per term is twenty-three books per student. Your boys are great readers. You must be so proud of them."

She handed us off to another teacher. "The children are on the run all day, with plenty of active sports. Supper at five. 'All-Ins' at seven o'clock, bedtime at eight, not an unreasonable hour after an active day. They get plenty of wholesome food, lots of rich fresh milk from our dairy."

"There's a continual soccer game on the field," one of the friendly dads told us. "Most of the kids play barefoot, but they're required to wear shoes to class and to meals. Everyone sleeps under mosquito nets. No screens, except in the dining room." The dads were impressed we had driven that beastly track through the forest. Most of them had flown in from various missions in their own planes. Some had made the long drive on the paved road from Kitwe.

After dinner, the little ones changed into pajamas and robes, and the older ones cleaned up a bit. Everyone gathered in the lounge. The young-sters sat together on the floor to sing carols. I could barely sing, a lump in my throat, all those sweet young voices. Some parents had prepared special numbers. Two boys played trumpets. We all listened to *Scrooge* on the phonograph. I never liked that story. A troop of little girls collected Mary Beth and Martha. Time for bed. The boys gave up their narrow cots to their parents and slept on mats on the floor in the dispensary.

The parents and teachers shared coffee and fruitcake. Many of the families had a long history of children at Sakeji. They introduced us to other parents, and we all talked about our children. Everyone spoke well of the place. I couldn't help but be impressed.

Peter and Tim had covered a year's work in three months. Peter had completed the fifth grade, and Tim the sixth. They would be promoted with their age group, into the sixth and seventh grades. This was very much to their advantage. Otherwise, they might lose a year when we returned, eventually, to American schools. I liked their teachers, and the teachers seemed to like my boys. Dedicated, cheerful, and lively, they were confident the boys could do the work. "All the boys idolize the young headmaster, Mr. Hess," Tim's teacher added. I had yet to meet him.

I fell in love with kindly old Dr. Hoyte, a pioneer missionary who had cut short his retirement in England when the school needed him. He seemed like an elderly grandfather, a comforter to a child who might need consolation. I tried not to think about January 23rd when the boys would return to Sakeji. I comforted myself, assured myself they were happy and would be well cared for.

Stewart and I were introduced to the traditional Sakeji breakfast, rice cakes, oatmeal, tea, toast, and marmalade. A jar of the notorious Marmite on every table. I passed. After breakfast, Stewart took the car over to the little store at a nearby farm, where he hoped to get the tire fixed. No luck.

I followed Tim and all the big kids down to the Sakeji River on their quest to gather greens to decorate the hall for the Christmas party. Most of them were already barefoot. Others shucked their shoes and waded as they gathered branches from the overhanging trees.

The land sloped down to the water, and the flow could be diverted through a canal into a concrete swimming pool and a smaller shallow wading pool. Below the pools, the water fed back into the stream. This ingenious arrangement assured fresh water for the twice-weekly swim day. They had even built a diving platform and a slide. The mud pool, where the river widened out, was irresistible. The big kids were allowed to take the three canoes out on the water. There were trees to climb, a rope swing, places to hide, everything children could possibly need to be happy, right there, five minutes from the school. In bright sunlight and deep shade, the river hummed along over rocks and sand, the happy barefoot children chattered.

I fell into conversation with a teacher, an American lady, probably in her fifties. She confided her joy to have the first and second graders in her care. She had never married, and here she was with all these little ones, who came to her as they would to their own mothers and showed her their treasures.

The big kids carried and dragged branches to decorate the halls. We followed them back up the hill, just in time for tea and biscuits served on the lawn. Three airplanes arrived, one after another. Paul the pilot came in the mission plane to pick up several students and deliver them to Kitwe. The second plane bore the brand of the South Africa General Mission, a group who worked, not in South Africa, I was assured, but in Rhodesia. The third plane was greeted with cheers. The Cartwrights had arrived. We were especially glad to see them. Our friendship went all the way back to West Hartford. Keith and Lucille had been among the first of the missionaries in training at the Hartford School of Missions to invite us to join them in the Congo. Just a week ago, Keith had flown into Jadotville to take Stewart and the girls sightseeing over the town. Their son, Johnny Jay, had helped Peter and Tim come to terms with Sakeji protocol.

All cleaned up and dressed in their best, the kids put on a show: relay races on the field in the center of the quadrangle. Everybody was summoned into the Main Hall, beautifully done up with greens and a lovely big Christmas tree from the forest. We sang carols, accompanied by the piano and violins and trumpets. Father Christmas made an entrance, jolly and clever and funny. The children gave three cheers. He passed out candy and toys. Everybody stood up and, sang "God Save the Queen." We filed into the dining hall for a hurried lunch.

A hard rain poured down for twenty minutes. "That isn't going to do that road much good," Stewart said. I envied those who had come by plane. Everyone was anxious to get underway. By one o'clock we were ready to go.

We joined the crowd to watch the planes take off. The first plane spewed muddy water, used all the runway, rose slowly into the air, and cleared the trees. We cheered and hollered and waved them on their way.

The second plane followed with no trouble at all and vanished in the cloudy sky.

The Cartwrights waved as they roared down the grassy runway. They couldn't seem to get up speed. "Go back," shouted someone in the crowd. "You aren't going to make it." The plane gave a burst of speed and rose abruptly into the air. The motor burped and missed. The little plane drifted silently down into the trees at the end of the runway. The right wing hit the stump of a big branch. The engine tore loose and shot out ahead. The fuselage caught in the branches. The plane cartwheeled, tipped up on its nose, and stopped upside down. It was like watching a movie in slow motion.

The doctor dads, four of them, sprang into action and ran toward the wreckage. Johnny Cartwright emerged from the trees and ran toward us. "A doctor," he yelled. "My mother needs a doctor." He bent over, trying to get his breath. "My sisters are all right," he panted. "My dad is trying to get my mother out of the plane."

There was an unspoken fear of fire. The men worked like demons to get Lucille free from the wreckage. She was caught by her ankle. Finally, they pulled her out of the plane and lowered her to the ground. She suffered a broken arm, a broken ankle, and cuts on her face and head. She was in shock. Keith said he was okay. "Don't worry about me. We've got to get Lucille to the hospital." The doctors conferred as they bandaged her and checked Keith and the two little daughters for cuts and bruises.

The nearest mission hospital was sixteen miles away. Someone offered a station wagon and Lucille was carefully laid on a mattress in the back, blankets tucked around her. Keith insisted he would drive. The doctors said no. One of them would drive, and one would ride in the back with her. Teachers assured Keith they would take care of his children. He climbed into the car and they drove away.

It seemed miraculous the children were unhurt. Johnny Jay told his story over and over to an attentive audience. He had kept his head through the whole thing, clamped his hand over his sister's mouth when she began to scream just before the crash.

Everyone was invited into the dining hall for tea. Word came from the hospital by short-wave radio that Lucille was resting comfortably, but the X-ray machine was broken. They would need to take her to a bigger hospital. Paul Pilot would bring the Methodist plane back and take her to Kitwe. Stewart was to leave immediately for Kolwezi, so that word of the accident would be sent out in the morning on the regular short-wave mission broadcast. We were instructed to take a more direct back-country road, rather than the way we had come. Heavy showers were predicted.

By midafternoon we were on our way, in convoy with another family, through uninhabited country, with no spare tire, over a track even worse than the one we had traveled, said to be a shorter route. Had that been only the previous day?

The children were quiet in the back seat. Too quiet.

"That was fun to see Santa this morning," I ventured.

Tim corrected me. "Father Christmas."

"I was glad he didn't bring along Zwarte Piet, the one who threatens to put coal in your wooden shoes if you aren't good. I guess the Brits don't do that." No response.

I tried again. "It was lovely to hear you all sing. That carol was new to me. "While Shepherds watch their flocks by night."

Peter took the bait. "Yeah, we have our own version of that song." He started to sing. "While shepherds washed their socks by night/all seated 'round the tub/the Angel of the Lord came out and they began to scrub/ They scrubbed and scrubbed and scrubbed and scrubbed until their socks were white/so Santa Claus could bring them toys on Christmas Eve that night."

"That's a good song," Mary Beth said. "Teach me that song."

We all learned it. We sang it over and over as we drove along until we got tired of it. We sang "Away in a Manger" and "O Little Town of Bethlehem."

The light faded into deep darkness. Headlights revealed vestiges of the track ahead. Following a downpour, we splashed along slowly and became hopelessly bogged down in the deepest, stickiest mud I ever hope to see. There's a special name in Africa for that morass, "black cotton." Strong men shudder at the name.

Our men and boys shucked their shoes and socks, rolled their pants up to the knee, and struggled for two hours to free us from the sticky muck. Had Ed Mathews not insisted we take his block and tackle, we would be there yet. The men hitched our car onto the trunk of a huge tree. Stewart put the car into low gear and gunned the motor. The motor whined in shrill protest. I held my breath. We inched forward and freed ourselves, only to bog down again.

The driver of the other car found sufficient traction in the grass along the track to pull us out of the mudhole. Then we just ignored the road and drove through the bush for a while until we got past the worst of it.

"This will make a good letter home," Stewart mused.

Tim said, "I wish we were home right now, writing a letter about it."

We arrived in Kolwezi before midnight. The resident missionaries put a pizza in the oven and made some phone calls. News of the accident would go out on the regular morning shortwave broadcast to all the mission stations. Hot baths all around, and beds for everybody.

In the morning, Stewart could hardly walk. He got the tire fixed, and we came home to Jadotville without incident. My family restored, I set the breakfast table. I scooped the oatmeal into six bowls and blinked back tears of joy.

Mary Beth piped up. "Mom, I want to go to Sakeji School. They have a playhouse and everything."

Tim glared at her. "Mary, you have no idea what you're talking about," he sneered. Peter looked at Tim, eyes wide.

Tim looked at Stewart, and then at me. "We're not going back."

Peter started to say something. Tim looked daggers at him. "You just shut up."

"Whoa there," Stewart said, "you can't talk to your brother like that. What do you mean, you're not going back? Of course you're going back."

"I'm not going back," Tim said.

"I thought you were happy there," I said. "Your letters were so cheerful. Did something happen?"

"Mom, the headmaster caned me. He hit me with his cane. Because I hadn't memorized my Bible verses." He tried so hard to hold back the tears.

"Would you tell me a little more about that?"

"We have to memorize Bible verses every day or we don't get any breakfast. He canes us. He caned me."

"That's terrible," I said. "We can't have that. I won't have that."

Peter found his voice. "He doesn't cane the girls. Only the boys."

"Oh, shut up, Peter," Tim said. "You never get caned. You just make nice."

"You didn't mention this in your letters," Stewart said. "You sounded so happy."

"Yes," I said. "Why didn't you tell us?"

"They read our letters," Tim said. "They tell us our parents are doing the Lord's work and we mustn't say anything that might distress them. They take that letter, and we have to write a different one. A cheerful letter."

Peter chimed in. "On Sunday afternoon we all get together in the library and write letters home. If they don't like what we write, we have to do them over."

"They censor your letters," I said. "That's terrible."

"Promise me you won't send me back," Tim said to me.

I thought of the Biblical word, beseech. Ruth and Naomi. "Beseech me not to leave thee."

My heart sank. "Tim, I can't promise that right now. I need to know more. But I can promise you, right now, the headmaster will never lay hands on you again. That is unforgivable."

I looked at Stewart. I shook my head. "We didn't know."

"Well, they have to go back. We don't have a choice."

"We always have a choice. We just have to decide how to handle this. We can't let that awful man punish Tim for not memorizing a Bible verse. The headmaster! Imagine! And he seemed so nice."

"Let's set it aside, for now. We only have them for six weeks. We can't let it spoil Christmas."

Chapter Nineteen

For two-and-a-half years, Moïse Tshombe, adroit shapeshifter and poster boy for the Methodists, kept Katanga independent from the rest of the Congo. In December 1962, he threatened to turn his mercenaries loose on the United Nations forces.

U Thant, elected to lead the United Nations after the death of Dag Hammarskjöld in a suspicious plane crash, finally lost patience with Tshombe and launched an offensive called Operation Grand Slam. Jadotville, with its strategic mining and ore-processing installations, was in the crosshairs of both armies. The Katanga troops threatened to destroy the city, street by street, rather than let it fall into the hands of the UN.

On the morning of December 28th, Stewart drove around town as he did early every day, checking in with the pastors. I hadn't even cleared the breakfast dishes when he rushed in the front door.

"We've got to leave. Right now. Ten minutes max. Just grab what you can and get the kids in the car. It's really bad."

Mary Beth carried a basketful of kittens. "We can't leave them here, they might get hurt," she pleaded, in vain.

Stewart drove fast through town, on our way to Mulungwishi. Mary Beth wailed in the back seat. Peter seemed subdued, not a single "knock-knock" joke. His face was flushed. I reached back to feel his forehead. He had a fever.

The Mulungwishi campus was unnaturally quiet. The students and pastors and teachers had gone to their villages for the holiday.

Was it just three days ago we had spent Christmas here? The children on the campus, black and white, had put on a simple Nativity pageant. Mary and Joseph tended a real baby in the manger. The boys in their bathrobes, turbans, and makeshift crowns on their heads, carried gifts of perfume bottles and jewelry boxes for the Christ Child. The other children were shepherds or angels with tinseled cardboard wings. We sang the familiar carols. I thought of the tenuous circumstances of that first Christmas. Mary and Joseph needed shelter for the birth and escaped to Egypt to save themselves and the baby from Herod's legions.

Andrea and I had helped the little girls shed their wings. Her family was headed for a few days in Rhodesia. She offered us their house.

"Spend the vacation here, with the others," she said. "You don't want to be all by yourselves in Jadotville."

I turned to Stewart. "What do you think? It would be nice to be here with everybody."

"I think I might be needed in Jadotville. After Christmas, I could bring you out here, and you and the kids can stay at Andrea's and enjoy yourselves."

We threaded our way home to Jadotville through the roadblocks on Christmas night.

Three days later, we fled back to Mulungwishi and settled into Andrea's house. I unpacked our suitcases. Stewart looked surprised to find his good suit in the closet. His only suit.

"Of all things, why did you bring my suit?"

I shrugged. "It just seemed the thing to do. You look so handsome in it. And it's the most expensive thing we own."

"We mustn't get attached to our worldly possessions."

I was ashamed to tell him the real reason. I didn't want to see that suit on one of those scruffy soldiers. This felt different from the other times we had fled from home in a hurry. This time we might lose everything. I couldn't tell him about a dream I'd had. Stewart in a coffin, dressed in his best suit, his shoes shined.

Peter's symptoms strongly indicated hepatitis. I walked with him down to the dispensary to consult with the campus nurse. The lab wasn't equipped to do the necessary tests. Contact with the clinic in Jadotville was out of the question, and the nurse couldn't give Peter any medication without a confirmed diagnosis. He recommended I put Peter to bed and keep him in isolation, give him vitamins to keep up his strength, and aspirin to bring down the fever. I remembered my own episode of hepatitis.

I heard the names long before I met the people: Doris and Woody. Woody and Doris. Those names were inseparable from Mulungwishi. Woody had served for many years as superintendent of the Ecole d'Apprentissage Pédagogique (Teacher Training School) and had founded the School of Theology. Doris was in charge of the Women's School. They had recently returned from an extended furlough in the States.

Doris was famous for her roses. Wild roses covered a lattice that arched over the front door of their sweet little cottage, and the fragrance of those flowers welcomed everyone.

I sensed a new energy when I visited the campus. If there was intra-tribal hostility, it was under control. Settled in at Andrea's, I had a perfect opportunity to get to know Woody and Doris.

Their daughter, Lorry, a teenager, attended a boarding school in Southern Rhodesia. She was home with her parents for the holidays. Everyone loved Lorry, especially all the little girls. She wore a red jacket, purchased in the States, with a feature never seen before by any of us: Velcro! We couldn't get enough of the sound as she pulled the coat open: "Thrupp." When Lorry outgrew the coat, she passed it on to Mary Beth. "Thrupp."

Ragged soldiers from the Katanga militia drifted through the campus all day. Some of them were sure to be deserters on their way to their villages. The layout of the mission made any sort of defense impossible. The houses were scattered over the hillsides, the school buildings and dormitories and church clustered in the central valley. A cross crowned the highest hill.

The missionary families would need to keep in close touch with each other. There were no phones, of course, and the African boys and girls who carried messages from house to house were gone. We monitored the BBC on shortwave radio.

Soldiers shuffled by on the road, singly and in small bunches, looking for transport. The mission vehicles included several Volkswagens, a couple of trucks, and vans. Stewart parked our big white Ford station wagon behind the house. He and Tim cut brush and tree limbs and piled them over the car. It looked absurd, decorated for some sort of arboreal procession.

That evening Woody declared a blackout. No exceptions. The night seemed unusually long, the smallest sound ominous. Woody was at our door at first light to collect Stewart and patrol the property. The single light at the entrance to the mission had been left on all night, as though it were a welcome sign.

All the missionary families were expected to gather for a communal breakfast. I mixed up a big batch of biscuits and put the kettle on for Nescafé. We had eggs, plenty of bananas, and mangoes. As I slid the first tray of biscuits into the oven, a tremendous deep *whoomph*, echoed across the valley. I thought the oven had exploded. A second boom and the ceiling light crashed to the floor behind me and scattered shards of glass across the floor. Peter, Mary Beth, and Martha appeared, wide-eyed and barefoot. I shooed them away from the broken glass. Twin towers of dense black smoke rose from the trees, not more than a half-mile to the West.

Stewart came up the hill and burst into the kitchen, breathless. "The bridges," he panted. "They've blown up the railroad bridge and the road bridge. They've cut off the soldiers' escape route." He looked around the kitchen. "Where's Tim?"

"I thought he was with you."

Woody came through the door and stopped short when he saw broken glass all over the floor. "The chandelier fell down," I said.

"I wouldn't exactly call it a chandelier," Stewart said, "more like a light fixture."

I shrugged and swept up the glass. Was something burning? I'd forgotten the biscuits. Stewart and Woody went out to search for Tim.

Peter said, "I feel better. Can I get dressed?"

"Where is your brother?" I asked him. Never one to conceal his thoughts, he struggled with something. I knelt, took hold of his shoulders, and looked directly into his eyes. "Peter, this is important. Your brother might be in danger."

He confessed. "We play army. We follow the soldiers. We carry sticks and pretend they're guns. I wasn't supposed to tell."

My heart was a stone in my chest. I dumped the charred biscuits into a paper bag for the chickens and started a new batch.

Stewart and Tim came up the hill. I ran outside and hugged Tim to me.

"We were just playing soldiers," he said. "We crawl on our bellies through the tall grass. They don't even know we're there." He wiggled free of my embrace. "They blew up the bridges. I saw it. Don't worry, Mom, we weren't in any danger."

Where had I heard that before?

"Promise me you won't do that again."

"Okay," he said. I believed him. He would never admit to being scared. He must have been really close to those bridges when the bombs went off. The soldiers would be desperate now, trapped on this side of the river.

Woody said we should all stay together. The electricity was off, but the kerosene stove still worked. The families straggled up the path, loaded with bundles, baskets, and bags of canned goods. Lorry carried her canary in a cage. Peter's room was declared off-limits, a quarantine impossible to enforce.

The house was full of people, sixteen of us: four missionary couples, eight lively children, the youngest a baby not yet a year old. We also housed several cats, a dog, a pet monkey, and the canary. I set the cage on top of a high cupboard. We gathered around the big coffee table, ate biscuits and leftover Christmas cookies, mangoes, and bananas, and drank Nescafé and cocoa. Doris brought a coffee cake. Peter looked on wistfully from the door of his isolation ward.

Nothing galvanizes people into action like close proximity to gunfire. A staccato burst from a machine gun, and the children dived under the coffee table. The two littlest girls crawled under a bureau. The rest of us took refuge where we could, behind furniture. The cats mewled, the monkey jumped around and chattered hysterically. The dog nudged his way under the bureau with the little girls.

"Mom," said Lorrie from under the table, "Don't let the cat get Budgie."

Her father told her to hush. Ten minutes passed. No more gunshots. We needed to find a better hiding place. We might be here all day. The concrete stairwell would be safer. The door at the foot of the stairs opened to the outside. I locked it, covered the window with a pillow, and propped a mattress against the door, supported by a couple of chairs. Would a mattress stop a bullet? Nobody was sure. We heard voices outside. Woody called for absolute silence. Whisper, if necessary. The soldiers were very close.

The monkey crouched at the top of the stairs. The little girls tried to divert the restless baby with finger games. I closed my eyes and pretended I was somewhere else. The concrete stairs were cold and unforgiving.

The children began to poke each other and giggle. Woody stood up and frowned at them. They settled down. The baby whimpered. His mother reached into her bag for a bottle and put the nipple into his mouth. He fussed for a moment, sucked noisily, and went to sleep. An hour passed. It seemed eons since the voices outside faded.

"I think we're safe now," Woody said quietly. "Let's offer a prayer of thanksgiving to the Lord for delivering us from danger." We bowed our heads. It wasn't a long prayer. He knew we were uncomfortable. I made a mental note to bring pillows next time.

"I think it's safe to go back to our homes," he said, finally, "but we all have to stay very quiet. Try not to attract attention. And may the Lord be with us."

The memory of that hour in the stairwell will be with me forever. When Mary Beth was in the sixth grade back in Putnam Avenue School in New Haven, her teacher was interested in her childhood in Africa. She wrote a story for him, called *Knee High to Africa*. It's a good story. She thought the time we spent in the stairwell, hiding from the soldiers, lasted for a week. What a revelation of how time is perceived and remembered. I'm appalled at the magnitude of her distress. Sometimes my guilt is almost more than I can bear.

The day wasn't over. In the afternoon Stewart walked around outside, keeping watch over the camouflaged station wagon. Soldiers came by in search of gasoline for their truck. Peter slept for a while. Mary Beth and Martha played with their dolls. Tim and I sat on the couch and read. I dozed off.

A sudden loud knock on the door jolted me awake. Tim sat up, startled. Mary Beth and Martha, their eyes wide with fear, cuddled close to me on the sofa. I put my finger to my lips and whispered for us to be very quiet. I had drawn the curtains across the windows. Nobody could see in, and we couldn't see outside. Whoever was out there continued to pound on the door.

A hoarse voice shouted. "*Hodi, madame, hodi.*"

I stood by the door. Tim stood beside me.

"*Ni nani?* [Who is it?]," I croaked.

"*Mama, ni mimi* [Madame, it's me]. The vegetable man. I have strawberries."

I eased the door open a crack. I knew that peddler. I opened the door wide. Mary Beth and Martha peeked into his basket. Strawberries, indeed, and green beans, some tired lettuce, a few tomatoes, and a wizzled papaya. I bought it all, pressed a wad of bills into his hand. We said, "*Asante sana*" to each other. I said, "*Kwenda vizuri,*" he said, "*Bakia vizuri.*"

I closed the door and leaned against it. "Who wants to help make strawberry shortcake?"

Peter said, "I think I got well." I took his temperature. No fever. He looked like himself. His eyes were clear. He was hungry. It seemed like a miracle. Later tests confirmed the diagnosis of hepatitis. Tim came down with it a couple of weeks later, when they were back at Sakeji School. No instant cure for him.

Stewart came in, and I started to tell him our news.

"No time for that now. Come outside. There's something you should see. History is being made out here."

We trooped out after him and joined the group gathered on the hillside that overlooked the road. Blue trucks rolled by below us, filled with United Nations soldiers in blue helmets. None of them looked up. I doubt if they knew we were there.

The cavalcade of the United Nations soldiers passed from my sight. We swept the branches off our car and drove home to Jadotville.

Our house was just as we had left it. Nothing missing, except electricity. The entire region was powerless. Our old kerosene stove could just about boil water. We had four kerosene lanterns and a charcoal-fueled iron. The price of charcoal increased tenfold. Gasoline was rationed. UN helicopters buzzed us every hour, keeping the peace, as the Blue Helmets swarmed the town. Troops from India this time were better behaved than the Moroccans. American equipment poured in to support the UN occupation, and Americans were now perceived to be enemies of the Katanga. Our best hope would be to remain as inconspicuous as possible.

The mines and processing plants were shut down, the railroad out of commission. The industrial din, the rumbles and rattles of the machinery, the toots and whistles of the trains, were silenced, and the powerful industrial lights were extinguished. The darkness was punctuated by campfires and cooking fires. The stars appeared. A moon such as I had never seen metamorphosed through its growth cycle to full brilliance. I could actually read by its light. Distant drums sent messages I couldn't translate.

The retreating soldiers had not only dynamited the bridges at Mulungwishi, but they had also destroyed the bridges south of us, across the Lufira River, cutting off rail and road access to Elisabethville and Northern Rhodesia.

I took stock of our supplies. Adversity was no stranger to me. Fifty pounds of powdered skim milk filled a barrel on the back porch. That should last a while. Burlap bags of Meals for Millions, a grey protein-rich powder, appeared for sale on the shelves of local merchants, clearly labeled, in English, "Gift of the United States, Not to be Sold." The Africans, suspicious of the charity of the *wazungu*, wouldn't touch the stuff. I spooned it into everything, oatmeal, bread, pancakes, even doughnuts. The Mulungwishi chickens continued to provide eggs. If the butcher had meat for sale, I bought it. I never questioned its origin. Stewart set up the charcoal picnic grill. When it rained, he put the grill in the fireplace.

"I can't imagine anyone cooking on these things for pleasure," he said.

More empty shelves in the shops, and more empty shops. Rumors of anything for sale brought a crowd of people, who stood in line for hours. The children took turns every morning at the bakery. On good days they came running home with a loaf or two, shouting. "Mom! Mom! We got bread today." For years to come, that would be a favorite sermon illustration. It never failed to wring a groan from a well-fed congregation.

Despite the challenges of daily life, or perhaps because of them, I look back on January 1963 with nostalgia. One evening, Martha, going on seven, stood on a crate to wash the dishes, a towel tied around her tiny waist. A kerosene lantern hung on the towel rack. Water heated on the sputtering kerosene stove.

By some miracle, we had escaped the depredations of the retreating army. Peter had recovered from hepatitis. Our home had been spared once again, our family of six intact under one roof, around the table. Amenities were gradually restored, limited power for two hours a day. Produce vendors appeared at the door.

Stewart and I tiptoed around the prospect of the boys going back to Sakeji, reluctant to reactivate the argument. Peter and Tim invented strategies to bypass the censorship of their weekly letters home, innocuous phrases to carry secret meanings. I would be sure to check under the postage stamps for messages. We spent long afternoons at the pool under the watchful eyes of the Union Minière guards.

In Elisabethville, United Nations soldiers were building a Bailey Bridge, a sort of giant erector set, assembled of pre-manufactured components. The project was on hold, waiting for components sent to India by mistake.

One evening, just after sunset, the pastor from Sandoa brought news that Ed Mathews was stranded on the far side of the Lufira. Ed and his family had been in Kitwe since Christmas. He heard a rumor that the bridge was repaired, filled his truck with supplies and food, and drove north to the river, only to discover that there was, as yet, no bridge. Stewart and Pastor Eli drove our Volkswagen down to the Lufira to help arrange transfer across the river. Hundreds of people had set up temporary shelters by the river. Men walked, or crawled, across on the ruins of the old bridge. The river was about fifty yards wide at this point. Trucks pulled up on the far side and unloaded supplies from Northern Rhodesia. Files of porters carried freight on their heads, making the perilous crossing. Empty trucks waited for their loads. The United Nations crew had their own small ferry to take personnel and supplies back and forth across the river.

"I could see Ed, across the river," Stewart said. "He sent a messenger across to warn me that it was too dangerous to cross in the dark. He asked me to bring the old truck from Mulungwishi, early in the morning, along with a crew to hand-carry loads on the makeshift bridge."

Ed spent the night in his truck to guard the food supplies. Around midnight, six men jumped on the truck and started to carry off boxes of food. Like most of the missionaries in our area, Ed wasn't armed. He whistled, the UN guards came, and the thieves fled. They were serious soldiers, Gurkhas, well-trained and well-disciplined. They wore sharp uniforms and wound their long hair and beards in turbans. The Africans didn't challenge their authority.

Stewart received a message that the missing parts for the bridge had arrived, and the construction would be completed by one o'clock the following afternoon.

"I think we should get down there, just in case. We can spend a few days in Kitwe and make arrangements to get the boys back to school."

By nine o'clock the next morning we were at the river, eager to watch the soldiers complete the bridge. Nobody believed the men could finish the job by one o'clock.

The Indian soldiers and officers worked with an air of competency and pride. We hadn't seen that before in any of the other UN cadres. These Gurkha engineers were all action. They ran, a dozen men in step, carrying heavy sections of the assemblage, and bolted them into place. Light rain fell. Mesmerized as the bridge materialized, we took photographs. We could have used a movie camera. The soldiers took pictures of us, including one of Stewart in his new red baseball cap, holding up Martha's little red plaid umbrella.

The friendly officers admired our children and pulled out photos of their families back in India. Their faces softened; their eyes took a faraway look. They presented Peter and Tim with a souvenir of the fighting, a large brass shell-casing about twelve inches long.

The rain stopped and the sun suddenly came out. We ate our sandwiches. The men laid the sections of planking in place for the roadbed and bolted them down. Finally, they set up the approaches to the bridge. I remembered the day at Samusamb when the guys struggled to erect the approaches to that abandoned bridge. We could have used a crew like this.

The major waved us into place, the first to cross the bridge. Stewart checked his watch. A quarter after one. Not bad. The soldiers beamed at us and saluted as we drove across. We cheered and waved.

An hour later we stopped at Lois and Maurice's house in Elisabethville. The American consul stood on the front porch, examining a bullet hole in the front window. The shell had landed in an upholstered chair inside that Lois had vacated a moment before. We didn't linger. We drove on to Northern Rhodesia.

The children were delighted to stay in Kitwe. They loved the Mine Mess, the cafeteria operated by the mining company, where they had sodas and ice cream at every meal. We shopped and window-shopped, took the kids to the park, and saw a movie, *West Side Story*. Late in the afternoon, the mission plane buzzed the guest house, and our holiday was over. We drove out to the airstrip to pick up Paul the pilot.

The next morning, Paul invited Stewart to come along on the flight to Sakeji. The windsock stood straight out, flapping in the breeze. Ominous clouds sailed across the sky. It didn't get easier to say goodbye to my sons. The plane took off into the wind, rose rapidly, headed west, shrank to a dot, and disappeared.

The afternoon dragged on. The sun was low in the sky when the plane buzzed the house, and the girls and I drove to the airstrip. Stewart looked a bit green as he climbed down from the little plane.

"A fast trip," he said, "too much wind. We played tag with thunderstorms. The Sakeji airstrip was muddy, and the staff just about had kittens watching us land. On the takeoff, the plane got stuck on the muddy runway. Tim and Peter helped push us out of the mud. We could still see the wreckage of the Christmas plane crash in the bushes and the treetops. On our way back, the plane suddenly hit an updraft. We went up a thousand feet a minute."

Paul conducted his careful walk-around examination of his plane. A small clip on the nosewheel had broken during the landing. "I can fix that," he said.

Chapter Twenty

The shortwave radio continued to bring the daily exchange of mission news. One thing I could depend on: things would get worse. One evening we heard the doctor at Kapanga calling for help. The soldiers stationed there had gone on a rampage, chased off the African administrators, and threatened the three missionary families on the station. "Please send help," the doctor pleaded over and over. "Please send help."

Help came twenty-four hours later. United Nations troops put a hundred of the rebels in jail. What would it be like to wait twenty-four hours for help?

In Elisabethville, Congolese soldiers, part of the African National Congress—Lumumba's group—ordered an elderly white man off the sidewalk. He refused. They shot him dead.

Back in the States, my mother was in the hospital, suffering from cancer. She was heartsick for me, as I was for her. I opened my heart to her in a letter.

"We can't go on here indefinitely spinning our wheels. Unless things change drastically, or Stewart gets a different job, like teaching in the seminary, we'll finish the school year and see how things look by June. I just want to have my family together and keep the cookie jar full for the kids. In any case, this year will not have been wasted, we're learning a lot! I feel about 110 years old. We'll pray about it, and I know you will, too."

When I read this today, I want to yell at the woman who wrote it. "Get out of there. What are you waiting for, the writing on the wall? Take your children and go home."

So why didn't we just leave?

We'd signed on with The Board to serve until they decided we would no longer serve. We were duty-bound to stay where they sent us, where God wanted us to be. Have you noticed that those who hold power claim God on their side?

We were trapped. Stewart couldn't escape his financial obligation to The Board for his Yale degree. Had I acceded to his wishes, and taken the children home to the States, The Board would have paid our passage and given me a stipend for six months. Is six months enough time for a mother of four children to find gainful employment? Where would we have settled? I didn't have a house in America. In our thirteen years of marriage, we had never owned a home. We began our life together in a dingy basement apartment. While Stewart was in seminary in Texas, we lived in student housing. The parsonage in West Hartford, fifteen feet from the church, was overseen by Swedish housewives whose standards of housekeeping were much higher than mine. Then that apartment in Belgium.

You understand the joy with which I'd settled into the house in Jadotville, as though I had a home of my own at last. Of course, it wasn't mine. It was mission property. And now the new doctrine of interchangeable housing made our occupancy subject to the whim of church committees. If an African family wanted the house, could I say no? I remembered the grubby old fellow who came to the door before Independence and claimed he had bought the house and me along with it.

One afternoon shortly before Easter, the girls and I were resting on the screened porch, our lessons over for the day. The girls dressed the kittens in doll clothes, their favorite thing, though probably not the kittens'.

Three boys, gangly adolescents in their early teens, clothed in the usual raggedy shorts and torn tee shirts, tattered sneakers, stood in the field in front of the house in the shade of the avocado tree. The school bell had released them ten minutes ago. Something about the boys' manner made me uneasy. They watched us carefully, spoke in low voices. They seemed to reach some decision, to set a plan set in motion.

The trio approached the house. I walked out to meet them by the scraggly juniper hedge. Mary Beth and Martha released the squirming kittens and followed me. Perhaps the boys wanted avocados? They could come back when the avocados were ripe. But they were not here for avocados.

The boys walked right up to where I stood, pulled down their pants, and urinated on my skirt. The warm stuff ran down my legs. They stood there and watched me. I pushed Mary Beth and Martha behind me. Pastor Joab stood outside the door of the school across the field talking to a couple of teachers.

"Run over there and get Pastor Joab," I told the girls, "Tell him to come. Go quickly, now."

They scampered across the playground. Joab turned to greet them, listened a moment, and hurried back with them to where I stood. The boys strolled away down the driveway, no rush. Joab yelled at them and they started to run. Mary Beth and Martha stood close to me, one on each side, careful not to touch my reeking skirt.

"I know those boys," Joab said. "Those boys are bad, always trouble. One of them is from our school. The others were expelled from the Catholic school. I'll give them a good scolding," he assured me. "It's a good thing you weren't hurt," he added, almost as an afterthought.

His concerned eyes looked into mine. He shook his head sadly and turned to go. I stretched out my hands to Mary Beth and Martha, and the three of us walked slowly back into the house. I was determined to remain calm, to minimize the impact of what my daughters had just witnessed. "I need to get cleaned up," I said.

They carried the kittens carefully into their bedroom, out of sight of the front yard. In the bathroom, I closed the door and turned on the hot water. The heater up on the wall roared into action. I took off my sneakers, socks, skirt, shirt, and underwear, and kicked everything into the corner. I never wanted to see those clothes again. I scrubbed myself over and over until my skin hurt. I stood up and let the water run down the drain. I filled the tub again.

When I turned off the water, I heard the girls' voices. Stewart had finally come home, too late for me. Let him hear it from them. I soaked and sobbed, and my tears fell into the soapy water. I washed my hair. The water cooled. I pulled the plug and wrapped myself in a clean towel.

Stewart knocked on the bathroom door. "Can I come in?"

I didn't want him to see me. I didn't want anyone to see me, unclean, shamed, humiliated, helpless, and furious. To think I had come here to help these people, to serve them. I wanted to do serious damage to those boys. I wanted Stewart to punish, to hurt them. I wanted Peter and Tim, far away at school. I wanted my mother. I towel-dried my hair, put on clean pajamas, and got into bed. I got out of bed, ripped off the sheets, and made up the bed with clean sheets and pillowcases. Mary Beth and Martha came in, wide-eyed, and climbed onto the bed with the kittens. Their sober faces full of concern.

Mary Beth said, "Are you all right. Mom?"

Martha said, "Those boys are bad."

I didn't want them to see me cry. "I'm all right, and yes, those boys are very, very bad. Get some books and I'll read to you."

Stewart looked in the door. "I'll fix us some supper."

We waited to talk until the girls were asleep.

Stewart said, "It's a good thing you weren't hurt."

Why did men keep saying I wasn't hurt? The boys had urinated on me. Wasn't that hurt enough? I started to cry and couldn't stop.

"I *was* hurt," I protested.

Stewart grimaced. "I meant physically hurt. I'm sure that was unpleasant."

"It was far more than unpleasant," I sobbed. "It was awful. Those boys should be punished."

"Calm down. It doesn't do any good to get so excited. You mustn't make such a big thing of this. Worse things happen to people every day. Think of that old white man in Elisabethville, the one who didn't get off the sidewalk fast enough."

"I *am* thinking of him, but this is *me*. Couldn't you just think about me for once? And the girls? How can we live where boys can just come into the yard and pee on me? What if they come into the house next time?"

"I'll talk to the school director."

"I'll go with you."

"That's not a good idea. I'll take Joab with me. He was there when it happened."

"No, I wailed, "*I* was there when it happened. Joab was there *after* it happened."

"But Joab recognized the boys. That's what matters."

I wanted to scream. "Those boys must be punished."

"I'll see what I can do." Stewart turned away from me. He didn't touch me. What is the protocol when the mother is urinated on while the daughters look on? Hundreds of Africans were suffering all around us. Another white man was dead. How did the degradation of one white woman figure in the great scheme of things?

Except, it was me.

Pastor Joab and the teachers decided it would be unfair to expel the boys and ruin their chances for a good life. What could they do without an education? After all, I hadn't been hurt. They gave the boys a good scolding.

I told Stewart to get rid of the clothes I had been wearing. I meant for him to destroy them. He gave them to Baba Samuel. No point in wasting good clothes. It made me sick to see them on Baba Samuel's wife.

I had to find a way to put this behind me. Ordinarily, I consoled myself by baking bread, a great way to work off aggression. I stirred dry yeast into warm water, measured flour and a bit of salt, mixed and kneaded the dough. I pounded it vigorously. "Take that," I muttered as I slammed the dough down. "Now aren't you sorry you did that?" I punished that dough, tossed it into the big yellow crock, covered it with a dishtowel, and set it in a warm spot to rise in the sun.

In the corner of the kitchen sat my latest acquisition, a Frigidaire wide-oven range, only a few years old. After Lois and Maurice were transferred to Elisabethville, their house became a temporary refuge for African families, desperate to escape the violence that erupted from time to time. No one was scheduled to move in for a while. I seized the opportunity to appropriate that stove in exchange for my old one. Baba Samuel gave it a thorough cleaning, and he and Stewart carried it into my kitchen. What satisfaction to see the old stove out the door.

I shaped the loaves for a second rising. They doubled in size, and my pressed finger left just a slight imprint. I turned on the oven. A river of cockroaches poured down the front of the stove and streamed across the kitchen in all directions.

"Help," I shouted. "Girls, come quick!" I stomped up and down on the crunchy beasts as fast as I could. The bugs came on, unabated, king-size African cockroaches. They gave off a nauseating sour smell as I stomped them.

"What is it, Mom?" asked Mary Beth. "What's wrong? Where did those bugs come from?"

"Quick. Help me stomp the bugs."

"Phew, they smell awful," Martha said.

The girls went right to work, judiciously smacking their little shoes down on the formidable insects. "Where did they come from?" Mary Beth asked again.

"The stove. Take a look."

"There are thousands of them," she said in awe.

"Yes, and we've got to get them all. Don't miss a one."

Mary Beth watched wide-eyed as I swatted one on the cabinet with my bare hand. I hastily moved the ready-to-bake loaves to safety in the refrigerator.

Stewart came in the back door. "What's going on? Are you dancing the twist?"

"Don't be funny. Get in here and help us kill these critters."

"What happened? Where did all these cockroaches come from?"

I pointed to the stove, where the flow of the loathsome creatures had slowed to a trickle.

"They were in the stove?"

"Bingo. Start stomping."

He got right into it. "We'll have to fumigate."

"Right. Both houses."

Mary Beth found the fly swatter and flailed away at the roaches seeking escape up the walls and on the counter. Whack! Whack! We seemed to be gaining a beachhead. Stewart got the broom and dustpan and began to sweep up the casualties.

"I never saw anything like it in my life," he said, as he emptied them into the garbage can. The kitchen floor was still covered. The bodies crunched under our feet.

Baba Samuel had spent hours cleaning that stove. How could he have missed all of this? Stewart said he didn't think they ever used the oven, except to store things. Grease accumulated under the burners. "Those critters thought they'd found cockroach heaven," he said.

"And they got chased out of paradise. Straight to hell. Does that make us God?"

"'Vengeance is Mine, saith the Lord.'"

I tried not to think about the ones who had escaped vengeance and were even now finding new homes behind the cabinets and in the dark corners of the cupboards. Would we ever be able to get rid of them? I opened the oven door, brushed out a few crispy creatures trapped there. Ignoring the smell of toasted roaches, I set the bread pans on the oven rack.

"Mom, are you going to cook in there, after all those bugs?" asked Mary Beth.

"Don't worry, honey, the bugs were incinerated. Like in the fiery furnace."

She knew her Bible stories. She looked thoughtful. "Only those guys in the Bible didn't get burned up. I guess God doesn't care about the cockroaches."

The wholesome smell of bread baking permeated the house.

A tall ladder leaned against the palm tree outside the back door. Oh, yes. Palm Sunday coming up. Every year men stripped the tree to decorate the churches. They never even asked. Didn't they have any notion of private property? The poor tree looked just awful for months, and as soon as it recovered, it was Palm Sunday again. Stewart came into the kitchen. "Now don't get upset. It's just a tree."

"Oh, sure. Like you don't get mad when the African kids steal the green mangoes and avocados."

"That's different," he said. "That's a waste of food. If they would just wait until the mangoes are ripe, they could have all they want. They just take one bite and spit it out and throw it on the ground. They need to learn to wait."

I slammed the plates onto the table. "This place drives me crazy. We have no privacy. People in and out of the house all the time, wicked boys in the yard, men on ladders chopping up the trees."

Stewart had the last word. "Well, the trees were here before we were. I'm sure when Bishop Springer lived here, he would have been happy for them to take the branches."

I had to admit the palm branches around the altar looked festive. I should have been more patient, more gracious. A better Christian.

New troubles arrived on schedule on Thursday morning, Holy Thursday, the day before Good Friday. A rumble of drums, faint at first, grew louder. The Luba Jeunesse rampaged down the street in battle dress, animal skins draped over their ragged clothes, fur caps on their heads, faces contorted as they roared challenges to their enemies. They brandished crude weapons: ancient muskets, machetes, and bicycle chains. The local Lundas took up the challenge, sent out their own young men. The street became a battlefield. In the mayhem, the United Nations forces—Indonesians this time—loaded their trucks, the Blue Shield on the doors, with a corps of Luba warriors from the camps in Kolwezi and Elisabethville. The commander of the UN forces bragged later his men never fired a shot. He declared himself a man of peace. "The word was stronger than the sword," he said. "All my men have to do is talk to the fighters, and they lay down their weapons."

On Palm Sunday afternoon, we took a picnic supper to Mulungwishi and stayed for the evening service in English. Doris urged us to come for the Easter sunrise service. "We gather on the hill at 5:30. Breakfast together afterward."

I offered to make hot cross buns for everybody.

In this season, just after the rains, the air was clear. A waxing moon illuminated our drive home. The soldiers at the roadblock didn't turn on their flashlights; they just opened the barrier and waved us through. Curfew kept everyone at home. The streets were deserted and ominously silent.

The house from which I had "borrowed" the stove was crammed with refugees from the fighting. The men asked Stewart to drive their wives to pick up some things from their homes. "They're too frightened to go themselves," Stewart said. "And the funny thing is, they are all Lubas."

Tomas, the literacy director for the mission, appeared at the back door, moaning and crying. Stewart went to the door.

"Oh, *bwana*," Tomas cried, "my wife and all my children are dead. The Jeunesse killed them."

Stewart sat down beside him, laid his hand on the man's arm. "Just tell me what happened."

Tomas seemed to pull himself together. "I was in the outhouse when the Jeunesse came. I heard them go into my house. I heard the noise of windows breaking. I ran into the bush and hid."

Stewart's voice grew stern. "You ran away? How do you know they're dead? Did you see the bodies?"

"No, *bwana*, I came here for your help."

"And you didn't even try to save your wife and children?" Stewart looked at me, shook his head. "Can you believe this?"

"All right, Let's go to the hospital. Maybe some of them survived."

Tomas refused to go with Stewart. He wouldn't go back home unless Stewart drove him there. Stewart refused. Tomas wandered off, crying noisily. Stewart came into the kitchen, disgusted. "Can you even conceive of such cowardice? I'll go over to the hospital and check on the wounded."

"Can we color the Easter eggs now?" Martha asked. The girls frosted and decorated Easter cookies while I rolled out dough for hot cross buns. They nibbled the currants when they thought I wasn't looking. Mary Beth sighed. She seemed awfully young to be sighing. "I wish we lived at Mulungwishi. Then I could play with my friends all the time."

Sometimes I wished that, too. Stewart had recently mentioned that might happen.

"When the Bartletts leave, there will be an opening to head up the seminary, and I might have a crack at it. It's a long shot. Don't say anything to the kids." If he were offered the position, would we stay? I didn't ask. I didn't want to know.

Stewart returned from the hospital, pale and shaken. I gave him a glass of water and he leaned against the refrigerator. The girls were in the bedroom, packing their Easter clothes for the overnight in Mulungwishi. Stewart spoke quietly so they wouldn't hear him.

"It's the worst thing I've ever seen," he said. "People hacked with machetes, whipped with chains from bicycles, shot by ancient *bundukis*. Every bed was occupied by at least two of the wounded. Men on the floor under the beds and in the corridors. Bodies everywhere. And blood. The doctors and nurses were doing their best. More and more wounded were carried in. Their screams and moans will haunt me forever. I found a few people I knew, but there wasn't much I could do to bring any comfort. I couldn't find Tomas' family."

He was overcome by the sheer numbers of the sufferers, as near to tears as I had ever seen him. I put my arms around him and held him until he stopped shaking.

Refugees streamed onto the mission property. We decided that, rather than drive out to Mulungwishi early Sunday morning in the dark for the sunrise service, we would go now and spend the night. I packed the hot cross buns into our largest Tupperware container. The sun was setting as we started out. In the brief dusk, fires blazed in the city. The smell of smoke followed us as we drove away.

The Bancrofts invited us to stay with them in the basement apartment where we had spent that memorable Christmas week. Andrea and I were considered cynics, short on belief. We thought of ourselves as realists. We didn't hold back with each other. We were ready to go home to America.

Andrea's little girls were delighted to be with Mary Beth and Martha. The girls asked to be excused from the supper table. Now we could talk freely about the uprising in Jadotville. Woody called "*Hodi,*" and he and Doris joined us around the table.

"What's going on in Jadotville?" Woody asked. "Can't you keep things under control?" He smiled, but I caught the sarcasm. Woody liked to brag that his Africans at Mulungwishi never gave him any trouble.

Stewart described the devastation at the hospital. He spoke softly so the girls in the next room wouldn't hear about the hideous injuries, the suffering, the deaths. His voice, husky, hesitant, so unlike his usual tone, revealed the depth of his distress. He told them how Tomas had abandoned his wife and children.

Woody wasn't surprised. "That sounds just like Tomas. Doris, do you remember when he first came here to school? He was timid as a rabbit, scared of his own shadow."

"His wife was definitely the strong one in that family," Doris said.

"When you left Jadotville, had things quieted down?" Woody asked.

"There were some fires burning," Stewart said, "but once the police moved in this afternoon, things calmed down. Most of the shooting stopped by dark." He stood up. "There is a curfew. I need to get back to see about the mission property. The other house was full of people who fled from their homes. They may need my protection."

So this had been his plan all along, to take the girls and me to safety and return home by himself, just like in 1960. Why hadn't I seen this coming? I turned to him, appalled.

"Surely you aren't going back tonight? It's dark. If it isn't safe for them, it isn't safe for you."

Woody said, "I'll go with Stewart."

"Good idea," Doris said.

Jeff said, "I'll come, too." Andrea looked at him, astonished.

"Stay where you are," Woody said. "You have a wife and children to think of."

"What about Stewart?" I protested. "He has a wife and children to think of, too."

"But Jadotville is my responsibility," Stewart said.

Woody nodded approval. As the senior missionary, his was the final word. Stewart's level look begged me not to make a scene in front of all these people. I turned away. I never thought we would part under these circumstances again. It was 1960 all over again.

Doris called to Woody. "Bye, honey, take care."

Stewart hesitated, came back, and gave me a quick kiss on the cheek. "I'll see you in the morning. Save me some hot cross buns."

He didn't have a choice. He had to go. That was his job. It was what the church in America paid him to do, to protect their property and care for the Christians. He couldn't say no to Woody, not if he hoped to succeed him as head of the seminary.

When Stewart left his family, he was a hero. The fact he liked being a hero was beside the point. He did what he had to do. This insight did not lessen my resentment. It was one thing to understand, another to accept. Stewart and Woody climbed into the car, slammed the door, and drove away.

Doris said, "Don't worry. They'll be all right. I should be getting home."

Andrea and Jeff and I offered to walk with her. She smiled. "I should know the way by now." Jeff reminded her to watch out for snakes. We watched her flashlight bob down the path.

The stars seemed unusually bright. The night was so still. I was accustomed to machinery rumbling day and night, and the garish industrial glow filling the night sky, hiding the stars. Here in the bush, the night birds called to each other. I took a deep breath of eucalyptus, plumeria, and woodsmoke. We passed the lighted windows of the dormitories and heard low voices of conversation and laughter, young people singing. It all seemed so peaceful.

"That's strange," Andrea said, after a moment. "No drums tonight."

The little girls chased each other around, giggled, and bounced on the beds. Andrea and I cleared off the table, cleaned up the kitchen, helped the girls into their jammies, and tucked them in. "But we're not sleepy," Linnie protested. They managed to stay awake for half an hour. We could hear them chattering.

"I wish you lived out here," Andrea said. It was becoming a refrain. "I don't know how you can stand to live in Jadotville, with all that fighting. It's so peaceful out here."

"I know; it's awful. I just wish we could all go home to America."

"What was that about? Woody didn't want Jeff to go with them?" Andrea asked. "I couldn't figure it out, but I was glad Jeff didn't go. They must be worried the mission might be looted if Stewart wasn't there."

The girls finally settled down. Torn apart by anguish, I couldn't get to sleep. How could Stewart leave me again like this? Didn't he care for us at all? Would we ever see him again? Where was God when I needed Him?

I must have slept. The alarm woke me at 4:30. The sunrise service would begin at a quarter after five. We dressed warmly, put on sweaters, and wrapped the sleepy girls in blankets. It was cold outside. The morning star seemed to signal better times ahead. We sat on the ground on the hillside—the mission community, the *wazungu*, seven women, three men, and four little girls. Several African men, seminary students, joined us. The eastern sky showed the faintest tint of pink. The dark, quiet valley stretched in front of us. The morning star faded and disappeared. A trumpet carried on the still air the clear notes of "I know that the Redeemer liveth." I would have enjoyed it more if I had been certain I still had a husband.

As if on cue, the sun appeared, the dawn of Easter Sunday. Immediately, I felt its warmth. We shed our sweaters. We sang the traditional hymns, in English, unaccompanied. Our voices seemed to vaporize in the gulf of air. "Jesus Christ is Risen today, Alleluia." I thought of Easters past, back home in America, the congregation belting out those triumphant words as the organ thundered. The fragrance of the lilies. Hats and gloves, new dresses. New shoes.

I helped to set out the celebratory Easter breakfast: fresh orange juice, coffee, and hot chocolate from the thermoses, brightly colored hard-boiled eggs. The Mulungwishi chickens had been unusually productive. Everyone got an egg. The hot cross buns were cold, but they were tasty, and everyone appreciated the effort. The girls took turns hiding Easter eggs and hunting for them. It was an almost perfect morning. We gathered the leftovers, bundled up the plates and cups, and stood around outside the church, waiting for the morning service to begin.

Stewart and Woody appeared, jaunty as ever. They didn't even get out of the car. "Just wanted to let you know we're all right," Stewart said, cheerily. "We're on our way to Kambove. I'm preaching there. Woody's going with me."

Doris waved to Woody. "Bye, honey, see you later."

And they were gone. I hadn't even had time to say anything. Stewart had not wanted to hear anything I might have said. He was there. Wasn't that enough?

We settled in a row on the hard, backless benches in the church for the endless Easter morning service. The girls preened in their ruffly dresses and petticoats. The young African women of the Ecole Ménagère (Home Economics School) preened, too, in their new outfits, all made from the same bright print cloth. The mission had an arrangement with the merchants in town to buy fabric wholesale, provided they bought the entire bolt. The young men wore clean cotton shirts, pressed trousers. Those who had neckties wore them. The church was crowded, every bench filled. People stood along the walls; others looked in through the window openings. The four little girls giggled and fidgeted and tickled each other. Andrea and I shushed them occasionally, but not seriously, and finally released them to go and play. The familiar hymns sounded again, this time in Swahili. "*Yesu a-li-fu-fu-ka,*" we sang, a translation of "Up from the grave He arose." The words sounded so silly to us; it was hard not to laugh. Pastor Joab preached for a long time. After all, it was Easter. Birds flew in and out of the windows, cheeping. Babies cried, and mothers nursed them. I tried to remember if I had ever believed in the Resurrection.

The Springers invited our family for Easter Sunday dinner. Aunt Helen, in her seventies, was a bit trembly. The bishop's face always lit up when he saw Martha.

Stewart arrived just in time for lunch, as he had promised. He had to be back in Kambove to preach the afternoon service. We decided to go with him. Bishop Springer and Aunt Helen received a royal welcome. Everyone loved them, honored them. The service lasted two hours, with baptisms. Mary Beth and Martha stretched out on the hard benches and slept. Exhausted by the emotion of the morning I dozed, to wake suddenly each time my head dropped down onto my chest.

We finally got home about five o'clock, not quite twenty-four hours since we left on Easter Eve. It seemed like years. Everything was just as we had left it. I went straight to bed. Stewart fixed the girls something to eat and tucked them into bed.

In the morning, Mary Beth and Martha brought us breakfast on trays. Martha peeled her prettiest Easter egg for me. They were so pleased with themselves. They crawled under the covers with me. We played with the kittens and listened to the news broadcasts until we decided it was safe to get up.

Chapter Twenty-One

The Union Minière workers went on strike early in May 1963 in an attempt to force the government in Léopoldville to get their troops out of Katanga. Congolese soldiers in Jadotville responded and killed a Belgian man. The number of Africans killed was invariably indefinite, while the Belgian count was specific, the victims identified by name. Most of the Europeans who were still in town were making plans to leave.

Stewart muttered to himself and pecked away at the Olivetti typewriter. He yanked the paper out of the machine, put in a new sheet, typed some more.

Curiosity got me. "What's up?"

"I'm writing to The Board. I'm sick and tired of all this nonsense. I'm asking to be reassigned to someplace we can do some significant work."

"It's about time. Can I read it?"

"Sure. I'll need you to type a clean copy."

He drummed his fingers on the desk. He raised his eyebrows. "Well, what do you think?"

"It's dynamite, I said. "I love that part about giving artificial respiration to a corpse. And the 'Valley of the Dry Bones.' Great stuff. Are you sure you want to send it?"

"What have we got to lose?"

"Good point. The worst they can do is send us home."

"Actually, the worst they can do is leave us here. But I'm pretty sure they'd let you and the kids go to the States."

I stared at him. "Not an option. We're a family. Go or stay, we're together."

"Okay," he said. "I'm going to the post office before I lose my nerve."

Nothing like an act of defiance to clear the air. He had lit the fuse. We'd have to wait for the explosion. How long had it been since I'd heard him whistling?

"Your birthday's coming up," Stewart said. "What do you say we go to Kitwe for a couple of days? Just you and me."

"What about the girls?"

"We can ask Maurice and Lois. They'd love to have them."

"Well, sure, let's ask them," I said, warming to his proposal. "It would be good to get away for a bit. Gosh, I'm going to be thirty-five."

He grinned. He seemed sort of jolly. "Well, you look pretty good to me." His eyes twinkled. I stepped into his arms and we held each other, in relief and hope, and a taste of freedom.

Northern Rhodesia, still under British control, seemed almost like America. We were a bit shy with each other; it had been so long since it was just the two of us. We went shopping. Stewart chose a dress for me, a stylish sheath in shades of yellow and orange. I treated myself to a real haircut in a beauty salon. We were carefree. We went to dinner at a fancy place, ignored the prices, ordered lobster tails and Baked Alaska. We didn't talk about The Work. Or The Letter. A small orchestra played, and we danced. It had been years since we danced together: it was a wonder we still knew how. It seemed almost illicit. I thought of Stewart's twenty-first birthday when we went dancing at the Blue Moon in Wichita. This felt like a new beginning.

In the morning I woke to a rush of blood. My menstrual periods had been unusually heavy, and now, for once, there was a doctor handy when I needed one. Dr. Fisher could see me that afternoon.

The doctor discovered a fibroid tumor the size of a grapefruit on my uterus. "There is some infection. You need a hysterectomy, without delay."

I was shocked at the gravity of my condition. Stewart frowned to hear the diagnosis and recommendation for immediate surgery.

Dr. Fisher was all too familiar with the arcane rules of the missionaries. "I know the mission doctor must be consulted before anything can be done. Contact him as soon as you can. Don't delay. If he agrees with my diagnosis, let me know immediately and I'll make the arrangements here."

What a relief to be in the care of this kind and competent doctor in his modern, fully equipped hospital.

Stewart stood up. But Dr. Fisher wasn't finished. "One more thing." Stewart sat down. Dr. Fisher continued, "You know, and I know, the Katanga is on the brink of collapse. It's dangerous, and it's not healthy for you, or your wife, or your children. I've treated a number of missionaries over the years, and I know how stubborn you can be. I appreciate the importance of your work, but your wife's health is at stake."

Stewart winced. He took a deep breath. "Thank you, doctor, for your help and advice," he said stiffly. Dr. Fisher looked steadily at Stewart and gave me a troubled smile.

Happiness was ephemeral, after all. That giddy couple on holiday seemed like ghosts of birthdays past. We had little to say on the drive back into the chaos of the Katanga. How would I phrase this news for Mary Beth and Martha? What about Peter and Tim? Their school term would finish in a couple of weeks.

In Elisabethville, Lois and Maurice heard my news with grave concern. In their long missionary career in Liberia and the Congo, they had experienced a lifetime of trouble, yet their hearts could still ache for beloved colleagues. They insisted we stay for supper. We prayed together.

In the morning, before we tackled our lessons, I spoke calmly to the girls, determined not to alarm them. I explained, as best I could, about a growth on my uterus. Martha snuggled closer and patted my arm. Mary Beth asked about that yew-ter-us.

We would need a new vocabulary.

"It's a place in the mother's tummy where the eggs are stored before they turn into babies."

She frowned, puzzled. "Sort of like a nest?"

"Something like that," I said, clumsy at explaining the details of reproduction. I didn't know that much about it myself, in spite of having given birth four times. Mary Beth looked up into my face.

"Does this mean I can't have a little brother?"

"I'm afraid so," I said.

"Maybe we could adopt a baby."

Stewart made contact on the shortwave radio with the mission doctor in Kapanga. The doctor told him to send me up there on the mission plane for the surgery. No big deal. He performed hysterectomies every day, he said. Stewart looked at me, eyebrows raised. I shook my head. I remembered the discomfort of the breast biopsy at the Kapanga hospital in 1958, without general anesthesia or a blood supply. I flashed on the scene at the doctor's dinner table, the sudden gush of blood staining my white blouse. The long wait for pathology, six months before I knew for sure there was no malignancy. Couldn't the doctor just fly down to Jadotville to examine me?

"Not possible. The paramount chief is dying." Several months ago, the doctor had gone to Kolwezi for Field Committee, leaving the chief in the care of his well-trained African nurses. The nurses feared the chief might die, and they would be blamed. They withheld his medication. By the time the doctor returned, the chief was barely alive.

Much was at stake. Years ago, Bishop Springer had baptized the chief's grandfather, and as long as the current chief did not recant, the entire tribe, thousands of souls, would automatically become Christians upon his death. The doctor didn't dare leave his bedside. He would send the mission plane for me, examine me and give the go-ahead for the surgery in Kitwe, and send me back to Jadotville. Paul, the pilot, would pick me up in his Cessna at the Jadotville airstrip.

Days passed. Twice we were alerted about a pending flight and waited for hours at the airstrip. False alarm each time. Stewart suggested, once the mission doctor gave his okay, I could fly to Johannesburg for the surgery. I narrowed my eyes and glared at him. I would rather die.

Why not go to a hospital in the States? I proposed to write to the chief of medical services for The Board, for permission to come to the States for the surgery.

"Good idea," Stewart said, seizing the opening. "Take the children with you. Stay there to recuperate. Or just stay there." He made airline reservations, just in case.

Another week passed. Was I the only one with a sense of urgency? I felt death stalking me. Dr. Fisher's warning echoed in my mind, the possibility of a malignancy. Indecision would kill me if cancer didn't.

The chief clung to life and could not be abandoned. Strange, the doctor had abandoned me without a qualm. Stewart came up with another possibility. One of the Belgian doctors, who was still at the government hospital across the street, had trained in the States for four months. "And he speaks good English," Stewart said.

"I hate that hospital," I grumped. "I have no respect for those Belgian doctors." Four years ago, one of them misdiagnosed my hepatitis as sunstroke. I finally turned yellow. I can still hear his triumphant cry, "*Voila, madame, c'est la jaunisse.*" Another of those doctors gave all six of us yellow fever shots with the same needle. Nevertheless, I trudged across the street. Desperate measures for desperate times.

The doctor was pleasant, and his English was fine. He prepared to examine me. He reached into the breast pocket of his white coat and pulled out a speculum. I tried not to think about where it might have been before he put it in his pocket. I looked around for an autoclave. He finished his exam and put the instrument back in his pocket.

"Yes, there is a fibroid tumor, but no cause for alarm, no need for a hysterectomy. You are, what, thirty-five? Young enough to bear more children. I can remove the tumor and you can recover at home with your family, cared for by the servants." All these doctors seemed to assume I had a retinue of well-trained servants, but there was only long-suffering Baba Samuel. I stared over the doctor's shoulder at the crucifix on the wall. So it was true about these Catholics. Forget the mother, save the baby. "I'll talk to my husband and get back to you."

Chapter Twenty-Two

Once again, we faced the long day's drive to Sakeji, on terrible roads through the bush. Red dust sifted into the car and permeated everything. We met only one car all day. At midday, we spread a blanket in the dusty road and ate our sandwiches.

In the late afternoon, we drove through the gates of the school and ran the gauntlet of kids. Tim and Peter appeared. My heart leaped up to see my boys, fit and tan, sweaty, and considerably taller. I hugged them both until they pulled away in embarrassment, lest their friends tease them. I vowed not to be separated from them again.

"It seems a shame to pull you guys out when you're doing so well," Stewart said.

"Forget it, Dad," Tim said. "We're not coming back. That was the deal, remember?"

Peter seemed less adamant. "I read twenty-three books this term," he offered.

"That's wonderful," I said. "That's more than I read this term."

"Yeah, I read *Lorna Doone* and *Ben Hur*." I suspected abridged editions but didn't ask.

"I read twenty-one books," Tim said, "and my class studied *Macbeth*."

The teachers gave good reports of the boys. Mr. Hess, the headmaster, came over to talk to us. Face to face with the villain who had caned my son, I gritted my teeth and forced a civil smile. "Your boys are doing very well," he said. "We look forward to having them with us again next term. I hope you will send your daughters, as well. We prefer to get them when they are in the early grades. The younger they are, the easier to break them to our system."

I managed a tight smile, resolved that my gentle little girls would never be "broken in."

Tim nudged me as Mr. Hess walked away. "Did you hear that, Mom? He actually said it. Believe me, you don't want that to happen to Mary Beth and Martha."

"It's not going to happen," I said. "I promised you, after you finished this term, that's it for Sakeji School." His shoulders relaxed.

Field Day began early the next morning, with races and tumbling and pyramid building. I never saw a healthier bunch of kids, the boys barefoot in white shorts and tee shirts, the girls in white blouses and baggy green bloomers.

All the children joined in the tug-of-war. Some of the little ones could barely reach the rope. In the father's race, two dads in kilts sped down the field, bare knees pumping. Mary Beth ran her first-ever race. She didn't realize she needed to break through the tape, and she stopped short at the finish line. Another girl zipped by and took the honors. "I didn't know," Mary Beth said, ruefully.

Peter's class presented a puppet show of *The Wind in the Willows*. Tim's class did *Robin Hood* in French. His teacher whispered to me that Tim had the best accent in the class. Hard-won, I thought, as I recalled those dark days in Belgium.

The headmaster presented prizes and we all stood and sang "God Save the Queen." The boys put their suitcases in the car, said goodbye to their friends, and we drove away.

"Well, that's our last trip to Sakeji," I said, as much to reassure myself as the boys. Stewart didn't say anything. Nothing would spoil this precious time with all the family together, not illness, not fears for the future.

Home at last in Jadotville, the boys moved back into their Wedgwood blue bedroom and met the newest clutch of kittens. They climbed into their bunk beds as though they had never been away.

Stewart, back from the post office, handed me a letter from the chief of medical services in New York. My hands shook as I opened it. I read it aloud to Stewart.

"I cannot in good conscience recommend that you come to the States at this time, only nine months into a four-year term. It would not be good stewardship of the money contributed by the American church. We have invested a great deal of time and money in the medical personnel on the mission field and they are certainly qualified to take care of the missionaries as well as the Africans. The excellent hospital in Southern Rhodesia at Nyadiri is the facility closest to you. I wish you and your family well."

"Can you believe this?" I raged to Stewart. "I thought he was my friend. And he has the gall to wish us well. I can't stand it."

"He's probably under a lot of pressure," Stewart sighed. "I should never have asked to be re-assigned." He canceled the airline reservations to the States. "It's just as well. We would have been really pressed to get ready in time." I wondered what lucky family would sit in those seats.

"Well, at least he gave me official permission for the surgery. How soon can we get on the road?"

"I'll need a couple of weeks to wind things up here, and the boys just got home. Let's visit some game parks along the way to Nyadiri. Who knows when we'll have another chance? We could see Victoria Falls again."

I shuddered at memories of the children capering along the slippery trails at the brink of the chasm, baboons chattering in the trees. Maybe there would be some railings by now.

"The strangest thing," I said to Stewart the next morning. "My eye hurts."

"Which one?"

"The left one. Would you take a look and see if there's something there?" He peered into my eye, pushed up my eyelid with his thumb.

"Ouch, that hurts."

"Sorry. It's definitely inflamed, but I don't see any foreign objects. Maybe you picked up something at the pool. They've been really sloppy about maintenance."

"Could be, but wouldn't that affect both eyes?"

"It might. It could be just a strain. You have been reading a lot."

Reading was my salvation. I could escape into a book and the world went away for a while. The next day the pain in my eye was worse.

"I can't take time to drive you to Kitwe, I've got way too much to do before we go to Nyadiri." He started out the door, stopped, turned back to me. "I hear they have a good eye man across the street at the hospital. You might go, let him have a look at it." He turned, to make his getaway. "I don't think you should let it go any longer," he said over his shoulder. The screen door slammed behind him.

Easy enough for him to say. But I'd give it a try. Couldn't hurt. Might help.

"Iritis," the doctor pronounced. "An inflammation of the iris. I'll give you an injection, and you must have one every day for two weeks. Stay quiet at home, rest, let the servants do the work. Do not travel. You will not have any permanent effects, but you must wear a patch over the eye." He paused. "And no reading."

No reading! Might as well be a death sentence. I watched as carefully as I could to see that he used a new needle for the shot in my arm.

"Wow! You look like the Hathaway shirt guy," Stewart said. He conjured up the popular advertising symbol, a debonair man with an eye patch and an immaculate white shirt.

"Thanks a lot," I grumped. "I feel like Job."

Peter came in just then. "Wow, Mom," he said, "you look like a pirate."

I retreated to the kitchen to start lunch. "I'll help you, Mom," Mary Beth said. "That black thing over your eye looks weird." She sat on the high stool and read the recipe to me while Martha set the table.

The boys helped me with the girls' lessons. We needed to finish the course so that when we went home to America the girls would be ready for the next grade. On chilly evenings, Stewart built a fire in the fireplace and popped corn and we listened to phonograph records. I knew them by heart by now, all four of them: *Rhapsodie Italienne, Swan Lake, Bach Organ Works*, and *Christmas in Europe*.

My mind raced like a hamster on a treadmill. Doctor Fisher in Kitwe said a complete hysterectomy immediately. The Doctor across the street in Jadotville would just take the tumor. The new mission doctor in Kapanga was dismissive. What would the doctor in Nyadiri do? Was it cancer? Did anyone care?

The pain in my eye eventually eased. I got rid of the patch and wore dark glasses. I still couldn't read. Mary Beth and Martha came down with some sort of bronchial bug and Mary Beth lost her voice. She and I were miserable; she couldn't chatter and I couldn't read. Tim read to the girls every morning. He and Peter were so fit from all that healthy living at Sakeji School that no germ had a chance with them. They didn't even wear their sweaters on the cool mornings and evenings.

When I no longer needed him, the mission doctor from Kapanga finally turned up. He had completed his vigil at the chief's deathbed, the conversion of the tribe secured. He examined me, reiterated there was no medical emergency. He checked my eyes, pronounced me ready for travel. He agreed with the doctor in New York that we should go to Nyadiri. Much better facilities there than his hospital at Kapanga.

"They never would have sent you to the States for this," he confirmed. I suspected he might have been in cahoots with the doctor in New York.

"I invited the doctor and his family to travel with us," Stewart said. "They plan to do the game parks, and I thought it would be great for us to go together. That big Land Rover of theirs will come in handy in the backcountry. He said he could fit us all in for game viewing."

"You expect me to spend a vacation with the man who collaborated with the doctor in New York? Who wouldn't give me permission to go to the States?"

He looked hurt. "I thought you'd be pleased, to have your own doctor on call if anything happens."

"Oh, great. I suppose if I start to hemorrhage, he can whip out his little knives and fix it."

"I wish you wouldn't be so difficult about this. You've had two doctors tell you this isn't a crisis situation. We'll spend a couple of weeks having a good time with the kids and then we'll check with the folks at Nyadiri."

"Let's switch places," I said. "Let's have me be the one who thinks everything is all right, and you be the one worried about me."

"I do worry about you, but it doesn't do any good to get hysterical."

"Maybe they'll remove the hysteria when they do the hysterectomy," I said, distracted by the similarity of the words. I wondered about their derivation.

"Don't you think we should make the most of the time with the boys? he said. "Before they...."

"Before they what? What were you going to say?"

"Well, if you're all right, and we stay another year, we might have to send the kids to Sakeji. You couldn't teach all four of them yourself, you know that."

"Look, we promised the boys if they finished this term they wouldn't have to go back. And didn't we agree the girls were too young? I thought we burned our bridges. Did I miss something?"

"I'm sure the boys would understand if the situation changed. They're old enough to know things don't always work out the way they want."

At that moment, I hated him. "And when will you be old enough to understand that?" I asked, furious. That surge of hatred frightened me.

We lapsed into our old roles as college debaters. I could out-argue him, but he could out-maneuver me. He took a step toward me and held out his arms. "It's silly to argue about something that probably won't happen. Surely you don't think I'd do anything to jeopardize your health."

Reluctantly I allowed him to embrace me. "That's more like it," he said. "You know how important you are to me."

A week later, I sat in the back of the doctor's Land Rover in the late afternoon with the seven kids, four of ours and three of theirs, bouncing along the rutted track through the game reserve, on our way back to the campsite. I had insisted on sitting in the back with the kids because I didn't want to talk to the doctor.

"How you doin' back there?" his wife called from the front seat.

"Fine," chorused the children, sated with a day of wildebeest, antelope, giraffes, elephants, water buffalo, hippos, and way too many zebras. Nauseated by the bucking of the car, I concentrated on watching the horizon through the open back of the Land Rover. Motion sickness can be contagious with a bunch of kids.

"What shall we fix for dinner?" the doctor's wife called. "I was thinking chili."

I faced away from the children, grabbed the nearest container, a Kleenex box half full of tissues, and threw up into it, as discreetly as I could manage.

"Whatcha doing, Mom?" asked Mary Beth.

I crumpled the box, stuffed it into a comer, and wiped my mouth on my sleeve before I turned back around. "I thought I saw some warthogs," I lied.

"Warthogs?" the doctor shouted. "Did you say warthogs? That's the only animal I haven't filmed today." A generation earlier, that would have been the only animal he hadn't shot today. He circled back.

As if on cue, a family of warthogs came around the bend, trotting toward us, fly-whisk tails erect, three little ones following the parents. Warthogs are about the size of pigs, ugly, bad-tempered, with razor-sharp curved tusks. The babies are so homely they're sort of cute. The doctor stopped the car, grabbed his movie camera, and stepped out into the road.

"Dad! You're not supposed to get out of the car," his oldest daughter called to him. "You always make us stay in the car."

"I'll be careful. This will just take a minute." He stepped away from the car and began to film. The big warthog charged him.

"Dad! Dad!" the kids yelled. "Look out! He's charging you."

He paid no attention. All the children joined in the uproar. They screamed at him to get back in the car. The warthog, head down, rapidly closed the space between them. He looked up, away from the eyepiece of the camera. I couldn't hear what he said as he turned and sprinted toward the car. His wife held the door open, he leaped onto the running board, dived into the car, and slammed the door.

"Why didn't you come when we yelled at you?" she asked.

"I didn't realize he was that close. He looked farther away in the viewfinder. Anyway, I'm okay. He didn't get me." Nobody said anything for a while as we drove back to the campsite, where we had left our car.

The doctor's wife and I chopped onions for the chili. "I hear you're having some female trouble," she said.

"Yes, I am," I sighed.

"I have trouble that way, too. I have really heavy periods, and I can't get my husband interested in doing anything about it. He says that's just women's lot in life. Eve's curse." Was it possible that callousness about "female trouble" was a prerequisite for service as a mission doctor? She ladled the chili into plastic bowls.

"Aren't you hungry?" Stewart asked me.

I turned away. "Not particularly, I'll just have some crackers and make some tea." He probably thought we were having a nice vacation.

In the morning, the doctor and his family left for their safari in South Africa and we were on our own. We drove for two days to the Nyadiri mission station in Southern Rhodesia, about thirty miles from Salisbury. Two months had passed since Dr. Fisher delivered his diagnosis. I could still hear the urgency in his voice and Stewart's dismissal. I had persevered, put aside my anger, and followed instructions. We arrived at the mission on a national holiday honoring the founding father, Cecil Rhodes. Though officially it was "Rhodes's Day" and the day after "Founders' Day," everyone called it "Rogues and Bounders." The order imposed on the country by the British was crumbling, and, before long, the colonies would fall like dominos, one after another. The missionaries at Nyadiri station had watched the Congo implode. They were eager to hear our stories and politely curious about our presence in their midst. After lunch, I presented to the mission doctor the letter from the doctor in New York. Surely he had advised the staff here that we were coming? Not so.

"I'm not sure what he had in mind," the mission doctor mused. "Our duty is to serve the Africans. We don't even provide medical care for our own families. We send them to the government hospital in Salisbury, for whites only. It's much better than the facilities they provide for the Africans. So the Africans come to us."

I looked at him in dismay. He rallied. "Of course, we can make an exception for you. And I'm sure we can find a place for your family to stay."

I knew I was expected to decline. "Thank you, but I can't ask you to do that." Hope evaporated once more, and despair loomed.

Stewart spoke up. "Perhaps you could refer us to a doctor in Salisbury."

"Not only that, I can recommend a place for you to stay. It's a vacation spot for missionary families. It's called Resthaven. We often go there when we need to take a break. It's about fifteen miles from Salisbury. It's run by a British couple, Mr. and Mrs. Briggs. I feel sure you would be comfortable there. "Shall I call and see if they can take you?" Stewart and I looked at each other. It wasn't what we expected, but it was something.

Chapter Twenty-Three

I couldn't have imagined a better refuge than Resthaven. The late afternoon sun shone on neat cottages scattered around the grounds. Children kicked a soccer ball around on the central green. We followed Mr. Briggs down the path to a little cottage. "A bit snug," he said, "but it's all I have at the moment. In a couple of days, I could move you to something larger and more comfortable." I assured him it would be fine.

"Mrs. Briggs and I invite all the children to come for tea at five o'clock. Your children are welcome to come and watch *Little Noddy*.

He noticed my confusion. "On the telly," he explained. "From Britain. I believe you Americans call them cartoons." All four children stared at him, wide-eyed. They could never have anticipated television.

"The nights are chilly at this altitude. I'll have the boy bring some firewood and I'll look in on you later, if I may, to see if you need anything."

He was hardly out of hearing when Mary Beth tugged at my skirt.

"Mom, He said he'd send the boy. You told us never to call them boys."

The day had been filled with emotional turmoil and confusion. Nothing had gone the way we expected. Later, the children tucked into bed, Stewart and I sat by the fire, reading. A light tap at the door,

"May I come in?" It was Mr. Briggs. "I won't stay, just want to make sure you have everything you need."

"Very thoughtful of you," Stewart said. "We're quite comfortable, thank you. It's good to be here."

The fire crackled. Mr. Briggs stood there, gravely studying me.

"I haven't asked how you came to be here," he said to me, "I believe you may be in some kind of trouble."

I started to cry. I couldn't stop. I sobbed. Finally, someone acknowledged my distress. I wept as I poured out my sorrows to this kind man. He listened intently to my tale of woe, no interruptions. Stewart handed me his handkerchief and sat silent. This was between me and Mr. Briggs. I came at last to the part where we were directed to Resthaven.

He smiled. "I believe I can help you. God sent you here, you know. I have an arrangement with a doctor in Salisbury, the finest surgeon in the Rhodesias. He's Jewish. He can arrange a bed for you in the government hospital at no cost. He's fond of missionaries. If you like, I'll phone him tomorrow and make an appointment for you to see him as soon as possible and decide what you want to do."

And just like that, everything fell into place. I trusted Dr. Rosen instinctively. I noticed impressive certificates and diplomas on the wall of his office. He was kind. He listened to me. I liked his eyes.

Dr. Rosen examined me and confirmed the need for a complete hysterectomy. "I can arrange a bed for you tomorrow, in the ward, at no cost to the mission. I have access to funds contributed for this purpose. With your permission, I'll perform the surgery the following day."

It seemed a miracle. Maybe God was watching over me after all.

The fire crackled that evening in our little cottage. The resolution had come so suddenly. I tried not to think about what might happen to the children if I didn't survive the surgery.

Stewart cleared his throat. "I have a gift for you."

I brightened at the prospect. Gifts were rare. I wondered what it would be. Something personal, for the hospital. A new nightgown, perhaps. Maybe a shawl. Or a book.

The children watched, breathless, to see how Mom liked the present from Dad.

"Open it," he prompted. "We all signed it."

He gave me a Bible.

When Stewart served a parish, it was his custom to present Bibles to those going into the hospital. But I wasn't a parishioner. I was a wife. What was he thinking? I studied the children's careful signatures. I smiled at them. I hugged the book to myself to show them I was pleased. I stammered my thanks.

That Bible traveled, unopened, for years, from bookshelf to bookshelf, from Africa to America, from Connecticut to New York, and back to Connecticut. Finally to California. I couldn't bear to look at it. Only recently did I repent. After all, his gift was well-intended. It was the best he could do, to acknowledge his apprehension, to suppress the thought of the family without a wife and mother. In his own inhibited way, he cared for me.

The first hospital days were filled with discomfort and pain. Dr. Rosen emerged occasionally from the fog. He assured me everything had gone well. Stewart appeared, briefly, from time to time. The children were fine and sent their love.

Gradually I became aware of the fifteen women with whom I shared the ward. Visiting hours were limited to half an hour in the afternoon and in the evening, and Stewart managed to get there almost every day, although he had a full agenda with the children and a fifteen-mile drive from Resthaven. Finally, I was allowed to get out of bed. Stewart shared his observation that all the women in the ward walked slowly, cradling their stomachs.

The color division was evident, as expected in this still-colonial country. White patients, white doctors and nurses, black orderlies, cleaners, and tray carriers. The other patients already suspected me of being a friend to the Africans. They figured out I was a missionary, as well as an American, therefore suspect.

The nurses were brisk, sometimes brusque, always efficient. The African staff smiled at me and murmured phrases of concern and good wishes. They invoked God's blessing. I looked forward to those friendly black faces, and I couldn't help but notice the discourtesy and scorn they endured from their "superiors." It would be several years before the winds of change blew through Southern Rhodesia, destroying the strict order of racial separation.

There was a large tumor, Dr. Rosen said, the size of a grapefruit, and several small ones. He'd removed my uterus. He described this as a partial hysterectomy. "You were frightfully anemic," he said. "We gave you three pints of blood."

It pleased me to know I now had African blood in my veins.

Children weren't allowed in the ward, but one afternoon, during the half-hour for visitors, four precious little faces peeked around the door at the far end of the ward. The attendant brought a wheelchair and I joined them out on the sun porch. We all talked at once, so much to tell. Mary Beth showed me the Band-Aid on her head. A butterfly bandage, she called it. She had run up the stairs outside the cottage, crashed into the wide-open casement window, and cut a gash in her head. Aside from that, they were all in fine shape, eager to tell me their adventures.

Stewart had given in to the boys' pleas for a BB gun. He looked a bit sheepish. We had discussed this, but I never agreed they should have one. Confronted with a done deal, I let it go. He was in charge of them now and doing an admirable job. I wasn't surprised he had taken the girls for haircuts. Hugs and kisses, sniffles, but no tears, and they were gone. I could hear their chatter in the stairwell.

Two nurses pushed a metal cart to my bedside, loaded with scissors and other sharp objects, dressings, and bandages. Time to take out the stitches. The older nurse wore a cap identifying her as Instructor. I hoped she would be the one. The young one looked scared to death. The Instructor nudged the not-instructor, gave her a stern look. Get on with it.

The trainee trembled. "I'm here to remove your stitches," she stammered.

They had to learn on somebody, and that would be me. I gave her what I hoped was an encouraging smile. Emboldened, she picked up the big scissors. I pulled up my nightgown and exposed my bandaged abdomen. She looked at the bandage.

"I've never done this before," she blurted. The older nurse glared at her.

"It's a first time for me, too," I said. She looked as though she might faint.

I hoped she would faint, so the experienced nurse could take over. No such luck. She took a deep breath. Then another one. Her hands shook. She tugged and pulled and snipped away. I grimaced and studied the ceiling. I tried not to move. Or groan.

At last, it was over. I couldn't tell which of us was more relieved. She wrapped me in fresh bandages, and the older one marched her away, pushing the odious cart, on her way to the next victim.

My fellow patients invited me to join them to knit baby clothes for indigent African babies. I accepted yarn and needles. It didn't seem to matter I didn't knit well. They unraveled my work and re-did the booties. I went back to reading books.

After ten days in the ward, I was more than ready to go home to my family A staph infection had come quietly into the room and worked its way down the line of beds toward me. I escaped just in time.

Stewart and I waited, side by side, not saying much, for our final meeting with Dr. Rosen. I studied the array of diplomas and certificates on the wall, more than ready to leave the hospital, eager to see the children. I didn't have much stamina yet, and my abdomen was quite tender. The ordeal was finally over.

Dr. Rosen took his seat across the desk. Those kind eyes studied me.

"I'm pleased with your progress. You must take time to recover your strength. Given time and care, you will be completely well." We smiled at each other. He turned to Stewart.

"Your wife has been through an ordeal. She needs peace and quiet. She must rest, not do any work for six months." He paused, looked intently at Stewart, as though to make sure he was listening. "You must not, in any account, take her back to the Congo. You and your family need to go home to the States, where your wife will have the care she needs."

Enormous gratitude and relief welled up in me. Perhaps it had not all been for nothing. After all the months of despair, the future opened before me. The Congo adventure, finally over. We could go home. I turned to Stewart and watched the color drain from his face. He looked stunned. For once, he struggled to find words.

"I'll see what we can do," he said, quietly, tentatively.

"I've had some experience with missionaries, you know. I appreciate your devotion to your work. But you must put your wife's recovery foremost. The Congo is no place for a family."

Dr. Rosen and Stewart stared at each other. It looked like an impasse. I waited.

"If you insist on going back to the Congo, you must see to it that the servants do all the work."

I imagined the doctor's impressive household staff, a retinue of faithful servants. I thought of faithful Baba Samuel, caring for our home, waiting for us to return.

Stewart broke the spell, pushed back his chair, and stood.

"Thank you, doctor. We appreciate all you have done for us." He reached across the desk to shake hands. He never liked to be told what to do.

"Don't forget all the good advice I just gave you."

Stewart helped me to my feet and steadied me, his hand under my elbow.

"Dr. Rosen, I'll never be able to thank you for all you have done for us," I said.

He came from behind his desk and took my hand in his. His hands had saved my life. He looked at me with compassion. "I'm glad I was here to help."

In the car, on our way back to Resthaven and the children, Stewart seemed preoccupied.

"Well," I asked him, "What do you think?"

Startled, he said, "What do you mean?"

"About what Dr. Rosen said, that we should go home to the States."

Stewart looked straight ahead, shook his head slowly from side to side. "You know how those doctors always exaggerate."

Now I was the one stunned and pale and silent.

Several days later, on the first day of August, we said goodbye to Resthaven and began our journey back to the Congo in our comfortable station wagon. We left our car in Kitwe to be serviced. I looked with dismay at the second-hand pickup truck Stewart had arranged to be purchased for Pastor Joab. Surely he didn't expect me to travel in this broken-down vehicle?

The boys helped him pile our boxes and suitcases into the bed of the truck, and climbed on top of the baggage. Mary Beth and Martha sat between Stewart and me, hot and sticky on the plastic-covered bench seat. We jolted along the familiar road back to the Congo as part of an armed convoy of United Nations soldiers, the daily northbound one-o'clock-in-the-afternoon run to Elisabethville. They anticipated more of the usual trouble on the road, snipers in the woods, renegade soldiers who dragged logs across the road to stop traffic.

I felt like a piece of baggage myself, a hostage there against my will, not even able to pull myself together to entertain the little girls. Every bump in the road intensified my discomfort. The boys, subdued, sprawled across the suitcases, their backs against the cab of the truck. I could hear them murmuring to each other. The BB-gun was well hidden inside a burlap bag, and they were forbidden to touch it. Listless, hope-less, I drowsed through the still heat of the afternoon. Red dust billowed up over us.

My reverie shattered at the sudden sound of a gunshot. The United Nations soldiers leaped out of their trucks and sprinted down the road, guns ready. In the back of the truck, Peter and Tim scrambled for cover, burrowing under suitcases and boxes. Mary Beth and Martha crouched under the dashboard. I just sat there, too dispirited to move. The convoy slowed and stopped. We waited. Stewart climbed out of the truck. He was back in minutes.

"False alarm. One of the trucks had a tire blowout, that's all." He went around the truck to talk to the boys. "You can come out now, it's okay." The soldiers changed the tire in record time, and the convoy moved slowly forward—the soldiers on alert, scanning the tall grass on each side of the road.

"Welcome to the Congo," Stewart muttered.

Chapter Twenty-Four

In Elisabethville, just before dark, Maurice and Lois welcomed us. What a comfort to see their dear faces again. They encouraged us to stay with them, at least for a couple of days. It seemed like old times to sit once more around their table and enjoy Lois's famous roast beef and Yorkshire pudding. Uncertain of its provenance, we had taken to calling it roast beast.

"I understand congratulations are in order, Stewart," Maurice said, as he served the plates. Stewart looked up, surprised, wary, as though he had been ambushed.

"I'm not sure what you mean."

"Is it possible you haven't heard? I understand you have been appointed director of the seminary at Mulungwishi."

Maurice turned to me. "Did you know about this?"

"No. I don't know anything about this." I looked at Stewart. "How long has this been going on?"

Stewart was clearly on the defensive. "I knew it was in the works. Woody encouraged me to put my name in for the appointment, but I didn't know it was official."

"When were you planning to tell me?"

"Well, I didn't see any point in talking about it when you were in the hospital, and it hadn't been decided yet. I didn't want to worry you."

"Oh dear," Maurice said. "I seem to have put my foot into it. I'm sorry."

"It's not your fault," I said. "Stewart should have consulted me when he decided he wanted that job."

"You're both exhausted, it's been a long day, and we have spoiled your homecoming," Lois said. "We didn't mean to let the cat out of the bag. It's a fine appointment, and we're happy for you." She turned to me. "I thought you always wanted to live at Mulungwishi."

"It's a lot to take in," I said. "Too much."

"Bishop Booth is due to return from the States any day," Maurice said. "He said he would fill you in on details of the appointment when he gets here. In the meantime, you'll be at home in Jadotville."

Confused, hurt, and furious, I didn't want to make a scene.

"It's been a long day," I said. "I think I'll go to bed."

"Your room is ready for you," Lois said. "Get your jammies on. I'll bring you a cup of tea."

She propped up pillows for me and sat on the bed while we drank our tea. She had long ago realized a cup of tea could usually calm things down, even if it couldn't help to solve the problem. She had seen me through a lot of crises. I wondered if she could help me this time.

"As we left the hospital yesterday," I told her, "the doctor told Stewart we needed to go home to America."

"What did Stewart say to that?"

"He said those doctors always exaggerate."

"Well, let's see what tomorrow brings. Right now, you need to get to sleep." She took my empty cup, fluffed the pillows, and tucked the covers around me.

"Maurice and I will pray with you about this," she said, as she turned off the light.

On Sunday, we went with Lois and Maurice to services in the big church the Methodists had built in Elisabethville. Some important government officials strolled up the center aisle with the minister and took seats on the platform. A guard of honor shambled up the aisle close behind. They were a double file of unkempt soldiers, a rabble of scruffy unshaved men in stained and wrinkled khaki. They leaned on their guns, talked, and joked with each other and belched loudly. They ogled the women in the congregation, adjusted their trousers, leaned on the pews. They stank of sweat and stale beer. I regretted my position on the aisle.

The preacher made the most of the opportunity to demonstrate his eloquence. The sermon seemed to last forever. At last, the band played a sort of march. On command to "Present Arms," guns pointed every which way. I felt sure those guns were loaded. I would have given anything not to be there. The rotund politicians were ushered out and the soldiers lurched after them, out of step. The music faded as they trudged away, down the street.

On the road to Jadotville that afternoon, we were stopped by heavy logs across the road. We had no papers for Joab's truck, and the soldiers were drunk and surly. Stewart talked his way through. We found our house occupied by guests from America, a minister and his wife, in town to preach a revival. I went to bed. Stewart and Baba Samuel took care of the children and the guests.

The tradition of "open house" at Jadotville was so deeply ingrained, I couldn't follow the doctor's orders to rest. People continued to show up and expected to be fed and housed. I was back in the kitchen. Stewart spent his days at Mulungwishi, busy with his new responsibilities at the School of Theology. Only two students had enrolled, but that did not discourage him. He was sure there would be others.

We were offered housing in the two-bedroom basement apartment at Mulungwishi in which we had spent the previous Christmas when the soldiers blew up the bridges. I couldn't imagine the six of us living there. Several of the missionaries volunteered to help me give the children their lessons. I couldn't possibly do it by myself. I felt helpless, a pawn in a game without rules.

The children seemed listless, not asking many questions. They played outside in the afternoon while I rested. Stewart took them to the Union Minière pool. I went with them, even went into the water, and paddled around a bit. In the evening they curled up on the bed close to me to read their books. Stewart led them through their prayers. "God bless Mommy."

We had been home in Jadotville less than a week. I was resting in the afternoon. Stewart came into the bedroom. "I have some news. There's a telegram from Sakeji School. It's from the headmaster."

I couldn't believe I was hearing this. What did Sakeji School want from me? As it turned out, they wanted my children.

"Because of my appointment at the seminary, the headmaster has consented to the urgent request by one of the missionaries to accept all four of our children at Sakeji. The term has already started, and the children are to be there as soon as we can pack up their things and arrange transportation."

"Did you know about this?"

He nodded, sheepishly.

"Who was it? Did you ask somebody to do this?"

"Actually, no, I didn't. One of our friends did it on his own."

"Some friend. And you didn't consult me?" I asked.

"He thought he was doing us a favor. He thought it would be easier for you without the children."

"Well, whoever he is, he doesn't know me very well."

"There was no point in getting you all upset until we knew for sure that Sakeji would take them. He said it was an answer to prayer. I thought you might be relieved they would be provided for."

I fell back on the pillows and sobbed. What would be the use of living if I didn't have my children? I pulled a pillow out from behind my head and beat it with my fists. How could anyone think I would be better off without them? I howled with rage and fury. How could Stewart dare to do this? I couldn't stop crying. I wasn't strong enough to put a stop to this. He could send them away. It was as though they were already gone. He stood there beside the bed and watched me, waited for me to say something.

"You can send my children away; I can't stop you. If you send them away, I will die."

Still, he waited. Finally, he seemed to make up his mind.

"I'll send a telegram to the headmaster and tell him the children will not be coming. I'll thank him for his offer. You realize we are burning our bridges. They will never take any of our children after this." He turned and walked out of the room.

After a while, I stopped crying. I was sick and tired of being helpless. I needed to get well, to be strong. I was determined not to die and become a sermon illustration, that poor, brave woman, that self-sacrificing mother who gave her life for The Work, leaving those four little children for her brave husband to raise alone.

I knew all about those stories. I'd read far too many books written by missionaries. Their long-suffering wives played a supporting role in those stories, as did the children. The wives were barely mentioned unless or until they died of malaria or blackwater fever. Or, too often, in childbirth. The brave widower carried on as best he could until he came home on furlough. He traveled around, preached his sad story, and sure enough, every time, some woman volunteered as the replacement wife and mother. All too often she met the same fate, worn out and undernourished, too far from home, too many babies to care for, her husband out saving souls. And then, inevitably, after she went Home to Jesus, he would find another.

I knew that story, and I'd be damned if some other woman was going to raise my children. I got out of bed, washed my face, put on my clothes, and went to the kitchen.

The daily evangelistic services continued, led by Stewart, Joab, and the minister from Maryland. Stewart drove Joab's pickup around, gathering up more sinners. They chalked up three-hundred-and-fourteen Decisions for Christ that week. "It was worth all the effort we put into it," he assured me. The local pastors would follow up.

Baba Samuel and I did our part. We put meals on the table for the family and visiting clergy. Every day it was more difficult to find food in the few stores in town. And every day we waited for Bishop Booth to come home to the Congo and resolve our dilemma.

The bishop and his wife were both in constant demand in the States for their insight on Congolese affairs and their deep personal knowledge of the history of the Congo. They always expressed themselves with eloquence, met with and advised highly placed diplomats at the United Nations. The bishop counseled top officials of The Board and found time to write a series of detailed letters to the families of the missionaries who were under his jurisdiction. My parents received those letters and preserved them. I have read those letters, full of concern and affection for his beloved flock of missionaries and Africans, with assurance we were in God's hands.

Late in August, we received word the bishop was on his way. He wanted to see Stewart and me right away. I confess I had some apprehension. I knew how important the seminary was to the bishop, and I knew his high regard for Stewart. He and Mrs. Booth had made enormous sacrifices in their lifelong work in the Congo. Mrs. Booth had endured long periods of ill health. Their labor in Africa meant separation from their children and grandchildren. In spite of all the demands of his position of leadership, he was always mindful of those who suffered. What would he expect from me?

I knew he cared for me. He and I had an especially warm friendship, ever since he won my heart with his admiration of the undercooked apple pie, all those years ago, when it all began. Now my fate was in his hands. Or, as he might say, in God's hands. This would be my last chance for deliverance.

And then Stewart and I were there, with him, in his familiar office, a simple room in what had been Elisabethville, and was now Lubumbashi. So many changes in those years, so much grief and suffering.

All that trouble had taken its toll on the three of us. The bishop was exhausted from his constant travels and the demands for his advice. He greeted us warmly, smiled at me, asked about my health. He listened carefully as I told him what Dr. Rosen had said, that if I was to recover, we must go home to America. He gave Stewart a sharp look. I held my breath, waiting for his response.

"Of course, you must follow the doctor's orders," he said at last. "Your health depends on that. I'm recommending a leave of absence."

My heart rejoiced. I started to cry. I waited to hear what Stewart would say.

"You know that some months ago we petitioned The Board for a leave of absence, which they denied," he said. "I've given some thought to what I might do in the event we returned home. I've kept up my contacts with colleagues in New York and Connecticut. Perhaps I can get a parish."

"That's certainly a possibility," the bishop said, carefully, "but I don't advise it for now. It would be too stressful for your wife and family. It would be impossible for her not to be involved in the work of the parish. I have something else in mind for you. This is a leave of absence, not a dismissal. I don't want to lose you two. I hope you can return to Africa one day when things calm down."

Stewart shifted in his seat. The bishop continued.

"I'm recommending The Board send you back to school to pursue a Ph.D. in Theology. Perhaps you'd go back to Yale; you already have connections, and you did well there with your Masters in African Studies. This will prepare you to return here and take the position you have been offered as head of the seminary at Mulungwishi. How does that strike you?"

Stewart may have overridden the doctor's advice, but this was different. The bishop's word was not to be denied. In his brilliant administrative style, he made it easy for Stewart to accede with his offer of two strong incentives: the opportunity for further study, and a future chance at the seminary.

"That's more than generous," Stewart said. "Thank you."

I took a deep breath and sat back in my chair. Deliverance.

The bishop turned to me.

"I have some idea of what this year has been for you," I said. "It means everything to me that in the midst of all your important work in diplomacy, you have taken time to find a solution for us. Thank you."

"You two are very dear to me," the bishop said. "You have done good work here for the church. But I admit, I'm going to miss your cheese soufflé."

He stood, and so did we. He turned to Stewart. "I'll write a letter to the general secretary for you to carry back to New York, with my recommendations for you."

My long ordeal was ended. We were free to go.

Chapter Twenty-Five

Great-Aunt Mary welcomed us back to her comfortable home in New Haven, and we settled in, safe in America. That last year in the Congo seemed like a bad dream. The children picked up their routines from the furlough year. Mary Beth, Martha, and Peter caught the school bus on the corner of Ridge Road to join their former classmates.

For Tim, the transition did not go well. The chaos and cacophony of Michael J. Whalen Junior High School overwhelmed him.

"The place is a zoo," Stewart said. "I hated to leave him. He looked as though he might cry. I think he would gladly have returned to Sakeji, had that been possible, but we don't have a choice. He'll just have to get used to it."

He never got used to it, but he learned to endure it. His attempts to make friends with the African American boys were violently rejected. They beat him up on the school bus.

I had days of leisure, hours to rest and regain my strength and composure. One afternoon, I waited at the window to watch Martha hop off the school bus. I savored the deep satisfaction my children were no longer in danger. Martha sauntered along, waded through the pile of autumn leaves on the lawn, kicked them with her little feet. She stopped, stood still for a moment, looked up, looked down. Suddenly she seemed to be paralyzed in fright. I opened the front door, stepped out, and called to her. She ran across the lawn. I hugged her to me as she wept.

"Martha, what is it? What happened?"

"Oh, Mom," she sobbed, "the leaves are falling off the trees."

"It's all right, honey," I said. I held her close. "That happens here, in the fall. It happens every year. The trees will get new leaves in the spring."

What other disasters had I forgotten to mention? Her tears subsided and her shudders eased as I hugged her. I comforted her with milk and cookies. How could I anticipate the other natural events that might terrorize her? What had I done to this dear child?

I'm ashamed to tell you this became a family joke on Martha. "Remember the day when Martha got scared when the leaves fell off the trees?" How long did it take for me to realize this wasn't funny, and Martha wasn't laughing?

Stewart and I had one last obligation, our exit interview with the chairman of The Board. I felt a bit shabby in the pristine lobby of the Interchurch Center on Riverside Drive in New York City. There hadn't been time to buy new clothes and shoes, and I needed a professional haircut.

On my first visit to the center years ago, when this Africa business was all new, I had been in awe of the marble walls, the bas-relief sculpture on the wall, representing men in all aspects of the mission—preachers, doctors, teachers, evangelists. I had hardly noticed the figure of a woman, her arms around some children. No longer in awe, I wondered how many churches Mr. Rockefeller could have built in the Congo for the price of all that marble.

I kept those thoughts to myself. We were here on legitimate business. We had an appointment with the general secretary. I resolved to be on good behavior. The elevator whisked us up to the seventeenth floor.

We were anticipated, but our welcome was tepid. Nobody seemed glad to see us. It seemed odd. I hadn't expected hostility.

A secretary handed us a sheaf of questionnaires, and we dutifully filled up the pages. Just the facts, none of the emotions. No place to mention danger, or fear, disappointment, or privation.

Physical exams first. The no-nonsense nurse glanced at my file as she led me away down the hall. "What's this? A hysterectomy? Why did you have a hysterectomy?"

Did she not know? I resisted the impulse to give a smart aleck response to such a silly question. Would any woman have a hysterectomy on a whim? I stammered something about a tumor on the ovaries. She cut me short. I followed her into the examination room.

"Take off your clothes. The doctor is waiting."

The doctor, a stranger to me, was not gentle. He seemed dubious of my answers to his questions.

Many years later, I requested that my medical files, which I had never seen, be sent to me. I read, for the first time, what the various doctors had written about me on that day in 1963:

"She had several terrifying experiences in Congo and has experienced fatigue, moodiness, irritability."

"Hysterectomy and general depression. Children separated at school. Living conditions, food. Attacked 2 times in yard, threw things at her, attempted to (illegible). "Seems a bit tense and says she nearly had a nervous breakdown but seems better."

"Generally good physical condition, all things considered. No recommendations for therapy."

I hoped the final interview with the chairman would go smoothly. After all, we had that letter from Bishop Booth.

Andrea Bancroft was also waiting for the general secretary. We had last seen her several weeks ago in Elisabethville when she and Jeff were leaving on furlough.

"Where's Jeff?" Stewart asked.

Andrea seemed reluctant to answer. There were other people in the waiting room, and she was obviously uncomfortable. "He stayed in Belgium to finish some research," she said in a low voice. "They're mad at me because he didn't come home with the girls and me."

The office door opened suddenly. She flinched when the chairman appeared. He did not look pleased. She disappeared into the inner sanctum. Stewart and I whispered together about the hostile reception. Maybe the chairman was just having a bad day. I paged through the magazines, *World Outlook* and *Africa Today*.

The door opened suddenly. Andrea came out, pale and shaken, struggling for control. She slowed, leaned down, and whispered to me, "Whatever happens, don't cry."

She'd wait for us downstairs in the cafeteria.

The chairman brusquely ushered us into his office. He took his seat behind the enormous desk. In the huge window, just over his shoulder, I could see the Hudson River and the Palisades, and the gargoyles on the carillon tower of Riverside Church next door. I flashed on the poor little mud churches in which the Africans worshipped.

The chairman gestured to us to sit down. Two folders lay on his pristine desktop. His and hers. He stared at us. We waited.

He broke the silence, "What brings you here?"

Stewart reached into his jacket pocket and placed the bishop's letter on the desk. Was it possible the chairman had not seen the letter?

"This may help to explain our situation," he offered. "It's from Bishop Booth."

The chairman cut him off. "I've seen the letter."

"Then you know the bishop appointed me to head up the seminary at Mulungwishi. I had to turn it down because of my wife's health. She's recovering from a hysterectomy. Bishop Booth recommended we return to America to recover, and for me to study for a Ph.D., to return to Africa when things settle down."

"And when do you think that might be?" the chairman asked. He was playing with us, a cat confronting two scared mice. "We just paid for you to get an expensive master's degree from Yale, and I sent you two out there for a four-year term. Now it's one year later, and you're back here, without my permission, and you expect me to pay for another expensive degree. Do you seriously think that's a good plan?"

"Well," Stewart said, "Bishop Booth thought ..."

The chairman slammed his hand down on the letter on his desk. "Do you see Bishop Booth in this room? No. *He* can't help you now. *Here's* what you're going to do. You're going to find yourself a church some-where and forget about ever going back overseas."

He was through with us. But I wasn't through with him. Could he just brush us off like this? Still, I was surprised to hear my own voice. "We were called to serve. When I get well, couldn't you send us someplace where we could live in safety and keep the children with us? Someplace where we could live like normal people?"

His cold blue eyes flashed fire. He gripped the edge of his desk.

"We're not interested in someone looking for an easy life," he sneered. "We need people who will go where they are sent and stay there until we tell them to leave. You left your post. How do I know you won't do that again?"

I felt dizzy. Of course he was furious. My will to survive had deprived him of a martyr. He could have used my death in Africa as a rallying cry for The Cause. If I could make the supreme sacrifice, others would dig deep into their pockets. If I were dead, he could use me. Alive, I was an impediment. I had been called by God and un-called by this angry man. I was no longer a missionary. I was free to chart my own course. Or so I thought.

Stewart stood up. I did, too. We hadn't been there for more than a few minutes, but it could have been a lifetime. Nobody shook hands or said "Goodbye," or "God bless." We stumbled out the door, through the waiting room, down the hall to the elevator.

We were alone in the elevator.

"Did he just fire us?" I asked.

"Seems that way."

"We're not missionaries anymore?"

"I guess not," he confirmed.

Andrea waited for us in the cafeteria. We had been through so much, it seemed appropriate to be together this day.

"I'll get us some coffee," Stewart said. He seemed distracted, but who wouldn't be, after what we had just been through?

"Why was he so mad at us?" I asked him.

"It's a long story," Stewart explained. "He's an old China hand, from a group of missionaries who were expelled by Chairman Mao. They're convinced if they had stayed at their posts, China wouldn't have gone to the Communists, and he's determined that history won't repeat itself in Africa."

"That sounds rather arrogant," Andrea offered.

"Do you think you can get a church?" I asked him.

"We'll see. I think I have some good connections."

I knew it wouldn't be easy. The bishop under whom he served in West Hartford had been furious when Stewart left, in the middle of a building program, to go to Africa. Insubordination doesn't sit well with bishops or chairmen—The Powers That Be.

"Did you cry?" Andrea asked me.

I shook my head. "No."

"Good girl."

"Would you wait for me for a few minutes?" Stewart said. "There's someone upstairs I want to see."

He was gone a long time, almost an hour.

"What took you so long?" I asked.

"I heard there was a job opening in recruitment and training of missionaries. I put in an application. My buddy will put in a good word for me. I think I'd be good at that."

"You mean you'd work for that guy who just fired us?"

"He might be your enemy," he said, "but he is not mine."

I held it against him for years. I might have been more understanding. He needed a job to support the children and me. He worked long hours, was good at what he did, and he traveled a lot.

I had my own work: to regain my health, learn to live in America, and help the children learn the rules in a place strange to them.

We had been home just six weeks. I had gone to bed early, and the children came in to say goodnight. I wanted to help them feel safe and secure, after so much stress and danger.

"We're going to be all right," I said and pointed to the telephone on the bedside table. "If we need help, or if anybody is sick, I can call the doctor, and he'll come."

"And they don't kill people in America," I added.

They nodded solemnly, kissed me, and went to bed. Stewart tucked them in and heard their prayers.

The following day, President Kennedy was assassinated.

Mary Beth came home from school in tears.

"But Mom," she said, "you promised."

I resolved to be more careful about making promises.

Epilogue—July 2021

Stewart accepted a position in the office of Missionary Personnel, and traveled extensively, as he had during our furlough year. We bought a house—our first—in New Rochelle, in an intentionally racially integrated neighborhood, a hotbed of advocates for peace and racial justice. I loved it. I joined Women Strike for Peace, got on the bus to demonstrate in Washington D.C. against Nixon's war in Vietnam.

Stewart took a leave of absence from the Interchurch Center to re-acquaint himself with the state of the local parish church in America. The pulpit in New Haven was open, and he hoped to be assigned. The Powers That Be, however, had not forgiven him for abandoning the West Hartford parish when we went to Africa. Instead, they gave him a congregation on the South Shore of Long Island. We sold the house I loved and moved into the parsonage. Many families in the church had left Brooklyn to escape the African Americans who were moving into their neighborhoods. On his first Sunday, Stewart preached on racial justice. The congregation eventually forgave him and loved him anyway. But they didn't love me, a peacenik. I tried. Lord knows, I tried. I taught Sunday school, sang in the choir, joined the Women's Society, helped with the youth group.

Dr. Martin Luther King Jr. was scheduled to preach, for the first time, against the war in Vietnam, at Riverside Church. I announced plans to take the train into the city to hear him and invited people to join me. There were no takers. Months later, Dr. King and Bobby Kennedy—champions of peace and justice—were murdered.

Someone in the hierarchy of the United Methodist Church proposed to make a documentary about a minister and his family who were in trouble with the congregation because of their opposition to the Vietnam War. Stewart and I agreed to do it. We were filmed sitting around the dinner table in the parsonage. The congregation liked the publicity, but not the content. They chastised Stewart and me. Eventually, they voted Stewart out of the pulpit and the family out of the parsonage. Another minister, a good friend, also participated in the film and was forced to leave his church. He left the ministry.

During high school, Peter spent a summer in Norway with the American Field Service. He and Tim spent months in France, at the Collège Cévenol in Le Chambon-sur-Lignon, an important center of passive resistance during the German occupation. The boys finished high school and went off to college. We moved back to New Rochelle and bought the house next door to the one we had sold.

Stewart was reinstated by The Board. Once again, he traveled constantly, all over the world. He worked his way up the ranks and became Secretary of Missionary Personnel. Martha spent a year in India at Woodstock School in the foothills of the Himalayas. Both girls went off to college.

I tiptoed into the world of employment. After a couple of false starts, two weeks as a travel agent, a few months as a teacher of Swahili in the Westchester Street Academy, I was hired as the adult program director in the YWCA in White Plains. I loved this job. I supervised a program for young mothers, "Holiday from Apron Strings." I changed the name to "Women on the Move." The YWCA provided childcare. First, an hour of exercise, then a break for coffee and snacks, and a speaker. Gloria Steinem came, and other feminists. We organized consciousness-raising groups, a brilliant, life-changing concept, telling our stories to strangers. I joined one of the groups.

A delegation of women came to the YWCA from Pace University in New York City, recruiting for the Graduate Management Program for Women, seeking undergraduates with a degree in the Liberal Arts who would earn an MBA to prepare to enter the corporate world. I applied and was accepted, with a full scholarship. I looked forward to a career as a YWCA executive.

I almost lost the opportunity. After years of successful examinations and biopsies, my luck ran out. I had a mastectomy. I recovered in time to join the MBA program and have been cancer-free since then. I was fifty. All those years as a minister's wife and a missionary were not ideal preparation for an MBA. My classmates, all much younger than I, regarded me as a project. They were a delight. They introduced me to bars. I had never been in a bar.

The math was a challenge. I learned to use a slide rule. I bought an expensive gadget—new on the market—an electronic calculator. My mother, once a math teacher, had been disappointed when I'd stopped short of calculus while I was in college. Calculus, she said, was the fun part. I declared a major in Business Economics and discovered that calculus was required. I sat through the lectures in a daze. I passed the course and kept my notebook so that I could remind myself I once performed calculus. I wrote a sonnet about it. Degree in hand, I set out to find a job.

Great-Aunt Mary moved into a beautiful residence for seniors and offered her home to Stewart and me. Empty nesters, we moved back to New Haven. Stewart said that now that I could support myself, he was free to go his own way. He was studying to be a Freudian therapist while continuing his duties at The Board. He took an apartment in New York City, to spare him taking the late train home to New Haven. I was not invited to that apartment. I never saw it. I was unaware that he was already in a serious relationship with another woman.

He wanted a divorce. I didn't want to be divorced. I had an MBA but didn't have a job. In my search for one, I did really well in interviews, but nothing was offered. A young woman in personnel in a bank in Boston took pity on me and explained that I was too old. I was grateful for her candor.

Stewart and I spent a miserable year. I applied for a position with a local bank that was launching an innovative program called Vistas for Women. They proposed to offer free financial counseling for women who were widowed or divorced. For months, they had searched for counselors—women like me, divorced or widowed—with knowledge of business.

I had some experience with computers and Fortran, with those tottery stacks of punched cards.

When Stewart moved out, Fortune smiled. I was to call that day for confirmation of my acceptance. Stewart left the house at 2:30. I called the bank, as instructed, at three o'clock. The job was mine. I felt sick with relief, delirious with joy. I had a private office and a secretary and a generous salary and benefits. I bought an Ultrasuede suit and nice shoes.

At five o'clock in the morning, I rose to study for the series of exams to be a Certified Financial Planner—new vocabulary for me, difficult exams, tricky questions. One by one, I passed the tests and was authorized to put CFP after my name. I joined the network of Women in Business. We were one of the two banks in the country to offer a program like this for women.

I participated in seminars all over the country and stayed in nice hotels. It was glorious. I felt like Cinderella. I traveled twice with a friend to France for a week of hot air ballooning.

After several years, my boss accepted a position in another city, and I was appointed to her post, as an assistant vice president. An officer of the bank! If my dad could see me now!

I joined the local International Association of Financial Planners and attended the annual national meetings. Corporate support for the Vistas for Women program began to erode, and personnel problems took the joy out of my work. A delegation from a bank in West Hartford invited me to set up a program for them. They offered a generous salary and a vice presidency. The offer was irresistible. I could not have anticipated the pitfalls waiting for me.

This was the era in which many banks morphed into investment companies. The program I developed—with color-coded questionnaires, notebooks, educational material—never left the warehouse. On the day it was to be distributed, I was informed the bank had decided not to use it. They escorted me to my new office, a windowless room. The district managers were preparing to be stock traders. To keep my job, I would need to pass the dreaded Series 7 exam. After weeks of intensive study of complicated things I didn't care to know, I passed the exam on my first attempt.

My daughter Martha urged me to come to California for Christmas. Listless with the usual winter cold, I climbed on a plane in an ice storm and landed in San Francisco in paradise. No snow anywhere. Scarlet cyclamen bloomed in oak barrels on the mall of the Stanford Shopping Center. I put my heavy coat in the closet and put on a cardigan sweater. Jolly Santas wore short-sleeved shirts. Suntanned people smiled at me and waved from convertibles. I fell in love with California. If only I could find a job there. Home again in frigid Connecticut, I scraped the ice off my car and went back to work.

The International Association of Financial Planners met in Idaho that year. I stood in line in the cafeteria, eavesdropping on a respectful group gathered around a nice-looking, well-dressed woman. I heard the magic word, "California," and edged into the group. She was looking for someone to replace one of her Certified Financial Planners, someone who had experience in retirement planning for college professors. The Vistas for Women program had added that counseling service back in New Haven. I edged even closer, introduced myself and entered the conversation. We knew many of the same people. She offered me a position in her boutique firm in San Luis Obispo. I noticed that when people said the name of that place, they fell into a sort of reverie.

The position she offered was not salaried, commissions only. I would inherit the portfolio of the man who was retiring. She invited me to come to San Luis Obispo to see the office. "I can see that you are a woman of impeccable taste," I said, "and you would not have an unattractive office. I have to be at work on Monday morning, in West Hartford. I can join you by the end of October, ready to go to work." We kept in touch. She told me later she'd never expected to see me again.

I resigned from my position as an officer of the bank, gave up a good salary, retirement benefits, and health insurance, for the opportunity to work in California on commission. I put my house on the market, hired a moving company, packed up the furniture, and drove my Honda across the country. Halfway across Missouri, the car radio caught my attention. The stock market crashed that day in October 1987. I stopped that night, as planned, at my brother's house in Kansas City.

"What will you do now?" he asked.

"Nothing to do but go on," I said. "I can always wait tables." I hoped that was a joke.

Had I not resigned from my position, I would have had to placate unhappy bank customers who had moved their savings accounts into mutual funds.

My daughter found a perfect garden apartment for me just south of San Luis Obispo, near the Spyglass Inn on Spyglass Drive at Shell Beach. At the end of the street was a small park where I often joined my neighbors to watch the sun set into the Pacific. If I stood on tiptoe on my patio, I could see the ocean. At night, the sound of the waves lapping the shore lulled me to sleep.

I was tired of finance. My daughter invited me to join her family in Sonoma County. I'd put money aside for retirement so that I could pursue my dream to write the Africa story. I turned on the Social Security spigot in 1990 when I was 62, resigned from the financial firm, and joined the family in Sebastopol. We converted the garage into a granny house. I drew the floorplan, borrowed my grandson's Legos to build a scale model for the contractor, and started writing.

For my first submission, I entered a contest to write a short story in fifty-five words. I placed second. The stories were published. I love the challenge of eliminating excess words. Concision, it's called. I joined a memoir class that met in St. Stephen's Episcopal Church, next door to the retirement community in which I now live.

The first time I read, Maudie, the woman-in-charge said. "You write like an English teacher."

"Well, I was an English teacher," I responded.

"We don't write like that anymore," Maudie said. People around the table gasped.

"How do we write?" I asked.

Maudie smiled. "Stick around," she said. "You'll see." Over the months that followed, other women, new to the class, received the same candid criticism. Most of them never came back. Maudie asked wonderful questions. In response to a piece I wrote about the Saturday produce market in Jadotville, I described the African women's clothes as "colorful."

"What color were those clothes?" Maudie asked. "You realize that none of us were there. You need to show us." Steve Boga, from the

Community Education program at Santa Rosa Junior College, took over the class. Maudie continued as the grammarian.

I found good friends in that class and great critique. I learned to eliminate that flowery first paragraph. Maudie edited a collection of our writing, published by a local small press. I contributed ten pages, a quick trip through the Congo experience. It reads like a synopsis of the book in your hands. I traveled to workshops and conferences and book fairs, reading my work to strangers. I no longer wrote like an English teacher.

Robin Pressman invited me to host a monthly program, "A Novel Idea" on the local Public Radio station, KRCB. Suzanne Lang produced the show. For each hour-long program, we focused on the work of one writer, time enough to explore the work in depth. Some of the writers were local, others were passing through on tour at Copperfield's Books store. Some were famous, others were not. They appreciated my thorough preparation for the interview. Some returned with their next book.

For many years, I sang with the Santa Rosa Symphonic Chorus all the great Requiems by Brahms, Mozart, and Verdi. I played my ukulele with the Ukestars, and, on occasion, played tub bass.

I volunteered one summer in Sitka, Alaska, in the admissions office at Sheldon Jackson College. I traveled thirty-three times all over the world with Elderhostel International. In a glorious adventure rafting down the Colorado River in the Grand Canyon, our boat flipped in Hermit Falls and I flew out of the raft into the river. I wrote about that, of course.

I was honored to serve on the Kaiser Permanente Arbitration Oversight Board for a dozen years. This board was composed of eminent physicians, nurses, hospital administrators, other medical professionals, and attorneys. I covered the bases on Medicare.

All this time, I wrote and re-wrote the Congo story. I filled binders with shorter pieces and essays. In a workshop in Santa Fe, I submitted my out-of-the-raft-into-the-river story to Phillip Lopate, author of *The Art of the Personal Essay*.

"Where did you learn to write like that?" he asked me. I had never experienced such validation. I asked Phillip where I could study with him.

"I teach in the low-residency master's degree program at Bennington," he said. "Ten days on campus, and then you go home and write."

"Oh, I could never get into Bennington," I blurted.
"Of course you can," he said. "I'll write a recommendation for you."
I almost fainted.
He smiled. "I look forward to seeing you there," he said.

On the day before I was to fly to Vermont to begin the prestigious master's degree in Writing and Literature, I tripped over the ironing board and injured my foot. A hairline fracture, as it turned out. I hobbled to the phone. The doctor recommended ice, elevation, and a cane. She saw no reason I should not go ahead with my travel plans. I was seventy-three years old. The prospect of gimping around the campus on a cane was not what I had in mind. Friends helped me get on the plane.

While I wasn't the only elder in the program, I was the only one using a cane. The rich curriculum, the lectures and readings by famous poets and writers, overwhelmed me. In workshops, I received critiques from young people who had no knowledge of the historical events I chronicled. I would need to add background information. Everyone said, some with envy, "You have a story." Every month I sent packets of writing to my assigned tutor for critique. Over the two years of the program, I had the best of the best. Susan Cheever, George Packer, Phillip Lopate, Sven Birkerts.

I presented my senior lecture, for which Susan Cheever suggested the title, "Lumumba and Me." I received my master's degree in Writing and Literature in June 2003. My thesis covered my first years in the Congo. Years later, Bennington College offered a post-graduate semester, and I was the first to take advantage of the opportunity. I studied with Peter Trachtenberg. Those ten mid-winter days on the campus were a bone-chilling ordeal of ice and snow. I bundled up and strapped crampons onto my boots.

Eight years ago, I left my beloved granny house and moved into Burbank Heights, a local retirement community. I continue to write and participate in critique groups. I was fortunate to find a perfect mentor, Skye Blaine. She coaches our memoir group, "SkyeWriters." We meet for several hours every Tuesday morning. During the pandemic, we met online. Skye and her husband, Boudewijn Boom, give me extraordinary support.

My children and nine grandchildren have done well for themselves. They made good choices in marriage partners. They keep in touch with one another, often vacation together. They are strong-minded and often disagree. There are fierce arguments and misunderstandings. They love one another. When tragedy strikes, when we suffer irredeemable loss, we mourn together, support and comfort one another as best we can. It's a sort of miracle they survived a childhood fraught with danger and violence. They are strong and compassionate, good citizens of the world. All credit goes to them.

They are well educated, college graduates, several with post-graduate degrees. I include the spouses of children and grandchildren in this roster of professions: educators and administrators; speech pathologists; international aid workers; an electronic engineer; civil engineers, both in alternative energy; epidemiologists; woodworkers; a financial advisor; a couple of organic farmers; several writers and artists; a designer; and a brand-new medical doctor. We are voracious readers.

There are five great-grands, so far, smart and cute and fast on their little feet.

I love you all, more than I can say.

Informal Guide to Some Swahili Words and Phrases

Swahili is a lovely language—flexible and logical. Each vowel and consonant has its own unique, simple sound. There is no gender. The Swahili spoken in the Katanga varies from the language spoken in other areas and is less formal. Here are some useful colloquial words and phrases found in this book:

People:
Mama: miss or missus. Plural: *wamama*
Bwana: mister. In colonial days: master. Plural: *bwanas*
Toto: child. Plural: *watoto*
Mazungu: white person, European. Plural: *wasungu*
Mwalimu: teacher
Yenu: everyone

Greetings:
Hodi: announcing one's presence: I'm at the door. May I come in?
Hiyambu, or *jambo*: hello
Response:
Karibu: come in. Literally: come near, approach

Question:
Habari? Habari gani? Literally: what is the news?
Response:
Habari njema, or *habari vizuri*: good news

Departure:
Kwenda vizuri: go well, goodbye
Response:
Baka vizuri: stay well, goodbye

Thank you:
Asante
Thanks a lot:
Asante sana
Huge thanks:
Akisante sana, or *akisante kabisa*

Gun:
Bunduki
Little antelope: *Dik-dik*
Bird, airplane: *Ndege*

About the Author

College graduate   The author today
1949   2021

Rosemary Manchester created her first book, *Kusoma Furaha*, in Swahili, for a literacy campaign in the Belgian Congo in 1960. She and her husband, parents of four small children, served as missionaries in the Congo from 1958 until 1963. This is her memoir about those years.

At the age of seventy-five, she received a master's degree in Writing and Literature from Bennington College. She lives in Sebastopol, California, where she recently celebrated her ninety-third birthday.

Colophon

This book is set in Minion Pro, 11.5 point.

Minion is a serif typeface designed by Robert Slimbach in 1990 for Adobe Systems and inspired by late Renaissance-era type.
…
As the name suggests, it is particularly intended as a font for body text in a classical style, neutral and practical while also slightly condensed to save space. Slimbach described the design as having "a simplified structure and moderate proportions." (Wikipedia)